Write as Spoken , Read as Written

WHAT'S YOUR NAME?

How to write your name in *Han'gŭl*
without learning the Korean language

ALBERT JUNG

Published by Good Governance Research
The JS Tower, 6, Teheran-ro 79-gil, Gangnam-gu
Seoul, Republic of Korea, 06158
research@goodgov.info

Hardcover ISBN: 979-11-990032-0-0 (03700)
Paperback ISBN: 979-11-990032-1-7 (03700)
eBook ISBN: 979-11-990032-2-4 (05700)

First Edition: 2024
Book Cover by Mark Karis
Illustrations by Albert Jung
Interior design by Good Governance Research

This publication is intended to provide accurate and authoritative information with respect to the subject matter covered. It is distributed with the understanding that the author and publisher are not engaged in rendering professional services. If legal, financial, or other expert assistance is required, the services of a competent professional should be sought.

Printed in the United States of America

To bring wide-reaching benefits

to the human world

Contents

Preface

This book is about *Han'gŭl* (or *Hangeul*), the writing system currently used to represent the Korean language. *Han'gŭl* has been used for hundreds of years in Korea, and it is still used today by tens of millions of Koreans and people globally who have learned the language. This book, however, argues that *Han'gŭl* offers more than just a means of writing Korean.

Indeed, *Han'gŭl* is an essential script for learning Korean, but learning the language is not a prerequisite for using the script. According to a 15th-century record of its creation,[1] this script was designed to be simple enough for anyone to learn and use to transcribe spoken sounds into written form. *Han'gŭl*, therefore, was developed to easily represent any spoken sound from any language.

---

[1] *Han'gŭl* was developed and completed by King Sejong in 1443. In 1446, three years following its creation, its development was documented in *the manual*, 訓民正音 훈민정음, 解例해례 (*Hun-min-jeong-eum*[hʊnminjʌŋɯ̆m], *Hae-rye*[hæɾje]), literally meaning *the proper sounds to enlighten people, with explanations and examples*. This

Unsurprisingly, *Han'gŭl* may be more suited to Korean or the languages around Korea spoken at the time of its creation than to languages typically written in the Roman script, such as English or French. Furthermore, the modern *Han'gŭl* script, refined over centuries by Koreans, may not match with your language well. However, if we could time travel to the 15th century, the era when *Han'gŭl* was born, and accurately restore the process by which Koreans have refined the script, using it to represent your language might not be so difficult.

You may still wonder whether this book is worth reading. Given that you are already familiar with a script representing your language, is there truly a need to learn *Han'gŭl*, no matter how easy it is? Besides, if you do not even plan to study Korean, what benefits could there be in learning *Han'gŭl*? The answer may be found in the expectation that this knowledge will resolve some inconveniences we've already grown accustomed to, as follows.

WHAT'S YOUR NAME?

Imagine a scenario in which you are introducing yourself. Typically, you begin by stating your name. You will emphasize certain letters, if necessary, to ensure that they are pronounced correctly. Sometimes you show your name written down from the start. In such cases, you would likely correct the other person's pronunciation if inaccurate, perhaps even having to repeat your name several times.

This, of course, can happen when using an English name in English-speaking regions. However, accurately conveying your name to someone unfamiliar with your language is considerably more challenging. This is a persistent issue for individuals from Asia, Africa, and sometimes even Europe. Often, instead of providing their native name, individuals resort to creating a *Romanized version* that sounds similar. They may even adopt a more accessible English name instead. This inconvenience impacts not only the person

manual was designated as National Treasure No. 70 of South Korea in 1962 and was additionally registered in UNESCO's Memory of the World in 1997.

to whom the name belongs but also those trying to pronounce foreign names. Even when a name is written in English clearly, determining the correct pronunciation can still be challenging.

You may think it unlikely that you will ever need to exchange names with someone from a foreign country or who speaks a different language. However, we often encounter the names of singers, actors, athletes, businesspeople, and politicians from around the world. Discussing these figures with those around us is quite common. Think of the names you've heard on TV or radio news, during sports broadcasts, or in your favorite internet videos. The experience of encountering foreign names is already shared, and understanding how to pronounce them correctly can be a rewarding journey.

Are you familiar with *Catherine Deneuve*, the elegant French actress? Have you seen any movies featuring the charismatic American actor *Djimon Hounsou* or the talented British actor *Chiwetel Ejiofor*? Are you aware of *Naguib Mahfouz*, the Egyptian novelist who, in 1988, became the first person from the Arab-speaking world to win the Nobel Prize in Literature? Even these widely recognized figures often have names that many find difficult to pronounce. This challenge is not limited to celebrities. What is your name? How would you introduce your name to people who might meet you or discover you through posts or photos on the internet?

Table 1. Try Reading the Names Below

Catherine Deneuve	French actor: *The Umbrellas of Cherbourg* (1964), *The Truth* (2019).
Djimon Hounsou	American actor: *Blood Diamond* (2006), *The King's Man* (2021).
Chiwetel Ejiofor	British actor: *12 Years a Slave* (2013), *The Man Who Fell to Earth* (2022).
Kylian Mbappé Lottin	French footballer: *Real Madrid CF* since 2024
Haile Gebrselassie (ኃይለ ገብረ ሥላሴ)	Ethiopian runner: set world records in the marathon in 2007 and 2008

Jacob Wallenberg	Swedish entrepreneur: Chairman of *Investor AB*
Jonas Gahr Støre	Norwegian politician: 36th Prime Minister and leader of the Labor Party of Norway
Naguib Mahfouz (نجيب محفوظ)	Egyptian novelist: *Children of Gebelawi*, winner of the 1988 Nobel Prize in Literature
JungKook Jeon (전정국)	Korean singer: member of BTS since 2013, singer of *Dreamers* (2022) and *Seven* (2023).

WHY GETTING NAMES RIGHT CAN BE CHALLENGING

Why do we find it difficult to accurately convey names? The language-script systems we use largely depend on shared agreements that link sounds to symbols. These agreements often change based on era and region, requiring us to learn how to read and write separately. For instance, in English, the same letters can be pronounced differently, which can make it difficult to know their pronunciation just by looking at the letters in written form. The *gh* in *enough* is pronounced as [f], whereas in *ghost*, it is pronounced as [g]. The two *A*s in *amazing* are not pronounced the same way. As a result, people often need to memorize how each English word is pronounced and spelled, which also applies to names.

The Spanish, German, and Russian languages maintain more consistent connections between sounds and letters than English. However, because Spanish and German use the same Roman alphabet as English, it is essential to identify to which language the written characters belong. Then, one must learn the customary ways those characters are read within that language's region. Russian, which employs the Cyrillic script, also requires learning how words are typically pronounced. Similarly, distinguishing between neighboring languages that use the same Cyrillic characters differently might be necessary. Ultimately, methods of reading characters stem from the relevant language and culture, or the shared agreements specific to each. Therefore, learning to read some of these characters will still be a similarly challenging process, even if there are fewer variations than in English.

For a commonly sharable method of reading written characters, we can't help but talk about the *International Phonetic Alphabet* (IPA), usually referred to as *phonetic symbols*. Introduced in 1888 by the *Phonetic Teacher's Association* (PTA), led by French linguist *Paul Passy*, the IPA has been continuously refined by scholars worldwide. This system was designed with the academic purpose of representing every possible sound in the world.

However, for ordinary people in everyday life, mastering over 80 consonants and their co-articulated letters, nearly 30 vowels, about 30 diacritics, and approximately 20 supplementary symbols for expressing supra-segmentals, tones, and accents is highly challenging.[2] Besides, except for cases that resemble Roman script, the shapes and pronunciations of all other symbols must be memorized individually. Even when focusing only on a few widely used languages, understanding the shapes and pronunciations of roughly 100 consonant and vowel symbols is essential. Learning this system is difficult, and with increasing reliance on typing on computers and mobile phones in our society rather than writing by hand, using such a complex script system in everyday life becomes cumbersome and inconvenient.

WOULD *HAN'GŬL* BE USEFUL FOR CONVEYING NAMES?

The *Han'gŭl* used today to write the Korean language certainly follows various shared agreements. However, it was originally designed to be easy for ordinary people to learn and use. The foundational principles of this script system allow it to represent any language from any era or region uniformly, regardless of their socio-cultural conventions. These rational principles of *Han'gŭl* are detailed in *the manual*, published three years after its creation in 1446.[3]

---

[2] Since the IPA was developed for languages based on the Roman alphabet, there are relatively few symbols needed for English and some Western European languages. However, to recognize pronunciations used by speakers from other linguistic regions, learning additional symbols and notations is necessary. The symbols' numbers referred to in the text adhere to the IPA 2020 edition.

[3] See Footnote 1.

According to this 15ᵗʰ-century record, *Han'gŭl* distinguishes between sounds *produced by moving mouth parts* and those that *connect these produced sounds*. The sounds made by moving mouth parts closely align with what modern linguistics identifies as consonants. These are represented by five basic letter shapes, each modeled after five parts of the mouth we use to make sounds. Following specific rules, additional strokes are added to these basic shapes to create twelve more letters. Moreover, these letters can be written side by side as *double* or *pair letters* to represent various adjacent sounds. The connecting sounds, which do not involve movement from the throat to the mouth, closely match what modern linguistics considers vowels. These sounds are categorized into three types based on the tongue's position and are represented by three basic letter shapes. Combining these creates eight more letters, which can also be joined to form *compound letters* to denote various adjacent sounds.

To summarize, *Han'gŭl* is designed to represent sounds based on how they are produced and the nature of those sounds. The shapes of the symbols are designed to evoke the act of making the sound and its properties. Moreover, the rules for writing and pronouncing *Han'gŭl* are independent of socially shared agreements and are systematically structured based on how humans produce sounds.

Therefore, you do not need to memorize numerous examples of Korean usage to learn how to read *Han'gŭl*. Once you learn how to pronounce each symbol and make characters with them, you can immediately start reading and writing *Han'gŭl*. In addition, anyone who has learned the basics of *Han'gŭl* can read what you write exactly as it is written.

However, the modern *Han'gŭl* used in Korea today does not fully reflect the original design explained above. It has been refined by Koreans to better align with their own language; merely transcribing sounds does not leverage the full potential of the writing system. It is necessary to understand the etymology and origins of words, and there must be a standard notation that enables effective communication despite regional dialect variations. In this regard, the spelling of words used in newspapers, broadcasts, education, and government offices may also need standardization. The current form of *Han'gŭl* is still actively being refined to meet these requirements. Notably, modern *Han'gŭl*, in use since the 1930s, has slightly deviated from its 15th-century origins. It is written and read differently, and it often fails to transcribe foreign pronunciations accurately.

Looking beyond these adjustments, the rational basis and utility of *Han'gŭl* are extremely valuable. The method for reading and writing the script is open and accessible, not confined to any specific language or culture. In addition, its character creation system is simple and systematic, enhancing its adaptability for representing new sounds. Thus, *Han'gŭl* can significantly assist you in reading and writing foreign languages, and it can help disseminate your native pronunciation more widely to people from other regions. Furthermore, it can serve as a handy tool for those who need to transcribe their native language using letters or scripts from others.

This book is not a Korean language textbook. It does not explain Korean expressions or Korean culture. Instead, you will discover that knowing Korean or Korean culture is not necessary for learning and using *Han'gŭl*. This book does not suggest replacing your beautiful native language or your familiar script system with Korean and *Han'gŭl*. It does not advise you to create a Korean name. There's no doubt that any language or script is superior to your own in your life. Every language and script is irreplaceable and unique, just like your name.

This book introduces *Han'gŭl* as an easy-to-learn and convenient auxiliary tool that can be used without social agreements when different languages intersect. It aims to alleviate some of the discomfort and effort involved in accurately knowing the names of others during interactions. While *Han'gŭl* cannot eliminate all difficulties, by the end of this book, you will have gained a valuable tool that aids communication with a diverse range of people, regardless of your previous language experience. Moreover, the more you use this tool, the more convenient it will become.

STRUCTURE OF THIS BOOK

This book introduces three methods for writing your name in *Han'gŭl*. The first method uses the modern *Han'gŭl* alphabet, which refers to the version that has been in use since the early 20th century and consists of 24 letters.[4] This modern version can be useful because it is well-supported on today's computers and smartphones. However, as previously mentioned, modern *Han'gŭl*, refined by Koreans for use in their language, is less flexible than its original version. You may find that the pronunciation does not perfectly match your name, and some notations may feel restrictive. Therefore, Chapter I includes the basics of modern *Han'gŭl* along with strategies for using it more flexibly, beyond the typical social agreements of modern Korean.

The second method utilizes the original *Han'gŭl* alphabet from the 15th century. This version consists of 28 letters and offers a broader range of notations, enabling the representation of many more sounds. However, it is not widely recognized today, and using it directly on modern devices like computers or smartphones can be challenging and inconvenient. While this method might better represent some pronunciations compared to the modern version, it still may not satisfy everyone. Nevertheless, Chapter II presents 15th-century *Han'gŭl* in its original form before it was refined over the centuries, providing deep insights and extensive possibilities.

The final method discusses various ways to notate several unique sounds from different languages using *Han'gŭl*. This approach draws on numerous historical attempts by Koreans to transliterate various sounds over the centuries. These examples utilize the 28 letters of the 15th-century version combined according to consistent rules. While no method can perfectly represent every sound from every world language——something unachievable with any script system——this third method represents a sincere effort to fulfill the original intent behind the creation of *Han'gŭl*.

---

[4] The *Han'gŭl* currently used in Korea underwent significant simplification in 1933 with the establishment of a standardized orthography. The further enactment of related laws in 1988 restricted its letters to 24 and banned certain combinations.

If, 600 years ago, the king who created *Han'gŭl* for the Koreans had been your ruler, what kind of script system might he have devised for you? Imagine if, after initially creating *Han'gŭl*, he had crafted a manual specifically for transcribing your spoken language or developed an *extended version* of *Han'gŭl* tailored to your language. What would that be like? Chapter III might just be the beginning of a multiverse journey to discover the version of *Han'gŭl* for yourself.

You may have already found online documents or videos about *how to use Han'gŭl* or even *write names in Han'gŭl*. However, these resources are generally designed to adhere to Korean regulations regarding the notation of foreign words.[5] This orthography is the result of Koreans determining how foreign words should be written and read in Korean newspapers, broadcasts, educational settings, or governmental offices. Should you adjust your name to fit this system? Through this book, you will learn how to write your name in *Han'gŭl* to closely match your own pronunciation. Someday, there may even be an easy way to fully use all 28 letters of 15th-century *Han'gŭl* alphabet on computers or smartphones. During your time with this book, I hope you enjoy discovering *Han'gŭl*.

HOW TO ENJOY THIS BOOK

Here are some tips on how to enjoy this book and make your experience easier, more informative, and last longer:

1) Begin by carefully looking at the illustrations and tables from the start to the end of the book:

---

[5] To be precise, this refers to a government decree in South Korea (i.e., 외래어표기법; lit. *The Regulation of Loanwords Orthography*), established to prevent confusion in the pronunciation of loanwords that have entered the Korean language. This regulation was first codified in 1986, building on manuscripts written by Korean linguists in 1933 and 1941, with initial institutionalization and subsequent amendments in 1948 and 1958. Originally addressing seven languages, including English, French, German, and Spanish, the orthography has since been expanded to provide guidelines for 21 languages across Europe and Asia.

The tables contain more words and pronunciations not fully explained in the text. Don't overthink or analyze them here; just read them out loud one by one as much as possible. Feel the sounds close to each other and far apart, distinguished differently from your familiar languages. Don't worry if you don't understand something——it's okay to skip over it now. Try to sketch how the *Han'gŭl* alphabet shares and carries the whole sound. You will find these activities alone already exciting and helpful enough to learn this new script.

2) Next, give the book's text a light read. It shouldn't take too long. If possible, try solving the *Quizzes*, and attempt to read the *Han'gŭl* words aloud in the *Examples* sections. Look around the tables again and notice if anything seems different from your initial impression. Try to refine your sketch from earlier. You may find yourself already writing your name in *Han'gŭl*.

3) If you wish to gain a deeper understanding of *Han'gŭl*, read the text again and look closely at the annotations. You may find fascinating or crucial information about linguistics, phonetics, and historical context:

The annotations in Chapter I contain information on modern phonetics, and those in Chapter II also show information on traditional East Asian phonetics. In Chapter III, they are filled with stories from the history of using *Han'gŭl* in Korea, and in Chapter IV, provide more stories from the long history of Korea surrounding *Han'gŭl*, with many historical *names*. All these annotations not only provide vital information for those who want to take their knowledge of *Han'gŭl* one step further but also offer valuable keywords as a starting point for communicating with experts surrounding you, such as teachers, researchers, or professors, or to navigate through the vast sea of information on the Internet.

4) If you enjoyed this book——share it with others! Read it together and exchange notes or messages in *Han'gŭl* with each other. Sharing *Han'gŭl* makes the experience even better.

List of Abbreviations:

Abbreviation	Definition
a.k.a.	also known as
cf.	compare
DE	German
e.g.	for example,
EN	English
ES	Spanish
FR	French
Fr.	Father as a title of a Christian priest
GA	General American
i.e.	that is
IF	in fact,
lit.	literally
Rev.	Reverend
RP	Received Pronunciation
Swe.	Swedish

CHAPTER I. WRITING NAMES IN
Modern *Han'gŭl*

Han'gŭl divides one spoken sound[1] into three parts: the top sound, the middle sound, and the bottom sound. These components are combined to form a single character, and this is the order in which the sounds are read.[2] In

---

[1] In most Korean language teaching materials and courses, these are typically taught as *syllables*. However, the term *syllable* originated in the 20th century, and it is inappropriate to apply the term directly to *Han'gŭl*, which was created in the 15th century. Although the tendency to write *Han'gŭl* in syllable blocks has increased since the mid-20th century, *Han'gŭl* has historically often been used independently of syllables, and this practice continues today. In addition, it cannot be overlooked that the criteria for syllable division vary across different languages. Here, in general everyday use, it is expressed as *one spoken sound*.

[2] In English-speaking contexts, the sounds at the top, the middle, and the bottom of *Han'gŭl* characters are usually translated as consonant, vowel, and final consonant, respectively. While this translation is not completely incorrect——given that letters at the top and the bottom of a *Han'gŭl* character are generally consonants, and those in the middle are vowels——the classification of *Han'gŭl* phonemes deviates from the modern linguistic distinction between consonants and vowels, based on different theoretical foundations. Therefore, the results of applying modern frameworks to ancient documents and translating them in such a way are inaccurate. The translation

other words, the top sound opens at the top, the middle sound takes over and relays in the middle, the bottom sound closes at the bottom, and all three sounds are pronounced together in a single character.

When creating a character in *Han'gŭl* to represent a single sound, two primary rules are followed for combining the top, the middle, and the bottom sound letters. First, the middle sound letter is positioned below or to the right of the top. Second, the bottom letter is placed below both the top and the middle.

Figure I-1. Two Rules for Combining *Han'gŭl* Letters

Rule 1. The middle sound letter is positioned below or to the right of the top.

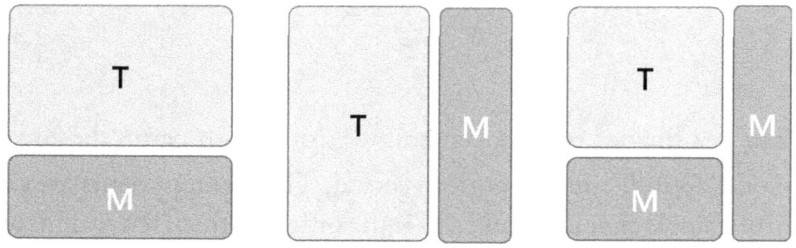

Rule 2. The bottom sound letter is placed below both the top and the middle.

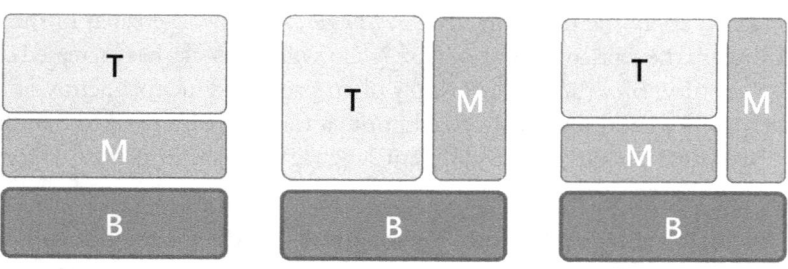

here aims to preserve the original content in the 15th-century *manual* by first translating the three positions of sounds in a character into everyday language and then describing them as *the order in which the sounds are read*. This also fits well with the historical context in which *Han'gŭl* was originally created as a vertical writing system (see 2. §3 of Chapter III for further information).

1. Writing Top Sounds

In *Han'gŭl*, top sound letters denote sounds produced by the movement of mouth parts (i.e., speech organs). These sounds fall into five categories: molar sounds, tongue sounds, lip sounds, tooth sounds, and throat sounds. The basic letters designed to mimic the appearance of these parts in the mouth as they produce sounds are ㄱ, ㄴ, ㅁ, ㅅ, and ㅇ (see Figure I-2).[3]

§1. Molar Sounds: ㄱ, ㅋ, ㄲ [4]

Han'gŭl molar sounds are produced near the molars, specifically at the back of the tongue, the rear part of the palate, and just in front of the throat (i.e., the uvular area).[5] The *Han'gŭl* letter for a basic molar sound, ㄱ, is designed to represent *the shape of the tongue's back blocking the throat*. The sound ㄱ is made by pressing the back of the tongue against the roof of the mouth and then releasing it, producing a sound similar to the [g] of g in *give* or *get*.[6]

---

[3] 기역[g̊ijʌg̚], 니은[niŭn], 미음[miŭm], 시옷[ɕiod̚], 이응[iŭŋ]. The names of each *Han'gŭl* letter are still partially unstandardized, so this information is for reference use only.

[4] 키읔[kʰiŭg̚], 쌍기역[ṣaŋgijʌg̚]* (or 쌍기윽[ṣaŋgiŭg̚], which literally means double-ㄱ.)

*The Korean prefix 쌍[ṣaŋ] generally indicates that the same element is doubled.

[5] The *Han'gŭl* molar sounds are considered dorsal consonants in modern phonetics. Dorsal consonants include palatal, velar, alveolo-palatal, and uvular consonants.

[6] In modern Korean, the ㄱ sound functions as a velar plosive, and appears as voiceless at the word-initial, voiced between vowels or near voiced consonants, and as an unreleased stop at the bottom of a character. Typically, the voiceless ㄱ is transcribed as a voiceless velar plosive [k]. However, in many languages, voiceless sounds are perceived as fortis, which can result in the mispronunciation of ㄱ as ㅋ or ㄲ when noted as [k]. This becomes problematic because, except in a certain dialects, ㄱ in

Figure I-2. *Han'gŭl* Top Sound Positions and 5 Basic Letters

5 basic letters in 5 categories of *Han'gŭl* top sounds:

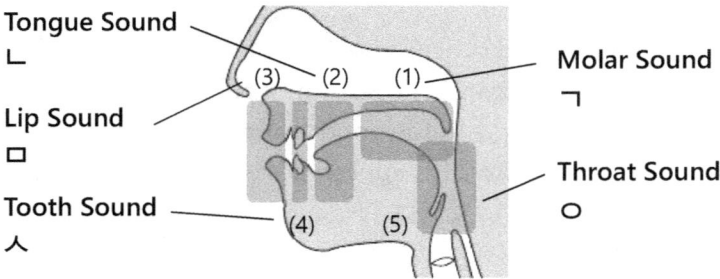

The letters are made by shaping sound-articulating organs.

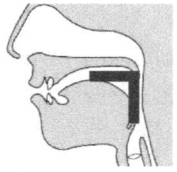 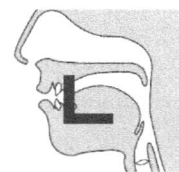 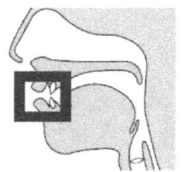

(1) The shape of the tongue's back blocking the throat

(2) The shape of the tongue sticking to the front of the mouth roof

(3) The shape of the mouth opening and closing (like a door)

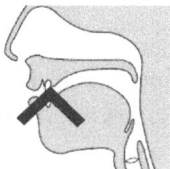 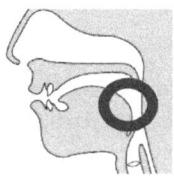

(4) The shape of the cross-section of front teeth

(5) The shape of the throat

Korean is always lenis, whether voiced or voiceless. Furthermore, in languages such as French and Spanish, where the [k] sound consistently resembles the ㄲ sound, using [k] for ㄱ leads to confusion between the representations of ㄱ and ㄲ in those languages. From this, some propose marking ㄲ as [k'], which corresponds to a velar ejective stop, also causing issues. Thus, this book indicates the voiced lenis ㄱ as [g], the voiceless lenis ㄱ as [g̊], the bottom ㄱ as [g̚], the tensed ㄱ (i.e., ㄲ) as [k], and the aspirated ㄱ (i.e., ㅋ) as [kʰ]. This approach is similarly applied to ㄷ-ㅌ-ㄸ, ㅂ-ㅍ-ㅃ, and ㅈ-ㅊ-ㅉ.

A more forceful exhalation for the same molar sound, denoted by adding a stroke, is represented as ㅋ. This ㅋ sound involves a stronger exhale and resembles the [kʰ] sound found in *kid*, *come*, or *queen*. When two ㄱ s get *tangled* together, a harder (or *thicker*) sound, represented by ㄲ, is produced.[7] The ㄲ sound retains the breath used in ㄱ but is made by applying additional force to the back of the tongue, similar to the [k] sound of *k* in *ski* or the Spanish *c* in *casa*.

Figure I-3. Modern Han'gŭl Molar Sounds: ㄱ, ㅋ, ㄲ

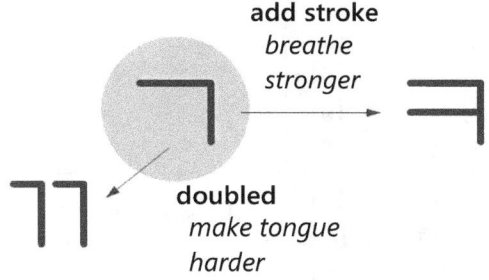

ㄱ	ㅋ	ㄲ
give	**c**ome	**s**ki
get	**q**ueen	*casa*

---

[7] The 15th-century *manual* describes the ㄲ sound with the term 凝응[ɯŋ], which connotes clotted, hardened, and slow, translated here as *tangled*. The interpretation of this description varies, considering it either as a tensed ㄱ——a tighter and more consolidated sound——or as a voiced ㄱ, characterized as both clotted and slow. Notably, one of the principal values of *Han'gŭl* is that anyone, even without additional societal agreements, should be able to easily read and pronounce the characters after learning the basics. Thus, in this book, ㄲ is viewed as a notation for a tense sound, created by applying additional force in the vocal apparatus with two overlapped ㄱs, and considered as the unaspirated fortis sound of ㄱ. This interpretation also extends to ㄸ, ㅃ, ㅆ, and ㅉ.

Table I-1. Modern Han'gǔl Molar Sounds: ㄱ, ㅋ, ㄲ

Han'gǔl (Korean)	ㄱ ([g̊], [g])		ㅋ ([kʰ])		ㄲ ([k])	
English	give agree	[g] [g]	kid choir queen	[k] [kʰ] [kʰ]	ski scramble	[k] [k]
French	garçon gain ronron	[g] [g] [ʁ]	krach très	[kʰ] [ʁ]	cabinet archange	[k] [k]
German	Gelände	[g]	kommen Käfig Quelle	[k] [k] [k]	-	-
Spanish	gracias Ágata amigo	[g] [g] [ɣ]	-	-	casa kilo quise	[k] [k] [k]
Russian	год герой господи!	[g] [gʲ] [ɣ]	Москва кино	[k] [kʲ]	кость короткий	[k] [k]

Various languages sometimes handle sound values uniquely, leading to cases where the sounds ㅋ and ㄲ might not be clearly distinguished, and ㄱ or ㅋ might be blended with the upcoming sound ㄹ or ㅎ. For instance, the [k] sound of *k* in ***Karen*** resembles ㅋ, whereas the [k] of *c* in *Jessica* often aligns more closely with ㄲ.[8] In addition, the [ʁ] sound of French *r* in *merci* or the German *r* in *hören* mimics a mix of ㄱ, ㄹ, or ㅎ, and the [x] or [χ] sounds of the Spanish *j* in *jardin* or *traje*, or in the German words *Buch* or *Dach* resemble a blend of ㅋ and ㅎ, all of which are absent in modern Korean. *Han'gǔl* was originally designed to combine two letters in such scenarios, but modern *Han'gǔl* does not commonly allow this.

---

[8] *Jessica*'s c ([k]) is usually articulated as ㄲ in American English (*GA*), French, or Spanish, and as ㅋ in British English (*RP*) or German.

Memorizing which letters from other languages match which *Han'gŭl* letters, as a rule, is problematic. *Han'gŭl* conveys *sound*, not letters. Thus, it is crucial to identify which *Han'gŭl* letters represent which sounds. Understanding the range of sounds each letter covers and conveys within the *Han'gŭl* alphabet system, as well as the differences between adjacent sounds, is more important than pinpointing the exact sound of each *Han'gŭl* letter.

For example, both English and Spanish speakers differentiate the sounds [g] and [k], produced near the molars. However, even with the same [k], a Spanish speaker might envision a different sound than an English speaker. Although the phonetic symbol [k] is defined as the same sound in both English and Spanish, the *c* in the English word *cut*[kʌt] and the *c* in the Spanish *casa*[kasa] are pronounced with distinctly different sounds.[9] Which *Han'gŭl* letter would best represent the letter *c* or the phonetic symbol [k]? What is conveyed, among the letter *c*, the phonetic symbol [k], or each sound itself, by ㅋ or ㄲ?

Han'gŭl divides the space inside the mouth into five areas to assign top sound letters. Among these, the molar sound letters in modern *Han'gŭl* are classified into three types: the lax ㄱ, the aspirated ㅋ, and the tense ㄲ. Now, reflect on a molar sound that is familiar to you. Without being restricted by spelling and phonetic symbols, decide which *Han'gŭl* letter, ㄱ, ㅋ, or ㄲ, would best represent the sound you have selected.

---

[9] [k] is voiceless velar plosive. In American Southwestern English, which interacts considerably with South American Spanish, speakers may not differentiate between the pronunciation of these two Cs. However, an individual who hears the *c* in *cut* or *cop* in British English and the *c* in *casa* or *coco* in European Spanish back-to-back will be able to identify the notable difference.

QUIZ FOR FUN!

Someone has mixed up *Han'gŭl* letters to match the sounds of their friends' names, including two from Spain. Let's restore them to their original names:[10]

Greㄱory	
ㄲarla	
ㅋristopher	
ㄱrace	
Marㄲos	
ㅋevin	

---

[10] Gregory, Carla, Christopher, Grace, Marcos, Kevin.

§2. Tongue Sounds: ㄴ, ㄷ, ㅌ, ㄸ, and ㄹ [11]

Han'gŭl tongue sounds are produced when the front or tip of the tongue touches the roof of the mouth (i.e., hard palate.)[12] The *Han'gŭl* letter for a basic tongue sound, ㄴ, is inspired by *the shape of the tongue sticking to the front of the mouth roof.* The sound ㄴ is created by pressing the tongue front against the mouth roof and then releasing it, producing sound through the nose. This sound resembles the [n] sound of n in *name* or *near*.[13]

While still a tongue sound, the sound that is *lighter and shorter* than ㄴ, produced without resonance, is designated as ㄷ by adding a stroke. The ㄷ sound is made by releasing the breath explosively without using the nose, similar to the [d] sound in *door* or *grade*.[14] A sound produced by expelling the breath more forcefully than ㄷ, created by adding one more stroke, is represented by ㅌ. This sound is akin to the [tʰ] in *top* or *attack*, or the [t] in *enter* or *retire*. Furthermore, a *tangled* sound of ㄷ is denoted as ㄸ, formed by combining two ㄷ s. The ㄸ sound involves maintaining the breath while applying force to the tongue against the mouth roof, similar to the [t] sound in *stop*, *stage*, or the two *T*s in the Spanish word *artista*.

---

[11] 니은[niŭn], 디귿[ḍigŭdˀ], 티읕[tʰiŭdˀ], 쌍디귿[ṣaŋdigŭdˀ] (i.e., double-ㄷ), 리을[ʎiŭl].

[12] In modern phonetics, *Han'gŭl* tongue sounds correspond to the coronal consonants* and appear as nasals or plosives.

*These are dental, alveolar, postalveolar, retroflex, and linguolabial consonants.

[13] In modern Korean, the ㄴ sound presents as an alveolar nasal [n] at the top, as a retroflex nasal [ɳ] at the bottom, and as an alveolo-palatal nasal [ɲ] when followed by [i] or [j]. Moreover, the ㄴ in Korean frequently exhibits a weaker nasal quality than the [n] in other languages, occasionally resembling an alveolar plosive [d].

[14] The ㄷ sound in modern Korean manifests as an alveolar plosive, occurring as voiceless [ḍ] at the word-initial, as voiced [d] between vowels or near voiced consonants, and as an alveolar unreleased stop [dˀ] at the bottom position. This book records the modern Korean ㄸ sound as [t] and ㅌ as [tʰ] (see Footnotes 6 and 7).

The letter ㄹ also fits into the tongue sound category, though it is somewhat different. *The manual* describes ㄹ as a *scattered and stretched* sound, distinct from other tongue sounds; thus, it has a unique letter shape.[15] In modern Korean, the ㄹ sound is made by attaching and then detaching the tongue tip, unlike ㄴ and ㄷ, which involve attaching the tongue front to the mouth roof. Generally, in Korea, the ㄹ sound closely resembles the [ɾ] of *tt* in *better* or *latter*, though sometimes it sounds similar to the [l] of *l* in *like* or *block*.[16]

When examining the tongue sound category across various languages, several sounds not used in modern Korean become apparent, depending on the position and movement of the tongue. For instance, the [ð] sound from *this* or *then*, which sounds similar to ㄷ, does not exist in modern Korean. Other sounds, such as the /r/ sound (i.e., [ɹ]) commonly heard in English, the /rr/ sound (i.e., [r]) in Spanish, the [r] sound in Russian words like **раз** or **играть**, or the [ʁ] sound found in French and German, are also absent in modern Korean.[17] These sounds are not satisfactorily represented in modern *Han'gŭl*.

---

[15] The ㄹ is the only *half-tongue sound* letter in *Han'gŭl*, but it is included here within the tongue sound category. *The manual* describes ㄹ using the term 舒서[ʂə], which suggests spreading, scattering, and slowing down, and the term 緩완[wan], which signifies being loose, slackening off, and relaxed. In modern phonetics, unlike ㄴ and ㄷ, *Han'gŭl* half-tongue sound (i.e., ㄹ) are created without fully pressing the tongue against the roof of the mouth and include all approximants, taps (or flaps), and lateral consonants produced between the hard palate and the tongue.

[16] In modern Korean, the ㄹ sound manifests as an alveolar lateral approximant [l] at the word-initial and as an alveolar tap [ɾ] at the word-medial, particularly between vowels. However, the ㄹ at the word-initial often resembles an alveolar tap [ɾ], exhibiting less tension in the tongue compared to the [l] typically found in English. Furthermore, ㄹ appears as a retroflex lateral approximant [ɭ] at the bottom and transitions to an alveolo-palatal lateral approximant [ʎ] when followed by [i] or [j].

[17] Rhotic consonants, commonly referred to as *R-like sounds*, include [r], [ɾ], [ɹ], [ɻ],

Figure I-4. Modern *Han'gŭl* Tongue Sounds: ㄴ, ㄷ, ㅌ, ㄸ, ㄹ

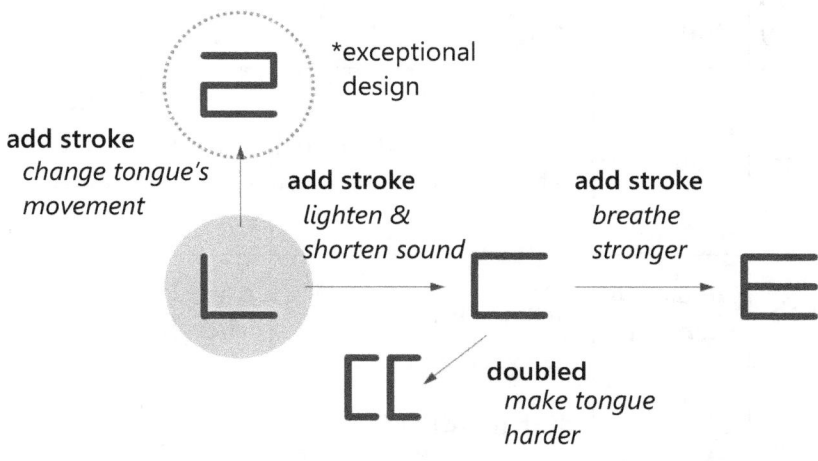

ㄴ	ㄷ	ㅌ	ㄸ	ㄹ
name	door	attack	stop *artista*	better like red

[ʀ], [ʁ], [ɾ], and [ɭ], among others. Generally, no more than two phonemes appear in any language. Thus, for convenience, the notation *r* is often used to represent the primary rhotic consonant in phonetic transcription. However, the IPA symbol [r] specifically indicates the alveolar trill, prevalent in Spanish and Russian. In English, the rhotic typically represented as /r/ is the alveolar approximant [ɹ]. Though the alveolar tap [ɾ] occasionally appears, it is widely regarded as a variant of [t], leading to the use of [t] in phonetic notation to differentiate it from /r/. Rhotic sounds in French and German are the uvular fricative [ʁ], with the uvular trill [ʀ] occasionally appearing as a variant.

Table I-2. Modern *Han'gŭl* Tongue Sounds: ㄴ, ㄷ, ㅌ, ㄸ, ㄹ

Han'gŭl (Korean)	ㄴ ([n], [ɲ])	ㄷ ([d̥], [d])	ㅌ ([tʰ])	ㄸ ([t])	ㄹ ([l], [ɾ], [ʎ])
English	name [n]	door [d] then [ð]	attack [tʰ] enter [t]	stop [t] stage [t]	like [l] red [ɹ] better [ɾ] million [ʎ]
French	nous [n] gagner [ɲ]	deux [d]	- -	tout [t] thé [t]	laisser [l]
German	Name [n] noch [n]	dürfen [d] oder [d]	Tag [t] Tochter [t]	- -	Liebe [l] raten [ʁ] rot [r]
Spanish	nada [n] cónyuge [ɲ] español [ñ]	dedo [d] dádiva [ð]	- -	artista [t] tardar [t]	hablar [l] bravo [ɾ] rumbo [r]
Russian	наш [n] нести [nʲ]	дать [d] женитьба [dʲ]	- -	то [t] тень [tʲ]	ложиться [ɫ] раз [r] лес [lʲ] рьяный [rʲ]

QUIZ FOR FUN!

Someone has mixed up *Han'gŭl* letters to match the sounds of their friends' names, including some from Spain and France. Let's restore them to their original names.[18]

ㄴancy	
Anㄸonio	
ㄹéon	
ㄷonald	
Anㄸoine	
ㄹarry	
Vicㅌoㄹia	
ㄷaniela	

---

[18] Nancy, Antonio, Léon, Donald, Antoine, Larry, Victoria, Daniela.

§3. Lip Sounds: ㅁ, ㅂ, ㅍ, ㅃ [19]

Han'gŭl lip sounds[20] are produced by opening and closing the mouth. The letter for a basic lip sound, ㅁ, is inspired by *the action of the mouth opening and closing*, similar to a door. The sound ㅁ, as produced by modern Koreans, involves sealing the lips and then releasing breath through the nose, closely resembling the [m] sound in words like *man* or *mother*.[21]

For a *lighter and shorter* sound than ㅁ, which is produced without resonance, the letter ㅂ is used with stretched strokes. This sound is made by releasing the breath explosively without using the nose, akin to the [b] sound in *bee* or *urban*.[22] A more forceful exhalation compared to ㅂ leads to the letter ㅍ. This sound involves pushing the breath out more powerfully, like the pronunciation of the $[p^h]$ in *poem* or *power* or the [p] in *panic* or *apart*. In addition, a *tangled* version of ㅂ is represented by ㅃ, formed by combining two ㅂ letters. This produces more robust sound, maintaining the breath as in ㅂ but with increased force from the lips. The sound is reminiscent of the [p] in English words like *expert* or *spy* and in Spanish terms such as *paella* or *peso*. It is also similar to the [b] in *boat* or *bus*.

---

[19] 미음[miŭm], 비읍[b̥iŭb˺], 피읖[pʰiŭb˺], 쌍비읍[s̥aŋbiŭb˺] (i.e., double-ㅂ).

[20] In modern phonetics, *Han'gŭl* lip sounds cover labial consonants, including both bilabials and labiodentals.

[21] In modern Korean, the ㅁ sound is consistently a bilabial nasal [m]. At the word-initial, this sound can occasionally emerge as a bilabial denasalized nasal [m̃], where its nasal quality is weaker compared to [m] in other languages. This variation some-times leads foreigners to perceive the sound as a voiced bilabial plosive [b].

[22] In modern Korean, the ㅂ sound is categorized as a bilabial plosive. At the word-initial, it is articulated as a voiceless [b̥], in the word-medial or between voiced sounds as a voiced [b], and at the bottom as a bilabial unreleased stop [b˺]. In addition, this book represents the modern Korean ㅍ sound as $[p^h]$ and the ㅃ sound as [p] (refer to Footnotes 6 and 7).

Figure I-5. Modern *Han'gŭl* Lip Sounds: ㅁ, ㅂ, ㅍ, ㅃ

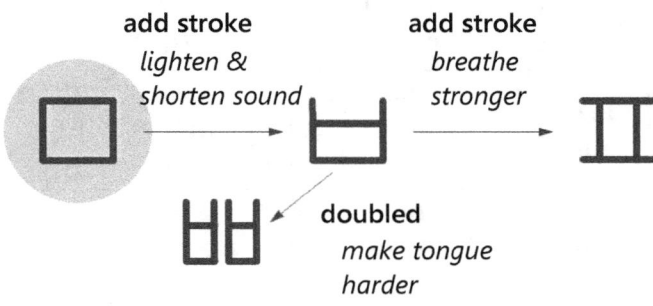

ㅁ	ㅂ	ㅍ	ㅃ
man	**b**ee urban	**p**oem	s**py** **b**us **p**eso

Table I-3. Modern *Han'gŭl* Lip Sounds: ㅁ, ㅂ, ㅍ, ㅃ

Han'gŭl (Korean)	ㅁ ([m])		ㅂ ([b̥], [b])		ㅍ ([pʰ])		ㅃ ([p])	
English	man smile	[m] [m]	bee urban valve	[b] [b] [v]	poem pie fish	[pʰ] [p] [f]	expert spy bus	[p] [p] [b]
French	ami	[m]	bien vous wagon	[b] [v] [v]	-	-	père pomme	[p] [p]
German	Mann	[m]	bei Vase was	[b] [v] [v]	Pack Pfeffer fade von Phänomen	[p] [p͡f] [f] [f] [f]	-	-
Spanish	madre grumete	[m] [m]	bestia vaca bebé curva vosotros	[b] [b] [β] [β] [v]	fase	[f]	paella peso opaco	[p] [p] [p]
Russian	муж мясо	[m] [mʲ]	бок белый вы его	[b] [bʲ] [v] [v]	форма Финал	[f] [fʲ]	под апрель пепел	[p] [p] [pʲ]

Some sounds utilized in various languages that are linked to the action of opening and closing the lips are not found in Korean. For instance, the [v] sound, common in English *valve*, French *vous*, or German *was*, as well as the [f] sound found in English *fish*, German *von*, or Spanish *fase*, do not exist in modern Korean. Furthermore, the [p͡f] sound in the German word *Pfeffer* and the [β] in Spanish *bebé*, which resemble [f] and [v] respectively, are also absent in Korean. Unsatisfactorily, all of these can only be represented by ㅂ or ㅍ in modern Hangul, respectively.

QUIZ FOR FUN!

This round includes friends from France, Spain, Germany, and the USA. As you proceed, try to correctly identify their original names.[23]

Alㅁa	
ㅍaul	
ㅃablo	
ㅂetty	
ㄱustav	
ㅋimㅂerly	
ㄷieㅌer	
ㅍeter	

---

[23] Alma, Paul, Pablo, Betty, Gustav, Kimberly, Dieter, Peter.

§4. Tooth Sounds: ㅅ, ㅈ, ㅊ, ㅆ, ㅉ [24]

Han'gŭl tooth sound[25] is produced by expelling breath between the upper and lower teeth. The *Han'gŭl* letter for a basic tooth sound, ㅅ, is designed to resemble *the cross-section of front teeth*. In modern Korean, the ㅅ sound is made without any nasal sounds by slightly lifting the front of the tongue toward the front of the mouth roof, allowing breath to escape through the gap between the teeth. This resembles the [s] sound in *scope* or *strike*. Typically, the ㅅ sound occurs when an *s* precedes a consonant.[26]

A *denser* sound than (or *grinded* sound of) ㅅ is formed by adding a stroke to create ㅈ.[27] The ㅈ sound involves pressing the tongue against the

---

[24] 시옷[ɕiod̚], 지읒[d͡ʑiɯd̚], 치읓[tɕʰiɯd̚], 쌍시옷[s͈aŋɕiod̚] (or double-ㅅ), 쌍지읒[s͈and͡ʑiɯd̚] (or double-ㅈ).

[25] In modern phonetics, *Han'gŭl* tooth sounds involve the space between the tongue and the hard palate (i.e., coronal consonant area) and encompass both affricates and fricatives.

[26] Korean textbooks generally depict the ㅅ sound as an alveolar fricative [s]. However, since [s] is often produced as a fortis sound in various languages, there is a frequent misinterpretation of the *Han'gŭl* ㅅ as the fortis sound ㅆ. While *Han'gŭl* differentiates between ㅅ and ㅆ, English and many European languages do not. For instance, in English, the letter *s* sounds like ㅅ before consonants (e.g., *strike*) and like ㅆ before vowels (e.g., *savage*), yet the phonetic symbol remains [s]. As a result, this book uses extended IPA symbols to distinguish modern Korean ㅅ as *weak s* (i.e., [s̠]) and ㅆ as *strong s* (i.e., [s̩]). Furthermore, the ㅅ sound does not become voiced in the word-medial and changes to an alveolo-palatal fricative [ɕ] when followed by [i] or [j]. In addition, all tooth sounds, including ㅅ, ㅈ, and ㅊ, manifest as an alveolar unreleased stop [d̚] at the bottom.

[27] *The manual* describes the ㅈ sound using the term 厲려[rjʌ], which suggests meanings such as grinded, fierce, and dignified, translated here as *denser*. This portrayal indicates that the affricate ㅈ sounds heavier and rougher than the fricative ㅅ. *The manual* also notes that, unlike the pairs ㄴ-ㄷ and ㅁ-ㅂ, the ㅅ-ㅈ pair does not exhibit a difference in *resonance* in stopping and releasing the sound. Therefore, ㅅ and ㅈ differ only in the placement of the tongue, not in the force exerted by the vocal

roof of the mouth and then releasing it, comparable to the [d͡ʒ] sound in *gene* or *jealous* or the [d͡z] in *birds*.[28] Moreover, a stronger breath sound than ㅈ is produced by adding another stroke, making ㅊ. Here, the breath is expelled more forcefully, like the [t͡ʃ] in *cheese* or *beach*, or the [t͡s] in *cats* or *shirts*.[29]

The *tangled* sound of ㅅ is represented as ㅆ. By applying more force to the tongue and exhaling more forcefully than when pronouncing ㅅ, this sound becomes ㅆ, similar to the [s] sound in *sea*, *sun*, or the Spanish *señor*. Typically, the ㅆ sound occurs before a vowel.[30] The *tangled* sound of ㅈ is indicated as ㅉ, where breath is maintained the same way as in ㅈ, but the tongue is used more forcefully to produce a stronger sound. This sound closely resembles the [t͡s] in *pizza*, the Z in Italian *grazia* or German *Zeit*, or the Ц in Russian **царь**.[31]

---

organs or the intensity of the breath. Indeed, in modern Korean, the ㅈ sound differs from ㅅ only in tongue placement, without any variation in the force or intensity of the breath.

[28] In modern Korean, the ㅈ sound is an alveolo-palatal sibilant affricate [d͡ʑ], which appears voiceless at the word-initial and voiced between vowels or near voiced consonants. In certain Korean dialects, North Korea, and the Manchuria region, it is realized as an alveolar affricate [d͡z]. Furthermore, ㅈ is pronounced as a postalveolar affricate [d͡ʒ] when preceding [w]. This book denotes the voiced ㅈ in modern Korean as [d͡ʑ], the voiceless ㅈ as [t͡ɕ], the ㅉ as [t͡ɕ], and the ㅊ as [t͡ɕʰ] (refer to Footnotes 6 and 7).

[29] Whereas ㅈ and ㅊ can directly represents [d͡ʒ] and [t͡ʃ], respectively, ㅅ represents [ʃ] only in combination with the appropriate middle sound (i.e., ㅣ). See 4. §4 of this chapter and 1. §2 of Chapter II for more information.

[30] Refer to Footnote 26.

[31] The ㅉ represents the unaspirated fortis sound of ㅈ, which often leads Koreans to hear the sounds [d͡ʑ], [d͡z], and [d͡ʒ] as ㅉ when they are stressed or accented (refer to Footnotes 7 and 28).

Figure I-6. Modern *Han'gŭl* Tooth Sounds: ㅅ, ㅈ, ㅊ, ㅆ, ㅉ

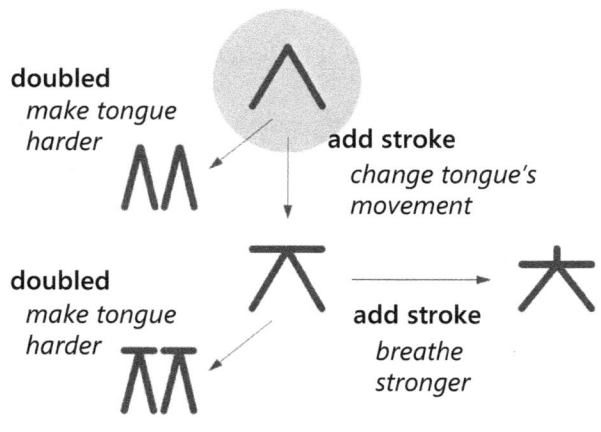

ㅅ	ㅈ	ㅊ	ㅆ	ㅉ
strike	**j**ealous bir**ds**	**ch**eese **c**ats	**s**ea *se**ñ**or*	pi**zz**a *gra**z**ia*

Tooth sounds are created by expelling breath between the upper and lower teeth. Unlike tongue sounds, where the tongue's front or tip touches the mouth roof and then detaches, tooth sounds are produced by creating a gap between teeth.[32] Some sounds in this category do not exist in modern Korean. For example, the [z] sound in *zoo*, or French *zèbre*, and the [θ] sound in *thin* or *thumb*, which can resemble ㅆ and sometimes sound like ㄸ, are not found in Korean.

---

[32] Both *Han'gŭl* tongue and tooth sounds are classified as coronal consonants in modern phonetics. These sounds are differentiated more by their production method than by their articulation location. Tongue sounds cover nasals and plosives, while the half-tongue sound includes approximants, taps/flaps, and laterals. Tooth sounds are mainly affricates and fricatives.

Table I-4. Modern *Han'gŭl* Tooth Sounds: ㅅ, ㅈ, ㅊ, ㅆ, ㅉ

Han'gŭl (Korean)	ㅅ ([s̪], [ɕ])	ㅈ ([d͡ʑ], [d͡ʑ], [d͡z])	ㅆ ([s̪])	ㅉ ([t͡ɕ])	ㅊ ([t͡ɕʰ])
English	scope [s] strike [s] sure [ʃ] emotion [ʃ]	zoo [z] birds [d͡z] beige [ʒ] giant [d͡ʒ]	sea [s] sun [s] census [s]	pizza [t͡s]	cats [t͡s] cheese [t͡ʃ] beach [t͡ʃ] tree [t/t͡ʃ]
French	artiste [s] espoir [s] cher [ʃ]	zéro [z] raison [z] jamais [ʒ] visage [ʒ] adjonction [d͡ʒ]	assez [s] ça [s] Saucisse [s]	- -	caoutchouc [t͡ʃ]
German	lassen [s] groß [s] schon [ʃ] Stadt [ʃ] Champagner [ʃ]	Sie [z] Genie [ʒ] Dschungel [d͡ʒ] Pidgin [d͡ʒ]	- -	Zeit [t͡s]	Cello [t͡ʃ] Celle [t͡s] Potsdam [t͡s]
Spanish	isla [s] mismo [s] riesgo [z]	cónyuge [ɟ͡ʝ]	señor [s] espita [s] xenón [s] cereal [s/θ] jazmín [θ]	- -	chubasco [t͡ʃ] muchas [t͡ʃ]
Russian	широкий [s̪] книжка [s̪] что [s̪] щека [ɕ:] считать [ɕ:]	заезжать [z] сбор [z] жизнь [zʲ] жест [z̪] вещдок [z̪:] джип [d͡z̪] дзюдо [d͡z̪ʲ]	собака [s] волосы [s] синий [sʲ]	плацдарм [d͡z] цена́ [t͡s] нравиться [t͡s] Цюрих [t͡sʲ]	лучше [t͡s̪] чай [t͡ɕ]

QUIZ FOR FUN!

You have a list of names from various countries, each interspersed with *Han'gŭl* letters. Next to each name is the country of origin. If you encounter any unfamiliar languages, feel free to skip them. Try to restore the names to their original forms as accurately as possible.[33]

Jaㅅon	U.S.	
ㄲarㅁen	Spain	
ㄱünㅌer	Germany	
Jeㅆica	U.K.	
Chriㅅta	Germany	
ㄴиㄲолай	Russia	
ㅆofia	Spain	
Huㄱo	France	
ㅁaㄹья	Russia	
ㅈarles	U.K.	
ㅁakㅆим	Russia	
ㅈoshua	U.S.	
Nanㅆy	U.K.	
ㅈade	France	
Patriㅉia	Germany	
ㄱaㅂriel	France	

---

[33] Jason, Carmen, Günter, Jessica, Christa, Николай, Sofia, Hugo, Дарья, Charles, Максим, Joshua, Nancy, Jade, Patrizia, Gabriel

§5. Throat Sounds: ㅇ, ㅎ [34]

The *Han'gŭl* throat sound's letter,[35] ㅇ, is modeled after *the shape of the throat.* ㅇ represents the most basic sound produced without using the tongue or lips.[36] A more forceful exhalation than ㅇ, with an added stroke, results in ㅎ.

In modern Korean, when the letter ㅇ appears as the top of a character, it generally leads directly to the middle sound, indicating that in modern *Han'gŭl*, the top ㅇ typically has no sound value. However, depending on the context, it may produce a sound similar to the [ʔ] heard in *uh-oh.*[37] Furthermore, when the breath is expelled more forcefully from ㅇ, it changes into ㅎ. This sound resembles the [h] found in *happy* or *high.*[38]

---

[34] 이응[iŭŋ], 히읗[çiŭd˺].

[35] Throat sounds in *Han'gŭl* are produced in the throat area, corresponding to laryngeal consonants in modern phonetics, which encompass pharyngeal, epiglottal, and glottal consonants.

[36] *The manual* characterizes ㅇ as *pure and vacant* and as *the most effortless sound.* Often, ㅇ is perceived merely as a placeholder ([∅]) at the top, serving to fill an empty space without contributing any sound value. However, this view complicates consistent explanations of ㅇ's various properties, uses, and its relationships with other letters as depicted in *the manual.* Ongoing research seeks to clarify the sound that 15th-century *Han'gŭl* intended to represent with ㅇ.

[37] In modern Korean, the term for *work,* 일, is voiced as [il̚], whereas *the number one,* 일, is voiced as [ʔil̚]. This articulation involves tension in the root of the tongue, leading scholars to speculate that, in the 15th century, this sound was distinguished using a now-obsolete letter ㆆ (refer to 1. §4. of Chapter II).

[38] In modern Korean, the ㅎ sound is identified as a voiceless glottal fricative [h], transitioning to a voiced glottal fricative [ɦ], following vowels or voiced consonants, and it becomes an alveolar unreleased stop [d˺], similar to ㄷ, at the bottom position. Furthermore, when followed by the consonants ㄱ, ㄷ, ㅂ, ㅅ, or ㅈ, it combines with them to produce ㅋ, ㅌ, ㅍ, ㅆ, and ㅊ, respectively (e.g., 좋다[조타]). When

Figure I-7. Modern Han'gŭl Throat Sounds: ㅇ, ㅎ

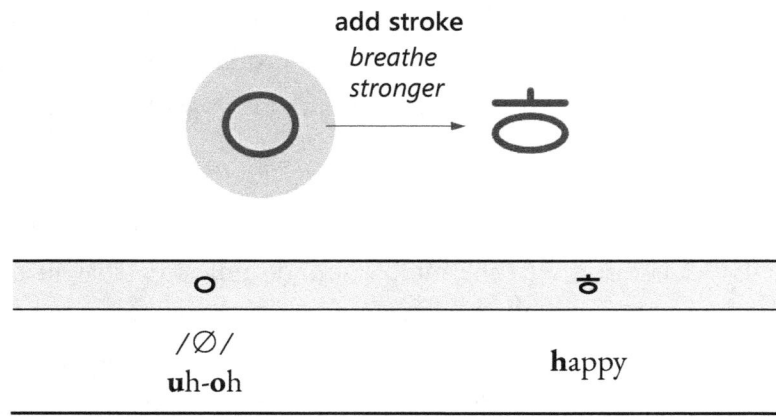

ㅇ	ㅎ
/∅/ **uh-oh**	**h**appy

In modern *Han'gŭl*, when vowels from words like *apple, egg, ice, open,* or *umbrella* are used without a preceding consonant, the slot for the top sound remains empty; this is where ㅇ is placed. In addition, sounds like the [w] in *wine* or French *oui*, the [ɥ] in French *aujourd'hui* or *huit*, and the [j] in *yes* or *hallelujah* also use ㅇ at the top position. These are consonants or semi-vowels in their respective languages but serve as definite middle sounds in *Han'gŭl*. The application of *Han'gŭl* ㅇ in these cases will be detailed in the subsequent section on middle sounds.

---

followed by ㄴ or ㅁ, the sound changes to ㄴ (e.g., 놓는[논는]), and disappears before a vowel (e.g., 좋아[조아]), leading to various allophones. In addition, ㅎ becomes a voiceless palatal fricative [ç] before [i], [j], and [y], a voiceless labialized bilabial fricative [ɸʷ] before [u] or [w], and a voiceless velar fricative [x] before [ɯ], [ʊ], and [ɥ].

Table I-5. Modern Han'gŭl Throat Sounds: ㅇ, ㅎ

Han'gŭl (Korean)	ㅇ ([∅]*, [ʔ]) *Top sound for all vowels		ㅎ ([h], [ɦ], [ç], [x])	
English	**uh-oh** certain	[ʔ] [ʔ]	**h**appy **h**igh	[h] [h]
French	-	-	-	-
German	beamtet beenden erinnern	[ʔ] [ʔ] [ʔ]	**H**ass dur**ch** A**ch**tung	[h] [ç] [χ]
Spanish	-	-	**g**eneral **j**amón Mé**x**ico	[x] [x] [x]
Russian	-	-	хо**д** Бо**г** **х**итрый	[x] [x] [xʲ]

QUIZ FOR FUN!

You have received another list of names from various countries with *Han'gŭl* letters mixed in. Review the list and try to restore the names to their original forms as accurately as possible.[39]

ㅆepㄱей	Russia	
ㄲamille	France	
ㅎenry	U.K.	
ㅎorㅎe	Spain	
Suㅈanne	Germany	
ㅎildeㄱard	Germany	
Aㄴacㄸaㅆия	Russia	
ㅁaㄷison	U.K.	
Aleㅎanㄷro	Spain	
ㅆaㅁantha	U.S.	
ㅁaël	France	
Anㄱeliㅋa	Germany	
ㅃолиㄴa	Russia	
ㅂalenㄸina	Spain	
ㄹouise	France	

---

[39] Сергей, Camille, Henry, Jorge, Susanne, Hildegard, Анастасия, Madison, Alejandro, Samantha, Maël, Angelika, Полина, Valentina, Louise.

2. Writing Middle Sounds

If the top sound letters depict the shape and movement of the vocal apparatus, then middle sound letters represent the quality of the sound. Since the qualities of sounds lack a physical shape that can be visually represented, middle sounds are depicted by symbols that convey the concept of *sound filling the entire world.*

§1. Filling the Whole World with ─, ∣, and · [40]

The sound produced when the tongue is at its lowest, maximizing the space inside the mouth, is considered the *deepest sound.* This is represented by · , evoking the *round sky* (or sun).[41] When the tongue contracts slightly, making the mouth space neither too broad nor too narrow, this produces a *neither deep nor shallow sound*, represented by ─, symbolizing *flat earth.* The sound created when the tongue does not contract at all, resulting in the narrowest space inside the mouth, is known as the *shallowest sound* and is denoted by ∣, representing a *standing human being.*[42]

---

[40] In *Han'gŭl*, middle sounds are named after their phonetic values (e.g., 으[ɯ], 이[i]). Although the name for · would traditionally be ᄋ, this letter is no longer in use, so such a name is hard to use now. As a result, it is typically referred to as 아래 아[arɛ ɑ] to differentiate it from ㅏ [a/ɑ]. However, 아래 means *under* or *below* in Korean, which some believe does not fully convey the importance of · , prompting others to call it 하늘 아[hanɯl ɑ] (refer to Footnote 41).

[41] *The sky* (하늘[hanɯl]) symbolizes deities, heaven, light, or the sun in the enduring legacy of Korean culture. The letter · , symbolizing *the sky*, is contrasted with ─, which represents *the earth*, and, together with ∣, symbolizing *human being*, forms a tripartite symbolic system that captures the sounds filling the entire world.

[42] The 15th-century *manual* states that the characteristics of sounds in *Han'gŭl* depend on the position of the tongue, specifically the shape of the space through which the

Figure I-8. Han'gŭl Middle Sound Symbols and 3 Basic Letters

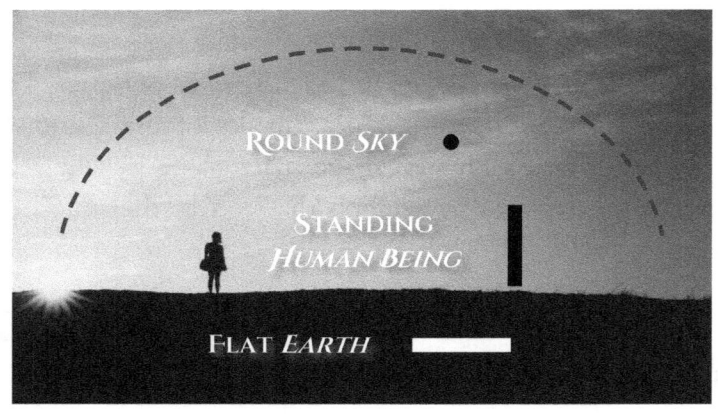

·	—		
This letter has not been used in modern Han'gŭl since the 1930s.	h**oo**k p**u**sh	free

The first three middle sound letters of *Han'gŭl* act as fundamental units for producing middle sounds, and they serve as symbols classifying their conceptual attributes. For example, *the sky* (i.e., ·) symbolizes upper, outward directions, brightness, or positive attributes, while *the earth* (i.e., —) signifies lower, inward directions, darkness, or negative attributes. *The human* (i.e., |) does not belong to either *the sky* or *the earth* and can be associated with the other two.

---

breath passes. Terms describing the state of the tongue in *the manual* are highly implicit, leading to varied interpretations by scholars (refer to Footnote 30 in Chapter II). Using an expression that remains most faithful to the original text while being more accessible, · is described as *with the lowest placement of the tongue*, — as *with the tongue drawn up and back*, and | as *with the most forward placement of the tongue* (Gnanadesikan, *The Writing Revolution*, John Wiley & Sons, 2009: p. 199).

Table I-6. Han'gŭl Middle Sound Symbols and 3 Basic Letters

Symbolic Meaning	Round *Sky*	Flat *Earth*	Standing *Human Being*
Original Symbol	•	—	|
Modern *Han'gŭl*	N/A	—	|
Tongue's Position	Lowest	Not low, not high	Highest
Size of Oral Cavity	Widest	Not wide, not narrow	Narrowest
Depth of Sound	Deepest	Not deep, not shallow	Shallowest
Aspect of Articulating Sound			
Conceptual Attribute	Upper Outward Brightness Positive	Lower Inward Darkness Negative	*free or no attribute*

Since the 20th century, the letter • , which symbolizes *the sky*, has ceased to be used,[43] and debates continue over its original sound value. Scholars are actively investigating its intended sound, guided by descriptions such as *deepest sound* and *sound made while the tongue is most contracted*, its

---

[43] In 1912, two years after Japan's colonization of Korea, • was removed from the list of letters for representing spoken language in elementary school spelling regulations, and by 1930, its use was also banned in written language. This decision was reportedly based on the belief among some *Han'gŭl* scholars that the phonetic value of • had been lost, leaving only its letter form. However, considering 1) • continued to be widely used until the 1930s; 2) standards for pronunciation could have been established or co-use permitted even though there had been overlap or confusion with other letters; 3) its phonetic value still appears in some regional dialects (i.e., *Jeju* Island); and, crucially, 4) its role as a fundamental letter symbolizing *the sky* in the creation of *Han'gŭl* is indispensable, the measures taken at the time appear not only irrational but also unnecessarily detrimental to the *Han'gŭl* system.

interactions with other letters, and historical uses spanning several centuries. Although • is a fundamental middle sound letter in *Han'gŭl*, it is not used in modern *Han'gŭl*. Its sound value will be discussed in the context of 15th-century *Han'gŭl*.

Like vowels in other languages, *Han'gŭl* middle sounds often have unclear boundaries and exhibit a broad range of vernacular pronunciations. This occurs because middle sounds are distinguished solely by the tongue's position (i.e., the shape of the space inside the mouth), height (i.e., the size of the space inside the mouth), and the shape of the lips, without distinctive movements of the vocal apparatus. In modern Korean, the — sound resembles the [ʊ] heard in *push* or *could*, or the double *o* in *book* or *hook*.[44] Moreover, — frequently appears naturally between consonants, such as between the *p* and *l* in *plus* or the *g* and *r* in *agree*.[45] The | sound in modern Korean is similar to the [i] in *happy*, *free*, or *idea* and closely matches the [j] in *you* or *year*.[46]

---

[44] In modern Korean, the sound — is pronounced as a high back unrounded vowel [ɯ] or a high central unrounded vowel [ɨ] (similar to the Russian ы). Typically, its standard pronunciation falls between these as a near-high near-back unrounded vowel [ʊ̈]. In Korea's southeastern regions, — is heard as a mid-central unrounded vowel [ə], and in the eastern mountainous and North Korean areas, as a near-high near-back rounded vowel [ʊ] or a high central rounded vowel [ʉ]. When transcribing foreign languages into Korean, the high-mid back unrounded vowel [ɤ] sometimes corresponds to — (e.g., Chinese 俄, Thai เออ).

[45] This becomes apparent when inserting an arbitrary vowel between the *p* and *l* of *plus* and comparing it to the typical pronunciation of *plus* (e.g., *polus* vs. *plus*). Extending and comparing the segment between *p* and *l* in both words reveals a flow of breath in *plus* that seems integral to the *p*. This phenomenon is also observed between the *g* and *r* in *agree* and between the *s* and *t* in *strike*. Pronouncing this extended sound clearly produces a resonance similar to —.

[46] In modern Korean, | is vocalized as a high front unrounded vowel [i]. In addition, all sounds represented as a voiced palatal approximant [j] are noted in Korean using | or a middle letter that combines with | (refer to §3. and §4). In transliterations into

Table I-7. Modern Han'gŭl Middle Sounds: ㅡ, ㅣ

Han'gŭl (Korean)	ㅡ ([ŭ], [ɯ], [ï], [ə], [ʊ], [ʉ])		ㅣ ([i], [j])	
Transcription into Korean[47]	[ə], [ɤ], [ʉ]		[i], [j]	
English	push could history	[ʊ] [ʊ] [ə]	happy free year mirror	[i] [iː] [j] [ɪ]
French	monsieur faisons ceux	[ə] [ə] [ø]	si régie payer hier	[i] [i] [j] [j]
German	Beschlag Name Gymnasium	[ə] [ə] [ʏ]	Berlin Jacke eben Bitte	[i] [j] [eː] [ɪ]
Spanish	-	-	di máquina ciudad ayer	[i] [i] [j] [j]
Russian	дышать жена	[ï] [ï]	воды линия часы четыре Майор	[ï] [ï] [ɪ] [ɪ] [j]

Korean from other languages, y (found in Spanish, Polish) or ы (in Russian) are often rendered as ㅣ.

[47] The *Transcription into Korean* section summarizes the guidelines for writing foreign words in Korean (i.e., 외래어표기법, see Footnote 5 in the Preface), as stated by the Korean government. Despite lacking legal binding power, this notation significantly influences practices in government offices, broadcasting, and educational sectors. While the term 외래어 typically denotes loanwords, this system extensively covers all foreign words, including proper nouns and names from various languages.

§2. *The Sky* (·) Creates ⊥, ┠, ┯, ┨ [48]

The sky · interacts with the other two middle sound symbols to create four more letters. A sound sharing attributes with *the sky* (·) when meeting *the earth* (—) produces the sound ⊥, articulated with *a more pursed mouth than* · . When *the sky* interacts with *the human* (│), it produces the sound ┠, articulated with *a more open mouth than* · . Similarly, a sound sharing attributes with *the earth* meets *the sky* to produce the sound ┯, articulated with *a more pursed mouth than* —. With *the human*, it produces ┨, articulated with *a more open mouth than* —.

In modern Korean, the sound ⊥ is akin to the [ɔ] in *force* or *north*, or the British pronunciation of *ou* in *thought*. It also appears as inside [oʊ] (=[o]+[ʊ]) in words like *hotel*, *note*, and *total*, similar to [o] in the French *saut*, German *oder*, or Spanish *sol*.[49] The sound ┠ resembles the [ɒ] in *cop*, *hot*, *not*, the [ɑ] in *palm*, *start*, or the [a] in French *patte* or *là*.[50] In modern Korean, the sound ┯ mirrors the [u] in *boot*, *goose*, or French *où*.[51] The sound ┨ closely matches the [ʌ] in *trust*, *unable*, the [ə] in *about*, *the*, or the [ɔ] in the American pronunciation of *thought* or *awesome*.[52]

---

[48] 오[o], 아[ɐ], 우[u], 어[ʌ].

[49] In modern Korean, ⊥ is articulated as a high-mid back rounded vowel [o] and is pronounced as a low-mid back rounded vowel [ɔ] in North Korean regions. When transcribing foreign languages, alongside [o] and [ɔ], the labial-velar approximant [w] is occasionally represented as ⊥ (refer to Footnote 51).

[50] ┠ in modern Korean typically spans a range from a near-low central vowel [ɐ] to a low central vowel [ä]. It can also manifest as a low back unrounded vowel [ɑ].

[51] ┯ in modern Korean is denoted as a high back rounded vowel [u]. In transcribing foreign languages, [u] is systematically rendered as ┯. In addition, the labial-velar approximant [w] is commonly transcribed as ┯ (refer to Footnote 49).

[52] The primary pronunciation of ┨ in Seoul in modern Korean is a low-mid back

Figure I-9. Modern Han'gŭl Middle Sounds: ㅗ, ㅏ, ㅜ, ㅓ

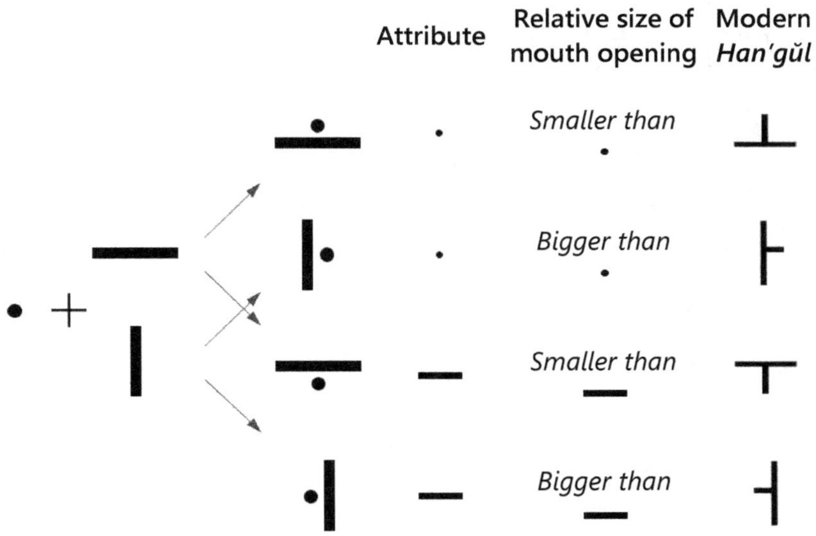

Attribute	Relative size of mouth opening	Modern Han'gŭl
•	Smaller than •	ㅗ
ㅏ•	Bigger than •	ㅏ
•	Smaller than —	ㅜ
•ㅏ —	Bigger than —	ㅓ

ㅗ	ㅏ	ㅜ	ㅓ
north boat *oder*	cow start	boot food	about awesome hurry the

unrounded vowel [ʌ], though it may be voiced differently depending on the region. In the central capital area, it may be voiced as a low-mid back rounded vowel [ɔ], a mid-central vowel [ə] in the southeastern and North Korean regions, or a high-mid back unrounded vowel [ɤ] in the southwestern regions and the former northwest dialects. However, looking closer, in the capital area and among older speakers, ㅓ frequently approaches the sound of —, and instances in North Korea where the phoneme ㅓ has shifted to ㅗ are noted. In the southeastern dialect, the distinction between ㅓ and — blurs, making it difficult for local speakers to differentiate these sounds. Therefore, determining whether variations of ㅓ in different dialects genuinely represent ㅓ or are effectively instances of — or ㅗ is challenging. When transcribing foreign languages, [ʌ], [ə], and [ɚ] are translated as ㅓ, while [ɔ] is rendered as ㅗ. As an exception, Hungarian *a* [ɒ] is occasionally transliterated as ㅓ.

Table I-8. Modern Han'gŭl Middle Sounds: ㅗ, ㅏ, ㅜ, ㅓ

Han'gŭl (Korean)	ㅗ ([o])		ㅏ ([ɑ], [ɐ], [ä])		ㅜ ([u])		ㅓ ([ʌ], [ɔ], [ə], [ɤ])	
Transcription into Korean	[o], [ɔ], [w]		[a], [ɑ]		[u], [w]		[ʌ], [ə]	
English	force north boat note	[ɔ] [ɔ] [o] [o(ʊ)]	cop start cow gauss hire	[ɑ] [ɑ] [a] [a] [a(ɪ)]	boot influence food push	[u] [u] [u:] [ʊ]	awesome hurry bird nurse history about serious the	[ɔ] [ʌ] [ɜ] [ɜ] [ə] [ə] [ə] [ə]
French	haut nôtre réseau sot	[o] [o] [o] [o]	patte femme glas	[a] [a] [ɑ]	coup roue poire	[u] [u] [w]	homme notre rhum sort	[ɔ] [ɔ] [ɔ] [ɔ]
German	Boot oder	[o:] [o]	das Speyer Staat	[a] [a] [a:]	Pointe Und Hut Gouache	[o̞] [ʊ] [u] [u̯]	kommen stalken immer Beschlag Hose	[ɔ] [ɔ] [ɐ] [ə] [ə]
Spanish	sol todo	[o] [o]	mal rata	[a] [a]	curable su aduanero fatuo	[u] [u] [w] [w]	-	-
Russian	облако радио	[o] [o]	палка какой Палка	[a] [ɐ] [ɑ]	пуля мужчина люди	[u] [ʊ] [ʉ]	облако собирать	[ə] [ə]

Previously, we noted that the [ɔ] sound in *thought* resembles ⊥ in British English and ㅓ in American English. Vowel sounds often vary based on region, context, or speaker, which explains why their boundaries can be ambiguous. For instance, the [ʊ] sound in words like *push* or *book* may correspond to either — or ㅜ, depending on the situation. Conversely, the [u] sound in *boot* generally corresponds to ㅜ and not to —. The [ə] sound in *history*, similarly, might be represented as either — or ㅓ, while the [ə] in *about*, the [ɛ] in *bird*, or the [ʌ] in *hurry* is commonly matched with ㅓ in modern Korean and not with —.

Let's look at how to transcribe sequences of two middle sounds (Table I-9). In such cases, two characters are written sequentially, but the top sound position of the second character is marked with ㅇ.[53] For example, the [ɔɪ] sound in *coil* or *boy* is transcribed as ⊥ㅣ (or ㅓㅣ). Similarly, the [oʊ] sound in *goal* or *note* is transcribed as ⊥우. The [aɪ] sound in *pie* or *nice* is likewise transcribed as ㅏㅣ, and the [aʊ] sound in *about*, *loud*, and *cow* is transcribed as ㅏ우.

In addition to the four previously mentioned examples, numerous combinations of *Han'gŭl* middle sounds are possible. In *Han'gŭl*, certain combinations, especially those incorporating the letter representing *the human* (ㅣ) or where sounds with similar attributes are combined, join two letters to create a new compound letter, pronounced as if it were a single sound. We will explore these letters next.

---

[53] The letter ㅇ is also used to indicate the top sound when there is no separate sound at the top position of the preceding character, e.g., 오이, 아이, etc. (refer to Footnote 36).

Table I-9. Modern Han'gŭl Middle Sounds: ㅗㅣ, ㅗㅜ, ㅏㅣ, ㅏㅜ

Han'gŭl (Korean)	ㅗㅣ (ㅗ+ㅣ)		ㅗㅜ (ㅗ+ㅜ)		ㅏㅣ (ㅏ+ㅣ)		ㅏㅜ (ㅏ+ㅜ)	
English	coil boy	[ɔɪ] [ɔɪ]	goal note	[oʊ] [oʊ]	hire nice pie	[aɪ] [aɪ] [aɪ]	about loud cow	[aʊ] [aʊ] [aʊ]
French	Pauillac	[oi]	-	-	ail gouvernail Travail	[aj] [aj] [aj]	-	-
German	neu äußern	[ɔɣ] [ɔɣ]	-	-	Ei Mai Meyer	[aɪ] [aɪ] [aɪ]	Auto Maus	[aʊ̯] [aʊ̯]
Spanish	estoy hoy oigo	[oi] [oi] [oi]	bou	[oʊ̯]	aire hay vaina	[ai] [ai] [ai]	causal aunque pausa	[aʊ̯] [au] [au]
Russian	большой тройка	[oj] [oj]	джоуль	[oʊ]	край давай	[aj] [aj]	наука	[ɐu]

QUIZ FOR FUN!

You're a guest at an event featuring attendees from multiple countries, including America, Britain, France, and Spain. Each person wears a name tag that shows their name and how it's pronounced in *Han'gŭl*. Since each individual provided their pronunciation, there's no need to check whether they are correct. While some characters may be unfamiliar, you can attempt to read some of the names. Based on the name tags, try to guess the nationality of each participant.[54]

Jessica	흐씨까	
Michael	미까옐ㄹ	
Thomas	타머ㅅ	
Thomas	토머ㅅ	
Thomas	토마	
Hugo	우고	

---

[54] Spanish, French, American, British, French, Spanish.

§3. *The Human* (ㅣ) Leads to ㅛ, ㅑ, ㅠ, ㅕ [55]

Previously, we discussed how the letter symbolizing *the sky* (·) has been combined with the other two middle sounds to create four new middle sounds. Now, the letter representing *the human* (ㅣ) influences the formation of four additional letters: specifically, when ㅣ precedes ㅗ, it creates ㅛ, and before ㅏ, it forms ㅑ. Likewise, when ㅣ appears before ㅜ, it results in ㅠ, and before ㅓ, it produces ㅕ.

In modern Korean, the sounds ㅛ, ㅑ, ㅠ, and ㅕ are each combinations of [j] with ㅗ, ㅏ, ㅜ, and ㅓ, respectively.[56] For example, the ㅛ sound is found in words like *yoga* or *yogurt* as [jo(ʊ)], or following [t͡ʃ], [d͡ʒ], or [ʃ] in *choke, joke,* or *show* as [o(ʊ)]. The ㅑ sound corresponds to [ja] (or [jɑ]) in *yard* or *yawn*, and is similar to the [ɑ] sound after [t͡ʃ], [d͡ʒ], and [ʃ] in *charming, java,* and *shop*. In addition, the ㅠ sound aligns with the [ju] in *beautiful* or matches the [u] following [t͡ʃ], [d͡ʒ], and [ʃ] in *fortune, shoe,* and *jukebox*. The ㅕ sound is akin to [jʌ] (or [jə]) in *young* or *yummy*, and parallels the [ʌ] (or [ə]) following [ʃ] in *chocolate, jumbo,* or *marshal*.

---

[55] 요[jo], 야[jɐ], 유[ju], 여[jʌ] (or [jə]).

[56] In modern Korean, at the word-initial, ㅛ is pronounced as [jo], ㅑ as [jɐ], and ㅠ as [ju]. In the word-medial, these sounds are articulated as [ʲo], [ʲɐ], and [ʲu], respectively. When transliterating Russian, ё is translated as ㅛ, я as ㅑ, and ю as ㅠ. The standard pronunciation of ㅕ in Seoul is [jʌ], but it commonly appears as [jə] across various regional dialects and as [jɔ] in North Korean regions. In the southeastern and southwestern regions, ㅕ is sometimes voiced as ㅐ or ㅔ.

Figure I-10. Modern Han'gŭl Middle Sounds: ㅛ, ㅑ, ㅠ, ㅕ

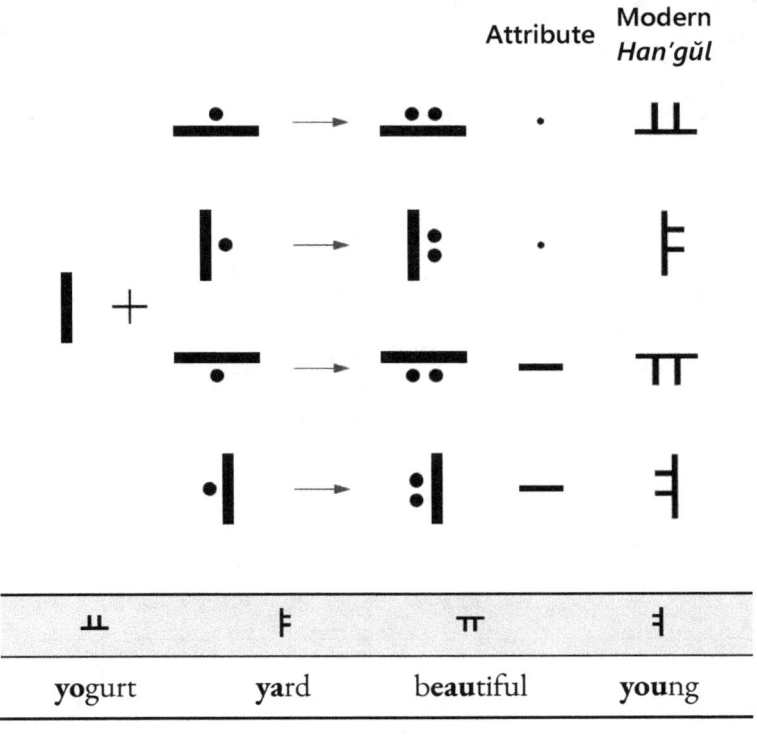

| Attribute | Modern Han'gŭl |

ㅛ	ㅑ	ㅠ	ㅕ
yogurt	**ya**rd	beautiful	**you**ng

In *Han'gŭl*, the sounds ㅛ, ㅑ, ㅠ, and ㅕ are always pronounced at once. This distinguishes them from ㅣ오, ㅣ아, ㅣ우, and ㅣ어. For example, the *yo*[jo] in ***yo**gurt* and *yu*[jʌ] in ***yu**mmy* are usually pronounced together. In contrast, the *illou*[ju] in French *ca**illou*** or *yo*[jo] in Spanish *apo**yo*** often emphasize the [j] sound separately. Similarly, the *yo*[joʊ] in *co**yo**te* and *eau*[ju] in ***beau**tiful* might either be pronounced smoothly or with the [j] distinguished, depending on the speaker or context. If pronounced smoothly, use ㅛ, ㅑ, ㅠ, or ㅕ; if distinguishing the ㅣ, then use ㅣ오, ㅣ아, ㅣ우, or ㅣ어.[57]

---

[57] Specifically, the sounds ㅛ, ㅑ, ㅠ, and ㅕ are produced by moving only the tongue while maintaining the lip shapes for ㅗ, ㅏ, ㅜ, and ㅓ, respectively. Conversely, the

Table I-10. Modern *Han'gŭl* Middle Sounds: ㅛ, ㅑ, ㅠ, ㅕ

Han'gŭl (Korean)	ㅛ ([jo])		ㅑ ([jæ])		ㅠ ([ju])		ㅕ ([jʌ], [jə], [jɔ])	
Transcription into Korean	[jɔ], [jo]		[ja], [jɑ]		[ju]		[jʌ], [jə]	
English	coyote yogurt choke joke show	[jo(ʊ)] [jo(ʊ)] [(t͡ʃ)o(ʊ)] [(d͡ʒ)o(ʊ)] [(ʃ)o(ʊ)]	beyond yard yawn charming java shop	[ja] [ja] [ja] [(t͡ʃ)a] [(d͡ʒ)a] [(ʃ)a]	beautiful use fortune jukebox shoe	[ju] [ju] [(t͡ʃ)u] [(d͡ʒ)u] [(ʃ)u]	young yummy chocolate jumbo marshal	[jʌ] [jʌ] [(t͡ʃ)ɔ] [(d͡ʒ)ʌ] [(ʃ)ə]
French	bestiau piaule chose	[jo] [jo] [(ʃ)o]	acariâtre paillasse	[ja] [ja]	caillou fioul duo juin	[ju] [ju] [ɥ] [ɥ]	mariol Niort	[jɔ] [jɔ]
German	Jod Marionette	[jo] [jo]	bejahen Jacke	[ja] [ja]	jubeln Jubiläum jucken	[ju] [ju] [jʊ]	Joch Jolle	[jɔ] [jɔ]
Spanish	apoyo ellos señora	[jo] [jo] [ɲ)o]	haya villa campaña	[ja] [ja] [(ɲ)a]	ayudar lluvia ceñudo	[ju] [ju] [(ɲ)u]	-	-
Russian	ёж шёпот мачо	[ʲo] [ʲo] [ʲə]		-	юг юбилей чуть	[ʲu] [ʲʉ] [ʲʉ]	-	-

---

sounds ㅣ오, ㅣ아, ㅣ우, and ㅣ어 involve altering the lip shape (refer to 2. §2 of Chapter II). From an auditory perspective, the notation varies depending on whether the ㅣ sound is distinctly heard.

QUIZ FOR FUN!

You noted some names at a previous event that, although spelled the same, were pronounced differently. They have been grouped based on the languages they use. Caught up in your focus on *Han'gŭl*, you forgot to write down the original names. There are still some letters you can't read, but try to fill in the blanks as best as you can.[58]

Name	English			Spanish
	루커ㅅ	류꺄	루카ㅅ	
	휴고		후고	우고
	싸샤	쌋샤		싸챠
	ㅅ띠븐		슈띠븐	
	제이컵	쟈껍	야콥	하꼽

---

[58] The top row, from left to right, includes French and German. The second row, from the top, includes Lucas, Hugo, Sacha, Steven, and Jacob (IF, *Jakob* in German and *Jacobo* in Spanish).

ONE MORE QUIZ!

You took photos of a few name tags written in Russian. Unfortunately, you don't know Russian at all, but reading *Han'gŭl* made you think you've seen similar names in English before. Write down the English names as they sound to you.[59]

Ксения	ㅋ씨니아	
Даня	다-냐	
Арина	아리나	
Тёма	띠요마	

---

[59] Ksenia, Danya, Arina, Tyoma.

§4. *The Human* (ㅣ) Helps Making ㅚ, ㅐ, ㅟ, ㅔ [60]

The middle sounds initially created by *the sky* (·) are refined with the help of *the human* (ㅣ), resulting in four additional middle sounds. When ㅗ combines with ㅣ, it becomes ㅚ, and when ㅏ meets ㅣ, it becomes ㅐ. Similarly, ㅜ with ㅣ turns into ㅟ, and ㅓ with ㅣ becomes ㅔ.

In modern Korean, the sound of ㅚ is closely related to the [ø] in the French *ceux* or the [œ] in the German *Köln*. It is also similar to the [we] in English words like ***weapon*** or ***wedge***.[61] Furthermore, ㅐ corresponds closely to the [æ] sound in English words like ***apple***, ***cat***, or ***fashion***.[62] The sound ㅟ in Korean is pronounced similarly to the [wi] in English ***we*** or French ***oui***, and it also resembles the [y] sound in the French *tu* or the German *über*.[63] Moreover, ㅔ matches the [e] sound in English words like *dress*, *let*, or *May*, and it is similar to the [ɛ] in *bed*, *pet*, or *tell*.[64]

---

[60] 외[ø], 애[ɛ], 위[y], 에[e].

[61] In modern Korean, ㅚ is a high-mid front rounded vowel [ø], and the pronunciation as a diphthong [we] is also acceptable. However, it is typically voiced as [we] or as a mid-front rounded [ø] in everyday speech, and the distinction between ㅚ, ㅙ, and ㅞ is becoming increasingly blurred. In southeastern and northeastern dialects, it is also voiced as a high-mid front unrounded vowel [e] (i.e., ㅔ). When transliterating foreign languages, both [ø] and the low-mid front rounded [œ] are represented as ㅚ.

[62] In modern Korean, ㅐ is a low-mid front unrounded vowel [ɛ]. In practice, ㅐ often merges with ㅔ [e] or shifts closer to a near-low front unrounded [æ], distancing itself from ㅔ. When transliterating foreign languages, [æ] is translated as ㅐ, and [ɛ] as ㅔ (refer to Footnote 64).

[63] In modern Korean, ㅟ is articulated as a high front rounded vowel [y], and the pronunciation of the diphthongs [wi] and [ɥi] is also acceptable. However, it is commonly pronounced as [wi], with the [y] pronunciation appearing occasionally, depending on the region and speaker. When transliterating foreign languages, [ɥ], [y], and [wi] are all rendered as ㅟ.

[64] The vowel ㅔ in modern Korean is a high-mid front unrounded vowel [e]. In daily use, however, it is often interchanged with ㅐ [ɛ] without distinction, or altered by

Figure I-11. Modern *Han'gŭl* Middle Sounds: ㅚ, ㅐ, ㅟ, ㅔ

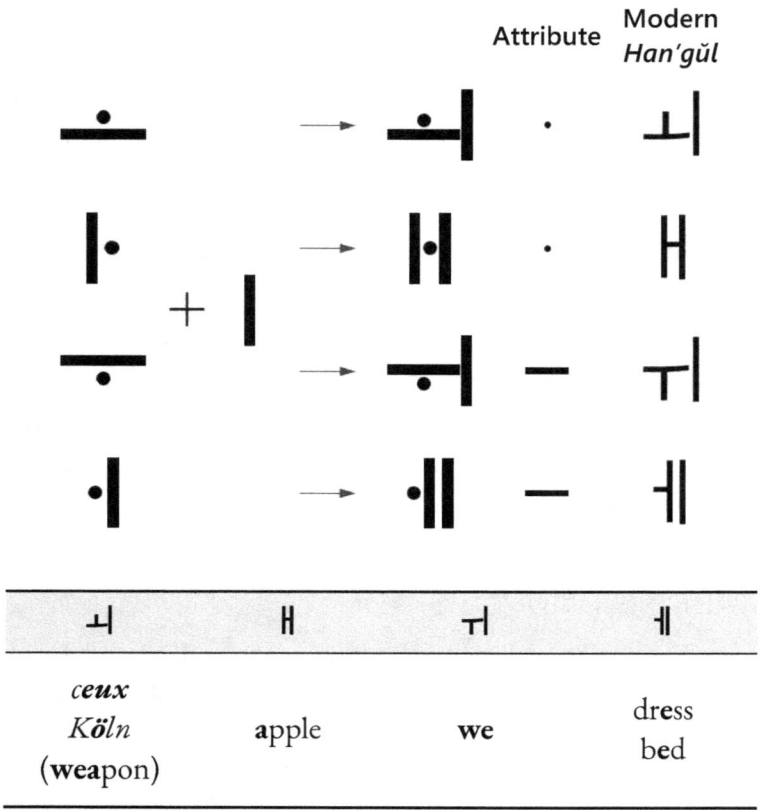

ㅚ	ㅐ	ㅟ	ㅔ
ceux *Köln* (**wea**pon)	apple	**we**	dress bed

Unlike the previously described sounds ㅛ, ㅑ, ㅠ, and ㅕ, the sounds ㅚ, ㅐ, ㅟ, and ㅔ in modern Korean generally do not include the ㅣ sound. However, while ㅚ, ㅐ, and ㅔ are distinct from ㅗㅣ, ㅏㅣ, and ㅓㅣ, the sound of ㅟ remains close to that of ㅜㅣ.

---

substituting with [i] or by prefixing with ㅣ [j], thereby enhancing its distinction (e.g. 네가→[니가], 너에게→[너예게]). In transliterating foreign languages, both [e] and [ɛ] are translated as ㅔ (refer to Footnote 62).

Table I-11. Modern *Han'gŭl* Middle Sounds: ㅚ, ㅐ, ㅟ, ㅔ

Han'gŭl (Korean)	ㅚ ([ø], [ø], [we])		ㅐ ([ɛ], [æ])		ㅟ ([y], [wi], [ɥi])		ㅔ ([e])	
Transcription into Korean	[ø], [œ] *[we]: ㅞ		[æ]		[ɥ], [y]		[e], [ɛ]	
English	weapon wedge	[we] [we]	apple bad cat	[æ] [æ] [æ]	we women	[wi] [wɪ]	dress May bake bed pet	[e] [e] [e(ɪ)] [ɛ] [ɛ]
French	ceux jeûne feuille	[ø] [ø] [œ]	baie fête maître peine	[ɛ] [ɛ] [ɛ] [ɛ]	début sûr huile enfoui	[y] [y] [ɥ] [wi]	été fée jeune sœur	[e] [e] [œ] [œ]
German	Möhre schön Köln öffnen	[ø] [ø] [œ] [œ]	Äpfelchen Ende Länge	[ɛ] [ɛ] [ɛ]	Büro üben	[y] [y]	Element	[e]
Spanish	-	-	-	-	huido güila	[wi] [wi]	beso guerra pique	[e] [e] [e]
Russian	-	-	-	-	-	-	жест этап этот	[ɛ] [ɛ] [ɛ]

QUIZ FOR FUN!

You have collected more names at a recent event. This time, identify the countries the participants are from——there are individuals from the U.S., the U.K., France, Germany, and Spain. Although there are still some letters you cannot read, try to fill in the blanks as much as possible.[65]

Name	U.S.			Germany	
	죠우세ㅍ	죠우제ㅍ		요제ㅍ	
	퍼얼	포올	뽈		빠울
		뤼쳐ㄷ			
	대니을			다니엘	
	퍼ㅌ뤼샤				빠ㄸ리띠아
			루위	루에ㅅ	
	다널ㄷ	도늘ㄷ			

---

[65] From left to right on the top row, answers are the U.K., France, and Spain. From the top, names in the first column are Joseph, Paul, Richard, Daniel, Patricia, Louis, and Donald.

§5. *The Human* (ㅣ) Helps Making ㅒ, ㅖ, ㅢ [66]

The letter ㅣ again follows the letters it led, ㅛ, ㅑ, ㅠ, and ㅕ, to create four new letters. Among these, modern *Han'gŭl* only uses ㅒ (i.e., ㅣ+ㅐ) and ㅖ (i.e., ㅣ+ㅔ).[67] In addition, *the human* interacts separately with *the earth* without *the sky* to further differentiate sounds. ㅣ appears before or after — to create *compound letters*, but modern *Han'gŭl* only uses ㅢ, where ㅣ follows —.

In modern Korean, the sound of ㅒ, which is ㅐ preceded by ㅣ, is similar to [jæ], resembling the [æ] that follows [t͡ʃ], [d͡ʒ], or [ʃ] in words like *channel, jacket*, or *shadow*.[68] The sound ㅖ, which is ㅔ preceded by ㅣ, is similar to [je], like the [ɛ] (or [e]) that follows [t͡ʃ], [d͡ʒ], or [ʃ] in words like *cherish, shell*, or *jealous*.[69] The sound ㅢ, which rapidly combines — and ㅣ,[70] closely resembles the [ɪ] in *historic, rabbit*, or *sing*.

---

[66] 얘[jɛ], 예[je], 의[ɰj]. (For the phonetic symbol of 의, refer to Footnote 70)

[67] In this arrangement, four letters can connect to eight combining sounds based on their combinations (i.e., ㅚ can link as ㅛ+ㅣ and ㅣ+ㅛ, ㅟ as ㅠ+ㅣ and ㅣ+ㅠ, ㅒ as ㅑ+ㅣ and ㅣ+ㅐ, and ㅖ as ㅕ+ㅣ and ㅣ+ㅔ). However, in modern Korean, apart from ㅣ+ㅐ (=ㅒ) and ㅣ+ㅔ (=ㅖ), the other six combinations are always written as two separate characters and not as ligatures (i.e., ㅛㅇㅣ, ㅠㅇㅣ, ㅑㅇㅣ, ㅕㅇㅣ, ㅣ외, and ㅣ위).

[68] In modern Korean, ㅒ combines ㅣ and ㅐ, pronounced as [jɛ], but it is often vocalized as [jæ] in practice, with the distinction from ㅖ [je] gradually diminishing. When transliterating foreign languages, [jæ] is translated as ㅒ.

[69] Similarly, ㅖ merges ㅣ and ㅔ, vocalized as [je]. However, in practice, its distinction from ㅒ [jɛ] is fading. Moreover, in various cases, by changing the sound to ㅖ [e], the vowels ㅐ, ㅔ, ㅒ, and ㅖ tend to become increasingly similar. When transliterating foreign languages, [je] is translated as ㅖ.

[70] In modern Korean, there is considerable debate about whether ㅢ is a falling diphthong [ɰj], a rising diphthong [ɰi], or a floating diphthong [ɰi]. Currently, ㅢ variably appears as —, ㅖ, or ㅣ, demonstrating substantial instability in its phonetic value.

Figure I-12. Modern *Han'gŭl* Middle Sounds: ㅒ, ㅖ, ㅢ

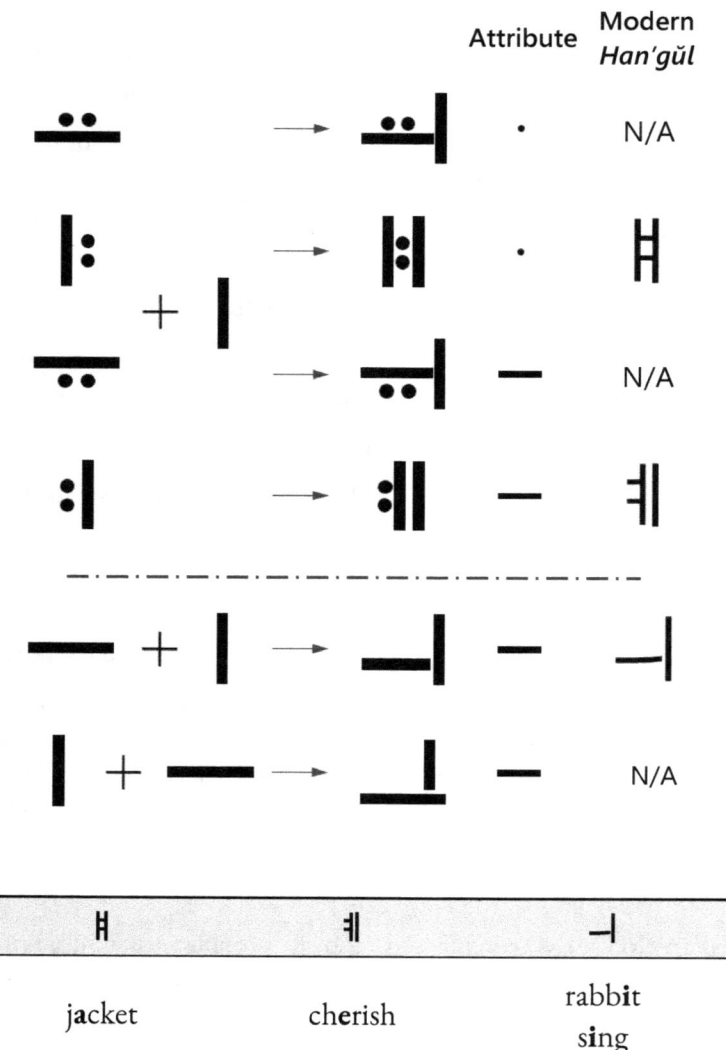

ㅒ	ㅖ	ㅢ
jacket	cherish	rabbit sing

Table I-12. Modern *Han'gŭl* Middle Sounds: ㅒ, ㅖ, ㅢ

Han'gŭl (Korean)	ㅒ ([jɛ], [jæ])		ㅖ ([je])		ㅢ ([ɰj], [ɥi], [ɰi])	
Transcription into Korean	[jæ]		[je], [jɛ]		-	
English	Yankee channel jacket shadow	[jæ] [(t͡ʃ)æ] [(d͡ʒ)æ] [(ʃ)æ]	yellow yes cherish jealous shell	[jɛ] [jɛ] [(t͡ʃ)ɛ] [(d͡ʒ)ɛ] [(ʃ)ɛ]	historic rabbit sing	[ɪ] [ɪ] [ɪ]
French	Ariège lierre	[jɛ] [jɛ]	janvier pied antérieur	[je] [je] [jœ]	-	-
German	jäh	[jɛ]	jeder Plädoyer	[je] [je]	bitte	[ɪ]
Spanish	-	-	llega oyente billete influyen muñeca	[ʝe] [ʝe] [jɛ] [jɛ] [(ɲ)e]	-	-
Russian	пять часть	[ʲæ] [ʲæ]	есть Ленин Алеф	[ʲe] [ʲe] [ʲɪ]	воды дымный Мыло шишка тяжёлый	[ɨ] [ɨ] [ɨ] [ɨ] [ɪ]

QUIZ FOR FUN!

Read the Russian names listed in *Han'gŭl* notation below and guess the English transliterations to fill in the blanks.[71]

Ирина	이리나	
Надежда	나지예쯔다	
Дмитрий	디미트리	
Евгений	예ㅂ기예니	
Гена	긔예나	
Верочка	븨에라ㅊ카	

---

[71] Irina, Nadezhda, Dmitry, Yevgeny, Gyena, Verochka.

§6. Letters Craft ㅘ, ㅝ; *The Human* Helps Make ㅙ, ㅞ [72]

Middle sound letters sharing similar attributes come together to create new sounds. *The sky* attribute combines ㅗ and ㅏ to form ㅘ, while *the earth* attribute combines ㅜ and ㅓ to form ㅝ. With further help from ㅣ, they create ㅙ and ㅞ.

In modern Korean, the sound of ㅘ, combining ㅗ and ㅏ, resembles the [wɑ] heard in *wash*, *swamp*, or *what*.[73] The sound of ㅝ, combining ㅜ and ㅓ, is akin to the [wʌ] in *one* or *wonderful*, the [wə] in *forward* or *worm*, or the [wɔ] in *want*, *war*, or *water*.[74] The sound of ㅙ, combining ㅗ and ㅐ, is similar to the [wæ] in *swag* or *wagon*.[75] The sound of ㅞ, combining ㅜ and ㅔ, matches the [we] in *weapon* or *wedge*.[76]

---

[72] 와[wɐ], 워[wʌ], 왜[wɛ], 웨[we].

[73] ㅘ in modern Korean is voiced as [wɐ]. Although the sound is a blend of ㅜ[w] and ㅏ[ɐ], the letter shape, as a result of merging letters with the same attributes, comes from combining ㅗ and ㅏ (e.g., ㅗ+ㅏ=ㅘ, ㅜ+ㅓ=ㅝ). In modern *Han'gŭl*, a ligature of ㅜ and ㅏ (i.e., ㅜㅏ) is not used independently, and especially when transliterating foreign languages, English [wa] (or [wɑ]) and French [wa] are rendered as ㅘ and ㅜ아, respectively.

[74] The Seoul pronunciation of ㅝ in modern Korean is [wʌ], with dialect variations appearing as [wə] in southeastern regions and [wɔ] in North Korea. When transliterating foreign languages, [wʌ], [wə], [wɔ], along with [wo], are all represented as ㅝ.

[75] ㅙ in modern Korean is voiced as [wɛ]. Over the past few decades, distinctions between ㅙ, ㅚ, and ㅞ have been fading. When transliterating foreign languages, [wɛ] is translated as ㅙ.

[76] In modern Korean, ㅞ is voiced as [we]. Over recent decades, there has been a trend toward convergence where ㅚ and ㅙ increasingly resemble ㅞ. When transliterating foreign languages, [we] is rendered as ㅞ.

Figure I-13. Modern *Han'gŭl* Middle Sounds: ㅘ, ㅝ, ㅙ, ㅞ

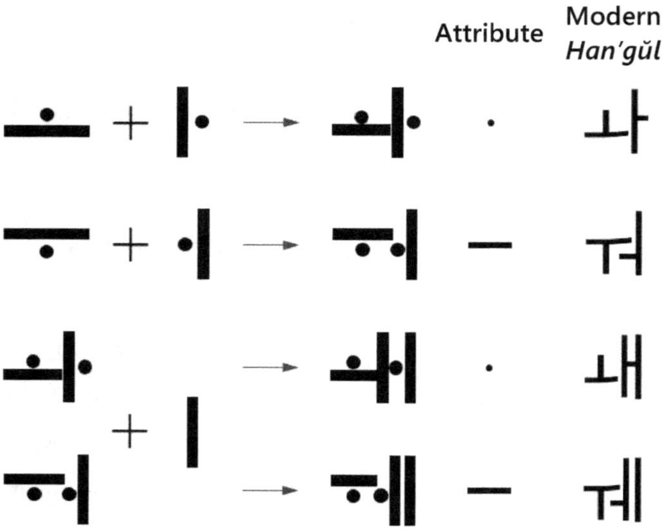

ㅘ	ㅝ	ㅙ	ㅞ
wash	forward want	swag	weapon

Table I-13. Modern *Han'gŭl* Middle Sounds: ㅘ, ㅙ, ㅝ, ㅞ

Han'gŭl (Korean)	ㅘ ([wæ])	ㅝ ([wʌ], [wə], [wɔ], [wo])	ㅙ ([wɛ])	ㅞ ([we])		
Transcription into Korean	[wɑ]	[wə], [wɔ], [wou]	[wæ]	[we]		
English	**wa**sp [wɑ] s**wa**mp [wɑ] q**ui**et [wa(ɪ)] **wi**ne [wa(ɪ)]	**forward** [wə] **one** [wʌ] **want** [wɔ]	s**wa**g [wæ] **wa**gon [wæ]	**wa**it [we] **wea**pon [we] **we**dge [we] **wa**ge [we(ɪ)]		

QUIZ FOR FUN!

You are helping with program operations at an international youth camp. The enthusiastic teacher, Ms. Elliott, has brought name tags written in beautiful *Han'gŭl* calligraphy for the children. She hurriedly hands you a paper box containing twelve name tags and a bundle of envelopes, asking you to pre-insert the tags for distribution. Each envelope is printed with a serial number, the child's native name, and their nationality. There is also a list organizing these details. The program is about to start. Please hurry![77]

No.	Name	Country	Name Tag No.
1	Brian	U.S.	
2	David	France	
3	Grace	U.K.	
4	Jack	U.S.	
5	Jade	France	
6	Jeffrey	U.S.	
7	José	Spain	
8	Julia	Germany	
9	Lucía	Spain	
10	Robert	U.K.	
11	Татьяна	Russia	
12	أميرة	Egypt	

---

[77] No. 1 – (5), 2 – (1), 3 – (12), 4 – (3), 5 – (8), 6 – (6), 7 – (10), 8 – (7), 9 – (11), 10 – (2), 11 – (4), 12 – (9).

List of Children's Names and Nationalities

No.	1.	Brian	U.S.
	2.	David	France
	3.	Grace	U.K.
	4.	Jack	U.S.
	5.	Jade	France
	6.	Jeffrey	U.S.
	7.	José	Spain
	8.	Julia	Germany
	9.	Lucía	Spain
	10.	Robert	U.K.
	11.	Татьяна	Russia
	12.	أميرة	Egypt

Ms. Elliott's Twelve Nametags

(1)

다뷔ㄷ

(2)

뤼버ㅌ

(3)

져-ㅋ

(4)

따·티야나

(5)

ㅂ롸·이은

(6)

제ㅍ뤼

(7)

율리아

(8)

야ㄷ

(9)

아·미라

(10)

호세

(11)

루씨아

(12)

ㄱ뤠이ㅆ

3. Writing Bottom Sounds

The bottom sound marks the edge of a single character. This represents the end of one spoken sound and signals a stop to the middle sound. Essentially, the bottom sound halts the flow of sound relayed by the middle sound. To tightly close the middle sound, use an appropriate bottom sound; to loosely extend it, leave the bottom sound position empty.

In *Han'gŭl*, top sound letters are also used at the bottom position, making the process of learning new letters for writing bottom sounds unnecessary. This simplicity should reassure you and boost your confidence in mastering the pronunciation of bottom sounds.

§1. Bottom Sounds ㄱ, ㅋ, and ㄲ

When ㄱ serves as a top sound, where the back of the tongue touches and then detaches from the mouth roof, as a bottom sound, it closes the middle sound by adhering the back of the tongue to the mouth roof. [78]

For example, in the word *dog*[dɔg], the *g*[g] is positioned to stop the *o*[ɔ] sound. However, when pronounced, a slight lingering sound (i.e., *audible release*) remains after the *g*[g]. [79] Here's how it's represented in *Han'gŭl*:

A. *dog*[dɔg˺] [80] 덕   B. *dog*[dɔg] 더ㄱ

---

[78] The bottom sound ㄱ in modern Korean is a velar unreleased stop [g˺] (refer to Footnote 6).

[79] In English and European languages, most word-final consonants display such *audible releases*.

[80] The diacritic [˺] signifies *with no audible release* and is applied to unreleased stop.

In Example A, ㄱ sharply cuts off the sound connected by the middle sound ㅓ, leaving no residual sound. In Example B, in contrast, the back of the tongue, initially attached to the mouth roof as if to make a top sound, slightly detaches, producing a lingering sound.[81] While ㄱ in A serves as a bottom sound, in B, ㄱ creates a distinct airflow separate from ㅓ, thus acting essentially as a top sound. This difference becomes more pronounced when another consonant follows.

A. *dog*[dɔg˺] 덕   B. *dog*[dɔg] 더ㄱ   C. *dogs*[dɔg˺s] 덕ㅅ

In Example C, the *g*[g˺] does not leave any sound because *s*[s] follows immediately after, stopping the *o*[ɔ] sound briefly before allowing the *s*[s] to emerge. This demonstrates the bottom sound ㄱ.

Now, let's compare the words *dogs* and *docks*.

A. *dogs*[dɔg˺s] 덕ㅅ   B. *docks*[dɔk˺s] 덕ㅅ (or 덕ㅅ)

In these examples, the [g˺] in *dogs* and the [k˺] in *docks* differ in phonetic symbols, and they are represented in *Han'gŭl* as ㄱ and ㅋ (or ㄲ), respectively, despite producing the same sound.[82] This occurs because the

---

[81] Due to the presence of an audible release, Korean speakers often attach a middle sound to a word-final consonant to form a single character. Commonly, ㅡ is added, which results in a pronunciation markedly different from the original, often creating an awkward sound (e.g., James제임스, Joyce죠이쓰). Such pronunciation distortions have become increasingly common within the standard orthography that mandates the use of a middle sound for all characters. This distortion also appears when notating the preceding consonant among two consecutive consonants (e.g., Scott스깥, Brenda브뤤다). In this book, word-final consonants or consonants followed by another consonant at the word-initial or medial are notated without a middle sound (e.g., James제임ㅅ, Joyce 죠이ㅆ, Scottㅅ깥, Brendaㅂ뤤다).

[82] The pronunciation of *dogs* that most people usually think of is [dɔgs], obviously different from *docks*[dɔks]. The *unreleased stop* sounds (e.g., [g˺] and [k˺] here) may look unfamiliar because they're not widely known, but they are surprisingly common sounds made every day, especially well shown when speaking quickly. They sound

movements and breath differences that usually distinguish the sounds of ㄱ, ㅋ, and ㄲ do not appear when these letters are used as bottom sounds. Therefore, when ㄱ, ㅋ, and ㄲ serve as bottom sounds, they all produce a sound similar to ㄱ.

However, there is no need to consistently rewrite *docks* as 덕ㅅ——it can also be written as 덬ㅅ (or 덖ㅅ).[83] This sound similarity in the bottom positions of ㄱ, ㅋ, and ㄲ does not necessitate a change in the representation of the sound in the word to ㄱ. Furthermore, if a vowel follows, the sounds of ㅋ and ㄲ should be revived in the next top sound position, where changing them to ㄱ might cause issues. As observed in the comparison between 덕 and 더ㄱ, when bottom sounds ㅋ and ㄲ lead into the next top sound, it is preferable to maintain their original representations. Of course, if they are used in the word-medial before a consonant, changing them to ㄱ is acceptable.

EXAMPLES	Douglas	덕을러ㅅ or 더글러ㅅ
	Nicolás (*ES*)	닉꼴라(ㅅ) or 니꼴라(ㅅ)
	Patrick	패ㅈ륔 or 패ㅈ뤼ㅋ
	Marceau (*FR*)	막ㅎ쑤

---

without any audible release at the end of a word, as if suddenly choked. Try to move the tongue in reverse order from sound [g].

[83] Modern *Han'gŭl* orthography for foreign words permits only seven letters (ㄱ, ㄴ, ㄹ, ㅁ, ㅂ, ㅅ, and ㅇ) at the bottom position. In this regard, *the manual* states that eight sounds (ㄱ, ㄴ, ㄷ, ㄹ, ㅁ, ㅂ, ㅅ, and ㆁ) are *sufficient* (足족[d͡ʒog]) and *not lacking* (不窮불궁[bulguŋ]), but it does not expressly prohibit the use of other letters for bottom sounds. This explanation indicates characteristics of bottom sounds rather than imposing restrictions on letter usage. The interpretation of this statement as a prohibitive rule emerged in the 1930s, although it is not applied in modern Korean orthography today. Nonetheless, the ongoing application of this rule to the *Han'gŭl* notation of foreign proper nouns and personal names is both absurd and groundless. This book does not adhere to this rule.

§2. Bottom Sounds ㄷ, ㅌ, ㄸ, ㅅ, ㅈ, ㅊ, ㅆ, ㅉ, and ㅎ

When ㄷ is used as a top sound, it is made by placing the front of the tongue against the upper gum and releasing it explosively. As a bottom sound, ㄷ stops the middle sound by keeping the tongue against the upper gum.[84] Similarly, ㅌ and ㄸ, as bottom sounds, produce the same effect as ㄷ. All tooth sounds, such as ㅅ, ㅈ, ㅊ, ㅆ, and ㅉ, along with the throat sound ㅎ, produce a sound akin to ㄷ when they serve as bottom sounds.

EXAMPLES	Edwin	엗윈 or 에ㄷ윈
	Becket	벡킽 or 베킽
	Hudson	헏슨
	Adam (*FR*)	앋동

§3. Bottom Sounds ㅂ, ㅍ, and ㅃ

As a top sound, ㅂ is produced by closing the lips and releasing the breath explosively. As a bottom sound, ㅂ stops the middle sound by closing the mouth.[85] Both ㅍ and ㅃ, when used as bottom sounds, mirror the sound of ㅂ.

EXAMPLES	Upton	업튼
	Rob	으랍
	Webster	웹ㅅ터-ㄹ
	Pippa	핖파

---

[84] The bottom sound ㄷ in modern Korean is a velar unreleased stop [d̚] (refer to Footnote 14).

[85] The bottom sound ㅂ in modern Korean is a bilabial unreleased stop [b̚] (refer to Footnote 22).

§4. Bottom Sounds ㄴ, ㅁ, and ㄹ

The ㄴ sound is produced, as a top sound, by placing the front of the tongue against the upper gum and resonating through the nasal passage. As a bottom sound, ㄴ continues to use the nose while closing the middle sound by maintaining the tongue's position against the upper gum, distinguishing it from ㄷ.[86] The sound ㅁ, generated by closing the lips and exhaling through the nose at a top position, also stops the middle sound by closing the open mouth when it acts as a bottom sound and continuing to use the nose, thereby differentiating it from ㅂ.[87] As a top sound, ㄹ is produced when the tongue tip is pressed against the upper gum and then released; as a bottom sound, it closes the middle sound by keeping the tongue tip in contact with the upper gum.[88]

EXAMPLES		
John	좐 (*GA*), 줜 (*RP*), 존 (*FR*), 욘 (*Swe.*)	
Ramsay	ㅇ램즤	
Hampton	햄튼	
Eloise	엘로위ㅅ	
Millie	밀리	

---

[86] The bottom sound ㄴ in modern Korean is a retroflex nasal [ɳ] (refer to Footnote 13). Unlike English or other European languages, which often feature an *audible release* of final nasals, Korean consistently produces these nasals as unreleased, similar to plosives. In contrast, French consistently releases final nasals audibly, as in the river *Seine*[sɛn], which should be written in *Han'gŭl* not as 쎄엔 but as 쎄엔ㄴ.

[87] In modern Korean, the bottom sound ㅁ is represented as a bilabial nasal [m] (refer to Footnotes 21).

[88] In modern Korean, the bottom sound ㄹ is a retroflex lateral approximant [ɭ] (refer to Footnote 16).

§5. Bottom Sound ㅇ

When ㅇ appears as a bottom sound, it produces an *ng*[ŋ] sound.[89] This occurs because the sound, previously represented by a different letter, is now denoted with ㅇ in modern *Han'gŭl*. We will discuss the 15th-century *Han'gŭl* alphabet that carried the sound value of the modern bottom ㅇ later (i.e., ㆁ).

The bottom sound ㅇ is especially common in French. For example, the [ɑ̃] sound in *sans* or *genre*, the [ɔ̃] sound in *son* or *réponse*, the [ɛ̃] sound in *brin* or *teint*, and the [œ̃] sound in *brun* or *grunge*, are all vowels in French. However, to write them in *Han'gŭl*, they must be represented using an appropriate middle sound in addition to the bottom sound ㅇ, such as 엉 (or 앙), 옹, 앙, and 웡 (or 욍), respectively.

EXAMPLES		
	Kingston	킹스뜬
	Langley	랭릭
	Gabin (*FR*)	갸방
	Nathan (*FR*)	나떵

---

[89] Velar nasal.

§6. 젯스카 or 제쎄카

Let's explore two different pronunciations for the name *Jessica* [d͡ʒesɪkə].

A. Jes-si-ca 젯스카   B. Je-ssi-ca 제쎄카

Although the two consecutive *Ss* in *Jessica* are represented by one sound (i.e., [s]), when pronounced quickly, Examples A and B sound the same. However, reading the parts separated by a hyphen reveals a variation in the length of *e* [e], attributed to the influence of the bottom sound. This raises the question: should the *ss* [s] sound in *Jessica* be attached to *Je*, or pronounced separately?

There is no definitive answer, as both approaches are possible.[90] The only thing to consider here is that in *Han'gŭl*, the bottom letter (i.e., ㅅ) causes an interruption in the middle sound (i.e., ㅖ). Of course, the preferred pronunciation would be whatever *Jessica* wants, which might even be 흐쎄까 or 예쎄까.[91]

---

[90] Depending on the region, context, and speaker, *Je* from the name *Jessica* can be pronounced as 제 or 졔, *ssi* as 시, 싀, 씨, or 쎄, and *ca* as 카 or 까. Therefore, *Jessica* can be variously written as 젯스카, 제쎄카, 졔쎄카, or 제시카, among other variations.

[91] In Spanish, *Je* from *Jessica* is pronounced as [xe] (i.e., 흐) or [je] (i.e., 예).

§7. Pair Letter

In modern *Han'gŭl*, a specific notation system is used exclusively for bottom sounds. This system, known as *pair letter*,[92] combines two different letters to function as one. Modern *Han'gŭl* limits the use of *pair letters* at the bottom position, allowing only the following eleven: they are ㄳ, ㄵ, ㄶ, ㄺ, ㄻ, ㄼ, ㄽ, ㄾ, ㄿ, ㅀ, and ㅄ.

In contemporary Korean, these letters are typically pronounced by articulating the first letter as the bottom sound and the second as the top of the next character. However, learning the letters can be complicated, as there are many exceptions. Originally, 15ᵗʰ-century *Han'gŭl* did not impose restrictions on these sounds, but rules limiting top and bottom sounds were applied beginning in the 1930s. These rules have shaped the current guidelines. This notation is not essential at this stage, so I will only note its existence.

We have now completed our exploration of the top, middle, and bottom sounds of modern *Han'gŭl*. Still, some sounds prove challenging to represent accurately using modern *Han'gŭl*. While it might be intriguing to learn about these in the context of 15ᵗʰ-century *Han'gŭl*, they are unfortunately not easy to express with the letters available on today's computers or smartphones. Before concluding Chapter I, let us review which pronunciations posed difficulties and investigate whether there are any last-resort measures——any port in a storm——to approximate these sounds as closely as possible using modern *Han'gŭl*.

---

[92] Several textbooks describe the bottom sound letter as a *final consonant* (refer to Footnote 2) and teach those combined letters in the text as a *double final consonant*. In this connection, top sounds ㄲ, ㄸ, ㅃ, ㅆ, and ㅉ are termed *double consonants*. However, as ㄲ and ㅆ are used both as top and bottom sounds, this translation leads to confusion. *The manual* introduces the notation as 竝書병서, meaning *write side by side*, distinguishing between 各自竝書각자병서, *write the same letters side by side*, and 合用竝書합용병서, *write different letters side by side*. Until the 19ᵗʰ century, there was no explicit prohibitive rule on this usage, but since the 1930s, certain letters have been restricted for use as top and bottom sounds. In this book, 각자병서 is translated as *double letter*, and 합용병서 as *pair letter*.

QUIZ FOR FUN!

The camp was a success last time, and Ms. Elliott was very pleased with you. She beamed and entrusted you with the name tags and envelopes, telling you to do it just like before. Will you do as well this time? Unfamiliar names seem to have increased, but there's no time to hesitate——let's hurry![93]

No.	Name	Country	Name Tag No.
1	Brandon	U.S.	
2	Camille	France	
3	Henri	France	
4	John	Norway	
5	Joseph	Germany	
6	Jürgen	Germany	
7	Kimberly	U.K.	
8	William	U.S.	
9	Виктор	Russia	
10	Миша	Russia	
11	خليل	Morocco	
12	אֵלִיָּהוּ	Israel	

---

[93] No. 1 – (7), 2 – (4), 3 – (12), 4 – (1), 5 – (6), 6 – (9), 7 – (3), 8 – (11), 9 – (8), 10 – (2), 11 – (10), 12 – (5).

List of Children's Names and Nationalities

No.			
No.	1.	Brandon	U.S.
	2.	Camille	France
	3.	Henri	France
	4.	John	Norway
	5.	Joseph	Germany
	6.	Jürgen	Germany
	7.	Kimberly	U.K.
	8.	William	U.S.
	9.	Виктор	Russia
	10.	Миша	Russia
	11.	خليل	Morocco
	12.	אֵלִיָּהוּ	Israel

Ms. Elliott's Twelve Nametags

(1)

욘

(2)

미샤

(3)

킴블리

(4)

까미

(5)

엘리야우

(6)

요제ㅍ

(7)

ㅂ뢘든

(8)

빅또ㄹ

(9)

유ㄹ겐

(10)

ㅋ할릴

(11)

윌리음

(12)

앙뤼

4. Difficult Sounds to Represent in Modern *Han'gŭl* (feat. Last Resort Solutions)

This section categorizes sounds that were challenging to represent during our examination of modern *Han'gŭl*. These include the *r* and *l* sounds, *th* sounds, *v* and *f* sounds, and finally, the *sh*, *j*, *ch*, and *z* sounds.

§1. *R* and *L* Sounds

As previously mentioned, the ㄹ sound appears as the [ɾ] sound in modern Korean, pronounced similarly to the *tt* in *better* or *latter*. Moreover, the letter ㄹ in modern *Han'gŭl* is, in fact, the only letter used to represent all *R*-like sounds and *l* sounds together. This makes representing the sound particularly inconvenient, as there is no separate notation for the rhotic [ɹ] sound, which is common in English. Emphasizing the *l* sound is also challenging.

(1) English *R* and *L*

When the English *r*[ɹ] sound appears before the vowels [ɑ], [ʌ], [æ], [e], or [i], it can be approximated by attaching ㅗ or ㅜ to ㄹ. For example, the [ɹɑ] sound in **r**o**b** can be written as 롸 (i.e., 로+ㅏ) instead of 라, and the [ɹʌ] sound in **r**u**sh** can be denoted as 뤄 (i.e., 루+ㅓ) instead of 러. Similarly, the [ɹæ] sound in **r**a**ndom** can be represented as 뢔 (i.e., 로+ㅐ) instead of 래, and the [ɹe] sound in **r**e**st** can be written as 뤠 (i.e., 루+ㅔ) instead of 레 for a closer approximation. Likewise, the [ɹi] sound in **v**e**r**y** can be denoted as 뤼 (i.e., 루+ㅣ) instead of 리.

EXAMPLES

Barbara	바-ㅂ롸
Robert	뤄버ㅌ
Brandon	ㅂ뢘든
Patricia	퍼ㅌ뤼샤

As you might've guessed, ㅗ and ㅜ represent sounds made with rounded lips. Thus, when ㄹ meets middle sounds such as ㅏ, ㅓ, ㅐ, ㅔ, or ㅣ, prefacing it with ㅗ or ㅜ helps the tongue move to produce a sound similar to the English [ɹ] when articulating ㄹ. However, when ㄹ encounters [o] or [u], it transforms into 로 or 루, respectively, and adding ㅗ or ㅜ does not significantly alter its movement to closely mimic [ɹ]. Therefore, we need a method to consistently produce the [ɹ] sound, no matter which vowel follows ㄹ.

In this regard, placing ㅇ before ㄹ, although not completely satisfactory, can create a sound quite similar to [ɹ]. For instance, the [ɹo] in **role** can be represented as ㅇ로, and the [ɹu] in **roof** as ㅇ루. This method can also further emphasize the [ɹ] sound by adding ㅇ before ㄹ. For instance, *rob* would be written as ㅇ롭 and *random* as ㅇ뢘덤. This approach involves producing the ㄹ sound with the mouth shape used for the middle sound ㅡ, allowing the tongue to move in a way that approaches the [ɹ] sound. To prevent the unusual pronunciation of 으 from becoming too prominent, only ㅇ is added to assist the following ㄹ.

EXAMPLES

Robert	ㅇ뤄버ㅌ
Rebecca	ㅇ뤄베카
Ryan	ㅇ롸이언
Roy	ㅇ뤄이 or ㅇ로이

Similarly, placing 을 before ㄹ causes the tongue to move in a way that comes very close to producing the *l* sound. For example, *club*[klʌb] can be written as 클럽 (i.e., ㅋ+을+ㄹ+업) and *plus*[plʌs] as 플러ㅅ (i.e., ㅍ+을+ㄹ +어ㅅ). This method uses the bottom sound ㄹ. However, when ㄹ appears at the word-initial, the preceding 을 sound is too noticeable. Hence, using one more ㄹ instead of 을 can more effectively emphasize the *l* sound at the word-initial. For instance, *lion*[laɪən] can be represented as ㄹ라이언 (i.e., ㄹ+라이+언), and *leg*[lɛg] as ㄹ레ㄱ (i.e., ㄹ+레ㄱ).

EXAMPLES	Linda	ㄹ린더
	William	윌리음
	Kimberly	킴벌리
	Larry	ㄹ래ㅇ뤼 or ㄹ래-뤼

Words that end with the vowel and the *r* sound can be particularly challenging to represent. British English, which often treats *r* as silent, presents less of a challenge compared to American English, where the sound of *r* is more pronounced. For instance, the words *where*[wɛɚ] and *near*[nɪɚ] could be transcribed as 웨어-ㄹ and 니어-ㄹ, respectively, using a hyphen to separate the elements. However, applying this method to the word *turn*[tɜɹn] results in 터-ㄹㄴ, which is both a hassle and awkward to pronounce. The optimal approach in modern *Han'gŭl* might be to treat sounds like [ɚ] and [ɜɹ] as silent, similar to British English, or use -ㄹ where necessary. If these solutions are unsatisfactory, it may be better to look toward 15th-century *Han'gŭl*, as we will in the upcoming chapter.

(2) Other *R*-like Sounds

The rhotic [ʁ] sound, as found in French or German, sounds like a combination of ㄱ and ㄹ. This sound involves friction deeper in the throat than is seen in ㄱ (i.e., closer to the uvula), sometimes producing a breathy sound akin to ㅎ preceding ㄱ.[94] Due to constraints in modern *Han'gŭl* on using multiple letters together, these sounds need to be written consecutively.

For instance, the [ʁ] sound is approximated as ㅎㄱ in French and ㄱㄹ in German. Although the precise sound may vary, and sometimes ㄹ alone is adequate, it is generally best to write according to the sound produced. Splitting a combined but single sound into two phonemic letters may feel awkward or unsatisfactory, but it is still a necessary compromise.

EXAMPLES	Gabriel (*FR*)	갸ㅂㅎ기엘ㄹ
	Gabriele (*DE*)	가브ㄱ리엘러
	Raphaël (*FR*)	ㄱ하빠엘ㄹ
	Raphael (*DE*)	ㄱ라파엘

The trilled rhotic [r] sound in Spanish and Russian, which may be reminiscent of the double ㄹ (i.e., ㄹㄹ), presents a challenge. While using ㄹㄹ in the word-medial is possible, this notation conflicts with the representation for the English *l*[l] sound at the word-initial. Adding an additional ㅇ before the double ㄹ for the initial [r] could clarify the pronunciation, but this also renders the transcription visually cluttered and more complex to write.

---

[94] The voiced uvular fricative [ʁ] is not an aspirated sound, but depending on the speaker or context, the exhalation produced by moving the back part of the tongue can manifest. This phenomenon also occurs with the voiceless uvular fricative [χ], commonly referred to as the *kh* sound. In French, both [ʁ] and [χ] are often notated as /ʁ/ (or /R/).

In reality, if different sounds and notations do not overlap within each language, universally using ㄹ or ㅇㄹ——essentially not distinguishing between [ɹ] and [r]——should not present a significant problem. Typically, ㄹ in the word-medial or ㅇㄹ at the initials would be utilized to produce the [ɹ] sound in English and the [r] sound in Spanish or Russian. If precise representation of [r] is necessary, it is acceptable to add an extra ㄹ, or for more emphasis, two, three, as many as you see fit.

EXAMPLES	Martina (*ES*)	마ㄹ띠나
	Rodrigo (*ES*)	ㅇ로ㄷ리고 or ㅇㄹ로ㄷ리고
	Александра	알릭싼ㄷ라 or 알릭싼ㄷㄹ라
	Виктор	빅또ㄹ or 빅또ㄹㄹ

§2. *TH* Sounds

As previously noted, the *th*[ð] in *this* or *then* sounds similar to ㄷ, and the *th*[θ] in *thin* or *thumb* resembles ㅆ or ㄸ. However, both [ð] and [θ] combine the characteristics of a tongue sound——where the sound is produced with the tongue's tip——and a tooth sound, characterized by exhaling air through a gap between the upper and lower teeth. Unlike [ʁ], which mixes two serial sounds, [ð] and [θ] should be produced at once as a single sound. No combination of any letters for tongue and tooth sounds makes it easy to produce a consistent sound.

Therefore, the best representation in modern *Han'gŭl* for [ð] is ㄷ, and for [θ], ㄸ or ㅆ. Currently, no alternatives exist.

EXAMPLES	Matthew	매띠유 (*GA*), 매튜 (*RP*)
	Anthony	앤ㄸ니 (*GA*), 앤ㅌ니 (*RP*)
	Elizabeth	을리즈베ㅆ
	Heather	헤더-ㄹ (*GA*), 헤더 (*RP*)

§3. *V* and *F* Sounds

Unlike sounds made by closing and opening both lips (i.e., lip sounds) or exhaling through a gap between the teeth (i.e., tooth sounds), [v] and [f] are created by exhaling air through a gap between the upper teeth and the lower lip. These sounds, sharing properties of lip and tooth sounds in *Han'gŭl*, are challenging to replicate with any letter combination, much like with [ð] and [θ].

As a result, [v] must be denoted as ㅂ and [f] as ㅍ in modern *Han'gŭl*. If ㅂ or ㅍ is followed by ㅣ, inserting the middle sound —— before it can help simulate the mouth shape when the upper teeth meet the lower lip. Placing ㅇ before ㅂ or ㅍ to soften the sound is another option. However, unlike ㄹ, the letter ㅇ does not enhance the sound of ㅂ or ㅍ, and it might even produce a separate sound, which is not ideal. Might 15th-century *Han'gŭl* offer better solutions? Let us move on for now.

EXAMPLES	Vincent	빈쓴ㅌ or 빈쓴ㅌ
	Olivia	올리비어 or 올리븨어
	Jennifer	졔니퍼
	Frank	ㅍ뤵ㅋ (cf. ㅇㅍ뤵ㅋ)

§4. *SH, J, CH,* and *Z* Sounds

Tooth sounds are produced between the upper and lower teeth, and they vary based on the tongue's position and the width of the gap through which air escapes. For instance, if the tongue is moved slightly backward from where the *s*[s] sound is made in words like *scope* or *strike*, the *sh*[ʃ] sound in *sheep* is produced. By further narrowing this gap and expelling breath more forcefully than for [s], the *ts*[t͡s] sound (as in *cats*) emerges. Moving the tongue back slightly from this *ts* position while further narrowing the gap results in the *ch*[t͡ʃ] sound in *cheese*. Similarly, by adjusting the tongue's position slightly back from where the *ds*[d͡z] sound in *birds* occurs, the *j*[d͡ʒ] sound in *jealous* is produced.[95]

However, modern *Han'gŭl* only offers ㅅ for *s*[s] and *sh*[ʃ], ㅈ for *ds*[d͡z] and *j*[d͡ʒ], and ㅊ for *ts*[t͡s] and *ch*[t͡ʃ]. To differentiate *sh, j,* and *ch* from *s, ds,* and *ts,* ㅣ must be added after ㅅ, ㅈ, and ㅊ. If ㅣ already follows ㅅ, ㅈ, or ㅊ, one can either enhance the *sh, j,* or *ch* sound by adding ㅜ before ㅣ (i.e., changing ㅣ to ㅟ) or clarify the *s, ds,* or *ts* sound by inserting ― before ㅣ (i.e., changing ㅣ to ㅢ).

EXAMPLES			
	Sean	셔ㄴ (셔=ㅅ+ㅣ+ㅓ)	(cf. 서ㄴ)
	Joe	죠우 (죠우=ㅈ+ㅣ+ㅗ우)	(cf. 조우)
	Richard	뤼쳐ㄷ (쳐=ㅊ+ㅣ+ㅓ)	(cf. 뤼처ㄷ)
	Jimmy	쥐미	(cf. 즤미)
	Washington	워슁튼	(cf. 워싕튼)
	Churchill	쳐-ㄹ췰	(cf. 쳐-ㄹ췰)

---

[95] The sound [s] is alveolar, and [ʃ] is postalveolar. Similarly, [d͡z] and [t͡s] are alveolar, while [d͡ʒ] and [t͡ʃ] are postalveolar.

A significant challenge occurs when *sh*, *j*, or *ch* precedes a consonant or occurs at the word final. Here, *sh*, *j*, and *ch* typically transition into the next top sound, yet merely using ㅅ, ㅈ, or ㅊ makes it difficult to differentiate the sounds from *s*, *ds*, or *ts*. As a result, to write *sh*, *j*, or *ch* in modern *Han'gŭl*, either preceding a consonant or at the word-final, one must reluctantly use ㅠ or ㅟ, which introduces an unusual middle sound and results in an awkward pronunciation. Could there be a better solution in 15ᵗʰ-century *Han'gŭl*? We will soon find out.

EXAMPLES		
Nash	내쉬 (=내+ㅅ+ㅟ)	(cf. 내ㅅ)
George	죠-ㄹ쥐 (=죠-ㄹ+ㅈ+ㅟ)	(cf. 죠-ㄹㅈ)
Ashton	애슈튼 or 애쉬튼	(cf. 애ㅅ튼)
	(=애+ㅅ+ㅠ/ㅟ+튼)	
Ashley	애슐리 (=애+ㅅ+ㅠ+을+리)	(cf. 애슬리)

Meanwhile, in the production of tooth sounds where the air is expelled through the gap between the upper and lower teeth, ㅈ and ㅊ involve sticking the tongue to the gums to block and then release the breath, whereas ㅅ does not.[96] However, if the vocal cords vibrate while producing the ㅅ sound without the tongue touching the gums, a sound similar to ㅈ emerges, akin to the *z*[z] sound in *zoo*. In modern *Han'gŭl*, the *z* sound cannot be distinctly differentiated. It is typically transcribed by using ㅈ, just like the *ds* sound, or by changing ㅣ to ㅢ when it precedes ㅣ.

EXAMPLES	
Blaze	블레이ㅈ
Hazel	헤이즐
Daisy	데이즤
Rosie	ㅇ로우즤

---

[96] In other words, ㅅ is a fricative, while ㅈ and ㅊ are affricates.

15th-Century *Han'gŭl*

Koreans have used *Han'gŭl* for centuries and have experimented with various orthographies. Although many traditional forms documented over the years were sorted and restricted by the 20th century, numerous records of them are still being passed down and so new discoveries are always being made. However, there is no need to examine all these now. Here, we will focus only on materials from the 15th century, such as *the manual* and other early records, those believed to have been written according to the initial intention and contents of *Han'gŭl*. From here we will identify what might be helpful to you.

Please note that there is no definitive way to confirm how the letters from the 15th-century *Han'gŭl* were pronounced at that time. We can only infer the sounds we recognize today by examining descriptions in *the manual* and the evolution of words with the same meanings across various records. Since actual sounds cannot be verified, scholarly opinions often diverge. Detailed explanations are included in the footnotes, so please refer to them if necessary.

1. 15th-Century Top Letters

The 15th-century top sound letters, no longer in use, are notable for three main features: soft lip sounds, more colorful tooth sounds, and highly functional ㄹ sounds. Moreover, this era saw a greater diversity in the use of *pair letters*, which combine two or three top letters.

§1. Soft Lip Sounds with ○ Below: ㅱ, ㅸ, ㅃ, ㆄ [1]

The manual describes soft lip sounds as being produced by *briefly closing the lips to expel a significant amount of breath*. Unlike sounds created by fully opening and closing the lips, these are made by releasing the breath through a gap between the lips, denoted by attaching ○ below the lip sound letter.

The 15th-century ㅱ sound was likely produced with less lip tension and closure compared to ㅁ, much like the *m* before [f] or [v] in the English *symphony* or the [ɱ] in Spanish *influir*.[2] The ㅸ sound, from the same era, produced with less closure than ㅂ, is thought to have resembled the [β] sound in the second *b* of Spanish *bebé* or the [v] commonly found in English *valve*, French *vous*, and German *was*.[3] The ㅃ sound, also made with less

---

[1] Soft lip sounds are designated by adding 여린 (lit., soft-) before the name (e.g., 여린 미음; soft-ㅁ).

[2] The sound of ㅱ, 여린 미음 (lit., soft-ㅁ), is generally considered a voiced labiodental nasal [ɱ]. Some also occasionally categorize it as a voiced labiodental approximant [ʋ].

[3] ㅸ (여린 비읍; soft-ㅂ) is typically perceived as either a voiced bilabial fricative [β] or a voiced labiodental fricative [v]. In rare instances, it is viewed as a labial-velar approximant [w]. Although some might liken unvoiced ㅂ to [p], leading to comparisons of ㅸ with [f], this book treats unvoiced ㅂ as [b̥], which is a voiceless bilabial plosive, and thus considers ㅸ as [v] (refer to Footnote 4 below and Footnotes 6, 7, and 22 in Chapter I).

closure than ㅃ, probably mirrored the [f] sound in the English *fish*, German *von*, and Spanish *fase*.[4] The ㆄ sound, which appears to have phased out and lost its original sound over time, is believed to have eventually become indistinguishable from the ㅹ sound (i.e., [f]).[5]

Figure II-1. 15th-Century *Han'gŭl* Lip Sounds: ㅱ, ㅸ, ㅹ, ㆄ

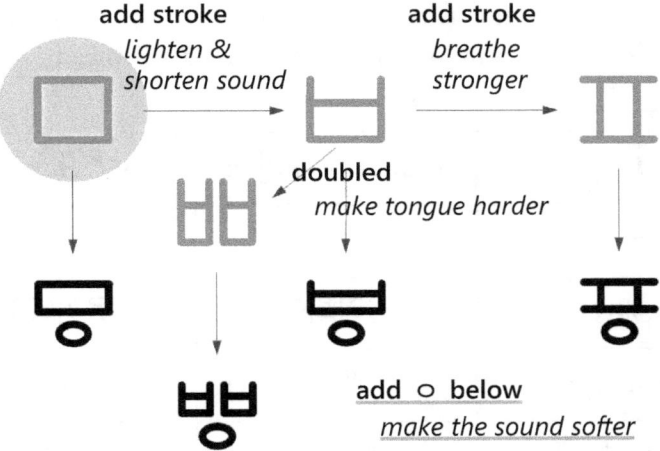

---

[4] ㅹ (여린 쌍비읍; soft-ㅃ) is identified as either a voiceless bilabial fricative [ɸ] or a voiceless labiodental fricative [f]. Although there are instances where voiced ㅃ is likened to [b], suggesting that ㅹ could be viewed as [v], this book defines voiced ㅃ as [ɓ], which is a voiced bilabial plosive, making ㅹ equivalent to [f] (refer to Footnote 3 above and Footnotes 6, 7, and 22 in Chapter I).

[5] ㆄ (여린 피읖; soft-ㅍ) is thought to have been once used for the aspirated voiceless labio-dental fricative [fʰ] and the aspirated voiceless bilabial fricative [ɸʰ], distinguished from [f] and [ɸ], respectively. These aspirated sounds are not currently in use anywhere, in any language, so it's hard to give examples, but [fʰ] can be said to make a harsher breath between the lips slightly apart, which is very similar to [ɸ], whereas [f] utilizes friction between the upper teeth and lower lip. The letter ㆄ has come to be used with ㅹ for denoting [f] and is usually preferred over ㅹ because of its writing convenience and the shape's clarity.

ㅱ	ㅸ	ㅹ / ㆄ
sy**m**phony *á**n**fora*	**v**alve *be**b**é*	**f**ish ***v**on*

EXAMPLES

Below is a comparison of names transcribed using [v] as the 15th-century *Han'gŭl* letter ㅸ and [f] as ㆄ, alongside their modern *Han'gŭl* equivalents. Let's examine how the sounds have evolved.

Name	Modern *Han'gŭl*	15C *Han'gŭl*
Vincent	빈쓴ㅌ	ᄫᅵᆫ쓴ㅌ
Olivia	올리비어	올리ᄫᅵ어
Jennifer	졔니퍼	졔니ᅗᅥ
Frank	ㅍ랭ㅋ	ㆄ랭ㅋ
Cliff	클리ㅍ	클리ㆄ
Faye	페이/풰이	ᅗᅦ이

§2. Tooth Sounds by Tongue Positions: ㅅ, ㅈ, ㅊ, ㅅ, ㅈ, ㅊ,[6] and ㅿ[7]

The king who developed 15th-century *Han'gŭl* and his team of dedicated scholars exerted significant effort to spread the writing system widely. They began by creating a foundational *Han'gŭl manual* and also the phonetics textbook.[8] They extended *Han'gŭl* application through the production of Buddhist scriptures, elementary education resources, and foreign language pronunciation dictionaries.

They used *Han'gŭl* for many purposes, including to differentiate the variety of tooth sounds occurring in Chinese. They crafted a method to denote these sounds based on tongue position. *The upper tooth sound*, produced when the tongue touches the upper teeth or gums, was represented with a longer stroke on the left side.[9] This sound was likely akin to the *s, ds,* and *ts* sounds.[10] Meanwhile, *the lower tooth sound*, produced when the tongue

---

[6] The sequence includes 윗시옷 (upper-ㅅ), 윗지읏 (upper-ㅈ), 윗치읓 (upper-ㅊ), 아래시옷 (lower-ㅅ), 아래지읒 (lower-ㅈ), and 아래치읓 (lower-ㅊ) (refer to Footnotes 9 and 11).

[7] 반시옷 (half-ㅅ).

[8] 四聲通攷사성통고, a phonetics textbook from the mid-15th century, was produced soon after the creation of *Han'gŭl*. *The textbook* elaborates on the content of the Chinese standard sounds book written in 1375 (i.e., 洪武正韻홍무정운). The task of creating this was undertaken by 申叔舟신숙주 (*Shin Suk-ju,* 1417–1475) under royal orders. Although the original text has not survived, 崔世珍최세진 (*Choe Sejin,* 1468–1542) revised the content and wrote a new one in 1517 (i.e., 四聲通解사성통해). The introductory remarks, transferred from the older version, include the notations for Chinese tooth sounds.

[9] Originally named 齒頭音치두음, this sound is described in *the textbook* (refer to Footnote 8) as being produced by *lifting the tongue* (擧舌거설) and *touching the tooth* (點齒 점치). The term *upper tooth sound* is used here to emphasize the position of the tongue.

[10] *The textbook* indicates that *the tongue touches the upper teeth* (refer to Footnotes 8 and 9); however, since Chinese lacks a definite dental sound in modern phonetics, this description likely refers to an alveolar sound, where the tongue contacts the alveolar ridge.

touches the lower teeth or gums, was represented with a longer stroke on the right side[11] and was probably similar to the *sh, j,* and *ch* sounds.[12]

This notation was only utilized to represent certain Chinese pronunciations. For Korean sounds, combining ㅅ, ㅈ, or ㅊ with the appropriate middle sounds was adequate. However, you may use this notation if needed. Notably, the lower tooth sounds prove useful when *sh, j,* and *ch* sounds occur before a consonant or at the word-final by helping to avoid awkward or unusual middle sounds.

The notation for upper and lower tooth sounds was added to the *Han'gŭl* system later and was not widely adopted, though it saw only limited use in specialized fields such as academia, trade, and diplomacy. However, there exists one more letter in the tooth sounds category, one that was created initially and used extensively but is no longer in use today: ㅿ.

The manual suggests that the relationship between ㅿ and ㅅ is akin to the relationship between ㄴ-ㄷ and ㅁ-ㅂ.[13] Thus, ㅿ likely represented a sonorous sound similar to the *z* sound (Figure II-3).[14]

---

[11] Originally named 整齒音정치음, this sound's production is described in *the textbook* (refer to Footnote 8) as involving *rolling the tongue* (卷舌권설) and *touching the mandible* (點顎점악). In the translation here, the focus is on the tongue's position, termed *lower tooth sound* to emphasize its placement.

[12] This sound is accurately a retroflex sound, though some interpretations are also extended to include alveolar-palatal sounds.

[13] ㅿ is the sole *half-tooth sound* letter, yet it is considered within the tooth sound category here. *The manual* groups ㅿ with properties similar to ㄴ, ㅁ, ㄹ, ㅇ, ㆁ, and ㆆ, noting that *(at the bottom position) five sounds form pairs based on their rates, binding slow with fast* (五音之緩急 亦各自爲對), implying that ㆁㄱ, ㄴㄷ, ㅁㅂ, ㅿㅅ, and ㅇㆆ all relate similarly. It is thus suggested that ㅿ has a similar relationship with ㅅ as ㄴ does with ㄷ and ㅁ with ㅂ. This means that ㅿ is a slower closing sound at the bottom than ㅅ, effectively adding resonance to the sound of ㅅ.

[14] The sound of ㅿ is widely believed to have been a voiced alveolar fricative [z], though some scholars also view it as a voiced postalveolar fricative [ʒ].

Figure II-2. 15th-Century *Han'gŭl* Tooth Sounds: ㅅ, ㅈ, ㅊ, ㅅ, ㅈ, and ㅊ[15]

| stretch left | | stretch right |
| move tongue forward | | move tongue backward |

Korean	ㅅ, ㅈ, ㅊ	
	Use without further distinction	
Chinese	ㅅ, ㅈ, ㅊ	ㅅ, ㅈ, ㅊ
	S, DS, TS Sounds	*SH, J, CH Sounds*

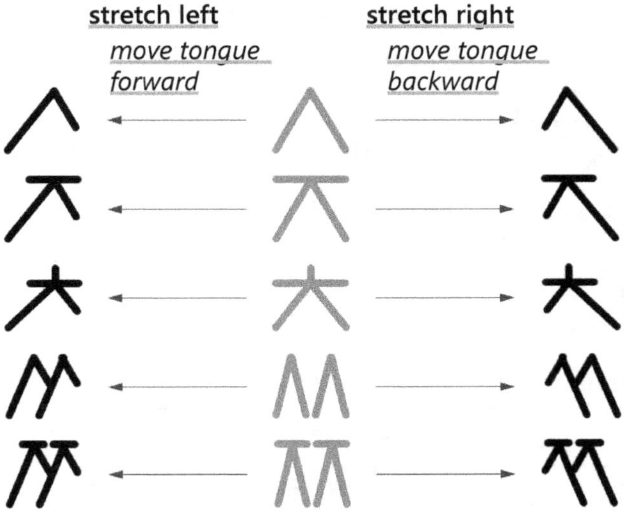

---

[15] 신숙주 asserts in *the textbook* that *In our country, the tooth sounds* ㅅ, ㅈ, *and* ㅊ *are situated between* 치두 (i.e., the dental ridge) *and* 정치 (i.e., the aligned teeth) (我國齒聲 ㅅㅈㅊ在齒頭整齒之間) (refer to Footnotes 8, 9, 11). This statement has various interpretations, but here it is perceived to mean: *In Korean,* ㅅ, ㅈ, *and* ㅊ *are broadly used, without distinction, from alveolar to palatal*. Notably, in the foreword to 東國正韻 동국정운 (*Dong-guk Jeong-un*; lit., the dictionary of Korean standard *Hanja** sounds, 1448, refer to Footnotes 13 in Chapter III), he commented that *Those sounds are not distinguished in our country because they are all naturally integrated* (於我國字音 未可分辨 亦當因其自然), adding that *There is no need to adhere to the 36 phonetic distinctions from old literatures* (何必泥於三十六字乎). Therefore, the term *between* 치두 *and* 정치 suggests *a flexible, non-discriminatory usage in Korean*, not a literal placement between two foreign sounds.

*See Footnote 12 in Chapter III for further information.

EXAMPLES

Below, we compare names using *sh, j,* and *ch* sounds transcribed with the 15th-century *Han'gŭl* lower tooth sounds ㅅ, ㅈ, and ㅊ to their modern spellings. Let's examine how the sounds differ.

Name	Modern *Han'gŭl*	15C *Han'gŭl*
Sean	셔ㄴ	서ㄴ/셔ㄴ
Joe	죠/죠우	조/조우/죠/죠우
Richard	뤼쳐ㄷ	뤼처ㄷ/뤼쳐ㄷ
Jimmy	쥐미	지미
Washington	워슁튼	워싱튼
Churchill	쳐-ㄹ췰	처-ㄹ칠/쳐-ㄹ칠
Nash	내쉬	내ㅅ
George	죠-ㄹ쥐	죠-ㄹㅈ
Ashton	애쉬튼	애ㅅ튼
Ashley	애슐리	애슬리

Figure II-3. 15th-Century *Han'gŭl* Tooth Sound: △

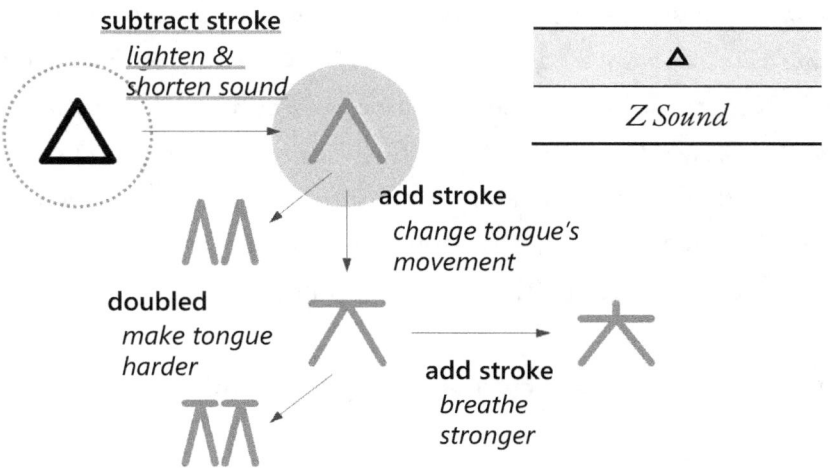

EXAMPLES

Here, we compare names using the *z* sound transcribed with the 15th-century *Han'gŭl* △ to their modern spellings. Let's explore how the sounds have changed.

Name	Modern *Han'gŭl*	15C *Han'gŭl*
Blaze	블레이ㅈ	블레이△
Hazel	헤이즐	헤이슬
Daisy	데이지	데이ㅿ
Rosie	ㅇ로우지	ㅇ로우ㅿ

§3. Tongue Sound Distinguishing *R*: ㆰ [16]

The manual advises: *There is a distinction between hard and soft sounds in* ㄹ, *so if you want to write a soft-*ㄹ *sound, write* ㅇ *below* ㄹ *like a soft lip sound.*[17] Next, the soft-ㄹ sound is described as *briefly attaching the tongue to the upper gums (and then detaching)*, which clearly explains the [ɾ] sound as heard in the *tt* of *better* or *latter*. In contrast to modern *Han'gŭl*, which uses a single ㄹ to represent [ɾ] at the top and [l] at the bottom, 15ᵗʰ-century *Han'gŭl* used ㄹ to denote [l] and ㅭ to distinguish [ɾ].

Figure II-4. 15ᵗʰ-Century *Han'gŭl* Tongue Sound: ㅭ

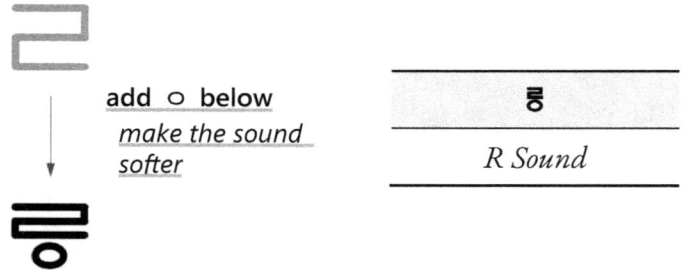

add ○ below
make the sound
softer

ㅭ

R Sound

---

[16] 여린 리을 (soft-ㄹ)

[17] In Middle Chinese phonetics, known at the time, the half-tongue sound (i.e., the onset of 來래) was always the *l* sound only, while the half-tooth sound (i.e., the onset of 日일) had undergone many changes. The half-tooth sound was an alveolo-palatal nasal [ȵ] originally, an alveolar flap [ɾ] from the 9ᵗʰ to the 10ᵗʰ century, and a retroflex flap [ɽ] from the 14ᵗʰ century on (王力; *Wang Li*, 漢語語音史, 中華書局, 2014: p. 163, 224, 458). In this regard, *the manual* explains, *(there are two types of half-tongue sounds, hard and soft, but) the sound classification in old literatures is always one, and there's no inconvenience in people's use without distinction* (然韻書字母唯一, 且國語雖不分輕重, 皆得成音). It shows that the *r* sound [ɾ] was identified in Korea at the time, although it used to occur as a half-tooth sound, as just an allophone of the half-tongue sound ㄹ. Thus, 15ᵗʰ-century *Han'gŭl* only treats soft-ㄹ (i.e., ㅭ) as a notation and does not distinguish it as another letter in alphabet. In addition, the half-tooth sound ㅿ is distinguished in conjunction with ㅅ, not ㄹ (refer to Footnote 14).

Since, in modern *Han'gŭl*, ㄹ can represent both [ɾ] and [l], ㄹㅇ can offer a way to denote other *R*-like sounds instead. For instance, it can represent the [ɹ] in English, as well as the [r] in Spanish and Russian. In addition, using ㄹㅇ can lead to satisfactory results for words in modern *Han'gŭl* that were difficult to transcribe because of *following r* sounds. However, a more suitable alternative is still necessary to represent the [ʁ] sound found in French and German.

EXAMPLES

Below is a comparison of names transcribed using the 15th-century *Han'gŭl* ㄹㅇ to represent *R*-like sounds, alongside their modern spellings. We have also incorporated several other 15th-century letters previously examined. Let's examine how the sounds differ.

Name	Modern *Han'gŭl*	15C *Han'gŭl*
Barbara	바-ㅂ롸	발ㅂ롸
Brandon	ㅂ랜든	ㅂ랜든
Kimberly	킴벌리	킴벓리
Rebecca	ㅇ뤄베카	뤄베카
Robert	ㅇ뤄버ㅌ	뤄벓ㅌ
Ryan	ㅇ라이언	롸이언
Jennifer	제니퍼	제니풔
Frank	ㅍ뢩ㅋ	퐁뢩ㅋ
George	죠-ㄹ쥐	조ㄹㅇㅈ/죯ㅈ
Rosie	ㅇ로우직	로우ㅿㅣ
Martina (*ES*)	마ㄹ띠나	마ㄹㅇ띠나
Rodrigo (*ES*)	ㅇ로ㄷ리고	로ㄷ뢰고
Александра	알릭싼ㄷ라 알릭싼ㄷㄹ라	알릭싼ㄷ롸
Виктор	빅또ㄹ/빅또ㄹㄹ	빅또ㄹㅇ
Верочка	븨에라ㅈ카	븽에롸ㅈ카
Сергей	쎄ㄹ게이	쎄ㄹㅇ게이

§4. Other 15th-Century Letters: ㆁ, ㆆ, ㆅ,[18] and More

15th-century *Han'gŭl* molar sounds consisted of four types of sounds: ㄱ, ㅋ, ㄲ, and ㆁ.[19] ㆁ is produced by blocking the throat with the back of the tongue and then releasing sound through the nose, as in the *ng* in *king* or *song*, or the *n* in *pink* or *bank*, which is commonly called the *ng* sound. Notably, ㆁ does not appear at the top position in Korean, and conversely, ㅇ originally had no sound value at the bottom. Thus, in modern *Han'gŭl*, these two letters are merged into one, i.e., ㅇ.

In English and most European languages, the top sound ㆁ does not exist as it does in Korean. In addition, modern *Han'gŭl* can represent the bottom sound ㆁ with ㅇ, which may render the letter ㆁ seemingly unnecessary. However, the top sound ㆁ is common in several dialects from southeastern China, in Thai, Vietnamese, some Philippine dialects, the Okinawan dialect of Japanese, some African languages including Swahili, and many Austronesian languages of the South Pacific. Understanding this sound could be useful, as it may appear at the top position in names from these regions.

---

[18] 옛이응 (old ㅇ), 여린 히읗 (soft-ㅎ), and 쌍히읗 (double-ㅎ).

[19] In 15th-century *Han'gŭl*, strokes were often added to letters to enhance the sound or add aspiration (e.g., ㄴㄷㅌ, ㅁㅂㅍ, ㅅㅈㅊ, and ㅇㆆㅎ). The sole exception was the molar sound ㆁ (e.g., ㆁㄱㅋ). *The manual* notes that although the production method of the ㆁ sound belongs to the molar sounds, *its sound resembles* ㅇ, *hence ancient texts frequently confuse the two* (而其聲與ㅇ相似，故韻書疑與喩多相混用). In this regard, Chinese phonetics depicted the onset value of 喩유 with sounds like [ɣ], [ʎ], or [j] until the 8th century, converging to [j] by the 9th century. By the 13th century, this value had started to mix with the long-standing [ŋ], the onset of 疑응, resulting in significant changes involving the onsets of 影영 (i.e., [∅], [j], [w]) and 吳우 (i.e., [w]) (*Wang Li, op. cit.*: p. 247, 288, 459–46, refer to Footnote 17). It is inferred that during the 15th century, when *Han'gŭl* was developed, ㆁ (i.e., the onset of 疑응) was considered a molar sound by articulation place and manner, but it was confused with ㅇ (i.e., the onset of 喩유) as *they shared similar sounds and were used interchangeably.*

Figure II-5. 15th-Century *Han'gŭl* Molar Sound: ㆁ

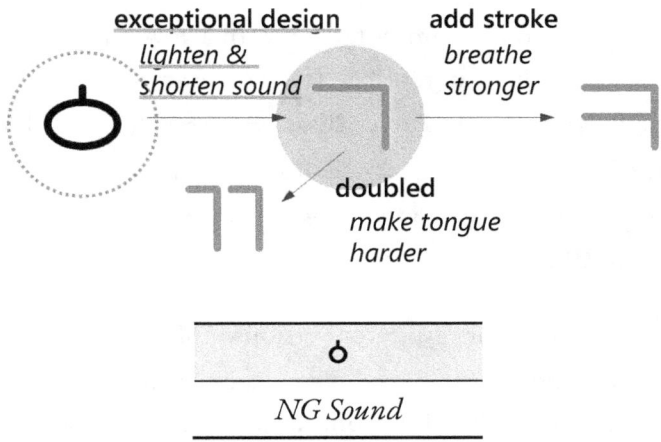

ㆁ

NG Sound

Below, we compare names using the *ng* sound transcribed with the 15th-century *Han'gŭl* ㆁ to their modern spellings. We also incorporate several other previously examined 15th-century letters. Let's see how the sounds have transformed.

Name	Modern *Han'gŭl*	15C *Han'gŭl*
Livingston	리빙ㅅ떤	리빙ㅅ떤
Gabin (*FR*)	갸방	갸방
Léon (*FR*)	레옹	레옹
Veronica Ngo[20] (Ngô Thanh Vân)	버뤄니카 응오 (응오타잉반)	버퉆니카 오 (오 타ㆁ반)
Dustin Nguyen[21] (Nguyễn Xuân Trí)	더ㅅ띤 응우인 (응우인쌰언찌)	더ㅅ띤 우인 (우인 쌰언찌)

---

[20] Vietnamese American Actress: *Star Wars: The Last Jedi* (2017), *The Old Guard* (2020), etc.

[21] Vietnamese American Actor: *Little Fish* (2005), *The Man with the Iron Fist 2* (2015), etc.

The 15th-century throat sound ㆆ, positioned between ㅇ and ㅎ, is likely to have represented the [ʔ] sound, as in **uh-oh**.[22] The ㆆ sound often appears as the top sound in names starting with a vowel and is also prevalent in English dialects where it replaces [t]. For example, *bottle of water* in northern Britain is pronounced precisely as 보어 오 워허. In addition, many speakers in the U.S. and the U.K. render *cat* as 캙 (or 캐ㆆ). In German, the ㆆ sound emphasizes a following vowel when vowels occur consecutively (e.g., *Beamter* as 버함터).

ㆅ is a tensed and more aspirated version of ㅎ.[23] This sound, which is tense and forceful, emanating directly from the throat, closely resembles the [ʔh] sound in the British English pronunciation of **hat**.[24] ㆅ proves helpful for transcribing Arabic sounds. For example, the initial sound of "حرف"

---

[22] In *the manual*, ㆆ is grouped with the throat sounds ㅇ and ㅎ, which involve adding a stroke to letters like ㄴㄷㅌ, ㅁㅂㅍ, and ㅅㅈㅊ. It also states that ㆆ shares similar relationship with ㅇ about closing loosely vs. quickly at the bottom position, as seen in ㆆㄱ, ㄴㄷ, ㅁㅂ, and ㅿㅅ (refer to Footnote 14). As a result, the sound of ㆆ is likely a glottal stop [ʔ], produced by obstructing airflow at the same place of articulation as ㅇ.

[23] *Han'gŭl* typically uses a double letter notation with sounds lacking aspiration and resonance (e.g., ㄱ→ㄲ, ㄷ→ㄸ, ㅂ→ㅃ, ㅅ→ㅆ, ㅈ→ㅉ) However, for throat sounds, ㅎ with aspiration is employed instead of ㆆ (i.e., ㅎ→ㆅ). *The manual* clarifies that, *because the sound of ㆆ is deeper* (ㆆ聲深), *it cannot get tangled* (不爲之凝), and ㅎ *has a shallower sound than* ㆆ (ㅎ比ㆆ聲淺), which allows it to get tangled (for interpretation of 凝ㆁ as *get tangled*, see Footnote 7 in Chapter I). In this regard, the friction in the glottal fricative [h] (i.e., ㅎ) spans a broad area from the glottis to the pharynx, making the articulation place of the glottal stop [ʔ] (i.e., ㆆ) deeper. Moreover, compared to [h], [ʔ] requires more effort or airflow to produce different sounds, suggesting that [ʔ] (i.e., ㆆ), being deeply placed, cannot be used for double letter sounds, hence the substitution of [h] (i.e., ㅎ).

[24] The sound of ㆅ is often viewed as either a voiceless uvular fricative [χ] (or voiceless velar fricative [x]), moving the friction site forward from [h] (i.e., ㅎ), or as a voiceless glottal affricate [ʔh] if it represents the doubled form of ㅎ. This book adopts the [ʔh] perspective for the sound of ㆅ.

(Harf), meaning *letter*, is more forceful than that of "هدف" (hadaf),[25] meaning *goal*, and can be distinguished by using ㆅ.

In addition to currently unused top sound letters, there is ㆀ,[26] and several pair letters. ㆀ does not have its own sound value; it is considered a shorthand for 이+ㅇ.[27] The pair letters noted in *the manual* include ㅶ, ㅼ, ㅴ, and ㅵ, which are thought to represent the consecutive pronunciation of each letter rather than having independent sound values of their own. It seems these examples were meant to show how to write the pair letters rather than to showcase specific usable ones.

Figure II-6. 15th-Century *Han'gŭl* Throat Sounds: ㆆ, ㆅ, ㆀ

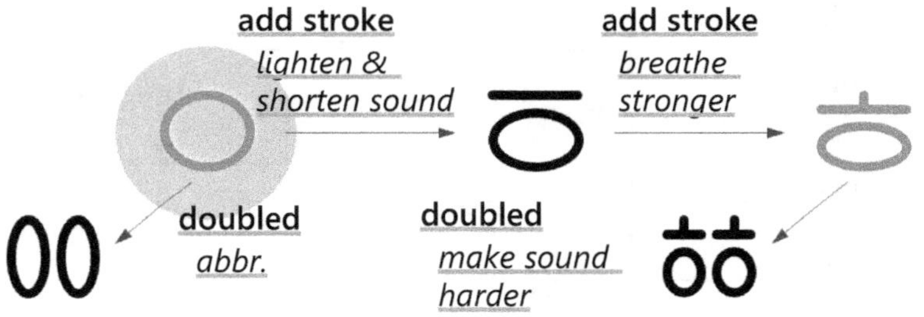

ㆆ	ㆅ	ㆀ
uh-**oh**	**h**at *tres* *Dach*	*abbr.* (이+ㅇ)

[25] The sound is a voiceless pharyngeal fricative [ħ], producing a rougher noise than the glottal fricative [h] (i.e., ㅎ) originating in the glottis.

[26] 쌍이응 (double-ㅇ).

[27] *The manual* explains that 괴여 *means that I love someone* (괴여爲我愛人而), and 괴ᅇᅧ *means someone loves me* (괴ᅇᅧ爲人愛我). Since subsequent records show that ㆀ appears only in passive predicates, it is regarded as a grammatical morpheme. Therefore, the sound of ㆀ is linked with the Korean passive affixes -이/-히/-리/-기, viewed as 이+ㅇ (i.e., 괴ᅇᅧ=괴이여).

EXAMPLES   Below is a comparison of names using the 15th-
century *Han'gŭl* ㆆ and ㆅ alongside their modern
spellings. Several other previously examined 15th-
century letters are also included. Let's see how the
sounds have changed.

Name	Modern *Han'gŭl*	15C *Han'gŭl*
Ann	앤	햔
Elton	엘튼	헬흔
Billy Eilish	빌리 아일리쉬	빌리 하일리ㅅ
Halsey	할씌	할쎄/핧쎄
Holmes	홈ㅈ	홈△/횸△
Muhammad (محمد)	무함마ㄷ	무햠마ㄷ
Haddad (حداد)	할다ㄷ	핳다ㄷ
Hashim (هاشم)	하쉼	하심[28]

---

[28] The top sound here is the glottal fricative [h], corresponding to ㅎ.

2. 15th-Century Mid-letters

§1. Finding the Lost Sky: ·[29]

As mentioned in the previous chapter, · is an essential letter in *Han'gŭl* middle sounds. Most modern *Han'gŭl* scholars focus on identifying this letter's sound in the 15th century. However, a detailed exploration of this debate is not necessary in this book. To effectively transcribe your name, following the explanations given in *the manual* to use · appropriately will be enough. In addition, it might prove more exciting if we could *find the lost sky*.

Let's begin by following *the manual*. According to the guide, the three basic letters of *Han'gŭl* middle sounds are differentiated by the tongue's position. · represents the tongue in its lowest position, — represents the tongue slightly lowered, and | represents the tongue not lowered at all, thus in its highest position.[30] Conveniently, modern *Han'gŭl* | is still clearly positioned where the tongue is raised to its highest and most forward in the mouth (i.e., [i]). The sound of | has remained unchanged over hundreds of years and should not cause confusion in other languages. Therefore, | serves well as a guidepost for *the manual*. Since the explanation for | and · are exactly opposite of each other, let us first assume that the sound of · is made by lowering the tongue as far back and down in the mouth as possible, opposite to |, akin to the [ɑ] sound in American English *hot* or British

---

[29] ·, a.k.a. 아래 아 or 하늘 아 (refer to Footnote 39 in Chapter I).

[30] *The manual* explains that · *results from lowering the tongue, producing a deep sound* (·舌縮而聲深), — *results from slightly lowering the tongue, producing a sound that is neither deep nor shallow* (—舌小縮而聲不深不淺), and | *involves not lowering the tongue, resulting in a shallow sound* (|舌不縮而聲淺). The underlined term 縮죽 in the original text, used to describe the state of the tongue, translates as to reduce, shrink, or draw back (refer to Footnote 42 in Chapter I).

English *palm*. Then, — would be positioned the other back end of the mouth (see Fig. II-7), mixing sounds with · and | by slightly lowering the tongue from the position of | .[31]

Figure II-7. Assuming · with — and |

(1) **15C *manual* describes three basic elements of *Han'gŭl* middle sound, as shown below:**

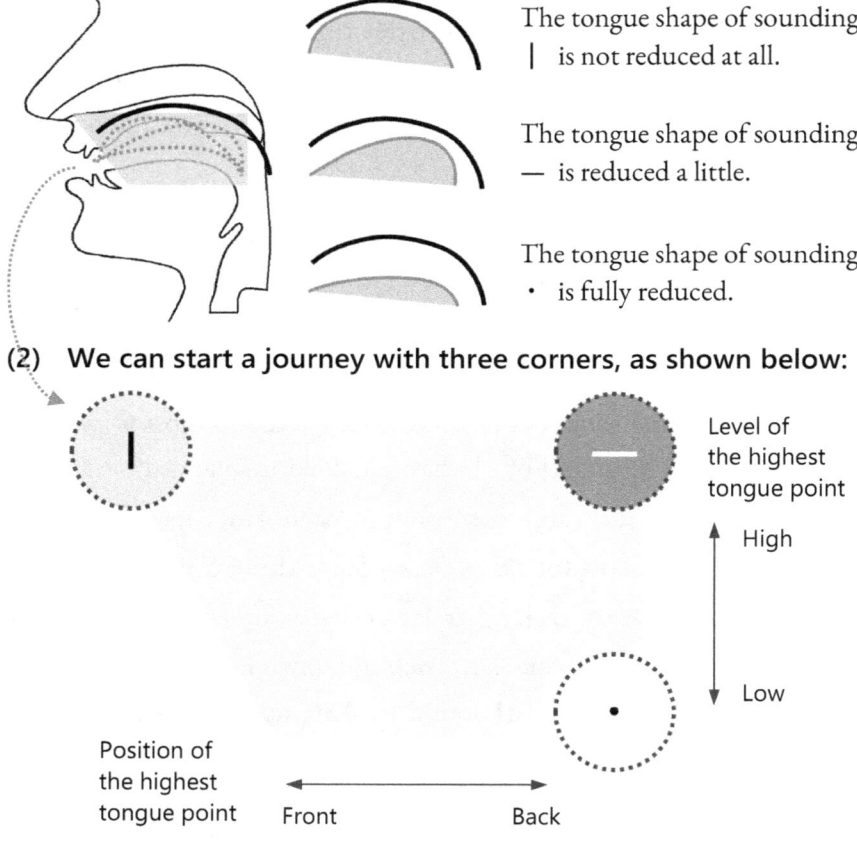

The tongue shape of sounding | is not reduced at all.

The tongue shape of sounding — is reduced a little.

The tongue shape of sounding · is fully reduced.

(2) **We can start a journey with three corners, as shown below:**

| | | — | Level of the highest tongue point

High

Low

Position of the highest tongue point   Front   Back

---

[31] When considering the curvature of the mouth and the three-dimensional shape of the tongue, a slight lowering of the front part of the tongue in a high front vowel, results in a high back vowel. Therefore, the high back unrounded vowel [ɯ] also fits the description of *a slightly lowered sound*. Observing the sound's depth along the curve from the mouth front to the throat along the upper surface of the tongue, [ɯ] qualifies as a sound that is *neither deep nor shallow*.

Now, let's differentiate the other middle sounds in *Han'gŭl* based on the definitive positions of ｜ and the assumed positions of ・ and —. According to *the manual*, ⊥ is pronounced by rounding and closing the mouth more than ・, symbolizing the meeting of *the sky* (・) and *the earth* (—).[32] We differentiate ⊥ by raising the tongue and narrowing the mouth in a rounded shape, as if *the sky* is approaching *the earth*.[33] *The manual* also describes ├ as being pronounced by opening the mouth more than ・, resembling the combination of ｜ and ・, signifying *the sky* and *the earth* waiting for *the human* (｜).[34] Thus, as if *the sky* is welcoming *the human*, we open the mouth further to distinguish ├.[35]

---

[32] *The manual* says ⊥ *is the same as* ・ *but with pursed lips* (⊥與・同而口蹙), *its shape results from combining* ・ *and* — (其形則・與—合而成), and *it embodies the will of the first meeting between the sky and the earth* (取天地初交之義也). Here, being *the same as* ・ suggests a positive attribute (refer to Figure I-10), and the underlined term 蹙축, meaning narrow or lessen, implies that *pursed lips* (口蹙구축) conveys rounding the lips and elevating the tongue to narrow the oral cavity.

[33] Since ・ comes first in the letter shape descriptions, it acts as the principal of action, thus translated as ・ *approaches* —. In the vowel quadrangle, the middle sound that results as ・ *approaches* — is either the low-mid back rounded vowel [ɔ] or the high-mid back rounded vowel [o].

[34] *The manual* explains that ├ *is the same as* ・ *but with an open mouth* (├與・同而口張), *its form is created by combining* ｜ *and* ・ (其形則｜與・合而成), and *it embodies the action of the sky and the earth on the material world, completed as the human arrives* (取天地之用發於事物待人而成也). Similar to the case with ⊥, being *the same as* ・ implies a positive attribute (refer to Figure I-10). The underlined term 張장 means to widen or enlarge, and given that the tongue is already at its lowest in ・, the phrase *open mouth* (口張구장) indicates that the mouth widens laterally while the tongue moves closer to the front of the mouth.

[35] Since ｜ comes first in the letter shape descriptions, it is regarded as the principal of action. However, as the letter implies *awaiting the human to complete it*, the translation is ・ *welcomes* ｜. In the vowel quadrangle, the sound produced as ・ *takes a step toward* ｜ is either the near-low central vowel [ɐ] or the low central unrounded vowel [ä].

Figure II-8. Blending to Pick out ⊥ and ┠

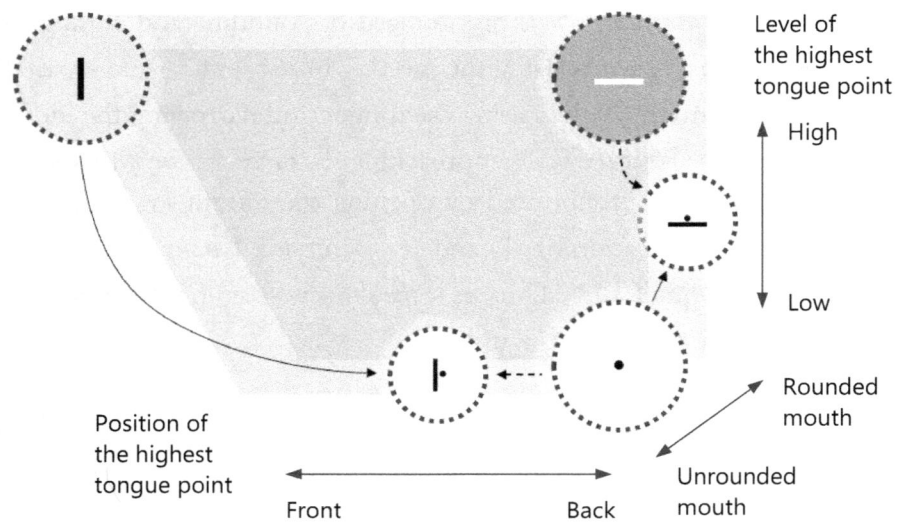

⊥ and ┠ share attributes with *the sky*. Now, we turn to the sounds that share attributes with *the earth*. *The manual* explains that ㅜ is pronounced by rounding and closing the mouth more than —, resembling the combination of — and ·, representing the meeting of *the sky* and *the earth* (like ⊥).[36] We distinguish ㅜ by rounding the lips and narrowing the mouth, as if *the earth* (—) is embracing *the sky* (·).[37] Furthermore, *the manual* states that ┤ is pronounced by opening the mouth more than —,

---

[36] *The manual* describes that ㅜ *is akin to* — *but involves pursed lips* (ㅜ與—同 而口蹙), and *its form is created by merging* — *and* · (其形則—與·合而成). *The manual also says it similarly encapsulates the will of the first meeting between the sky and the earth* (亦取天地初交之義也). The statement *akin to* — signifies a sound attribute (refer to Figure I-10), and *pursed lips* (口蹙구축) implies adding rounded-ness to the already elevated tongue position in — (refer to Footnote 32).

[37] Since — is mentioned first in the description of the letter shape, it is viewed as the principal of action. However, as the ground cannot move, the translation adopted is — *stays in its place while enclosing* ·. In the vowel quadrangle, when rounding the lips from the position of —, the sound produced, which is closer to — than to ⊥, is the high back rounded vowel [u].

resembling the combination of · and ｜, indicating *the sky* and *the earth* waiting for *the human* (like ㅏ).[38] Therefore, as if *the sky* is moving toward *the human* (｜) while closer to *the earth*, we open the mouth and raise the tongue to distinguish ㅓ.[39]

Figure II-9. Blending to Pick out ㅜ and ㅓ

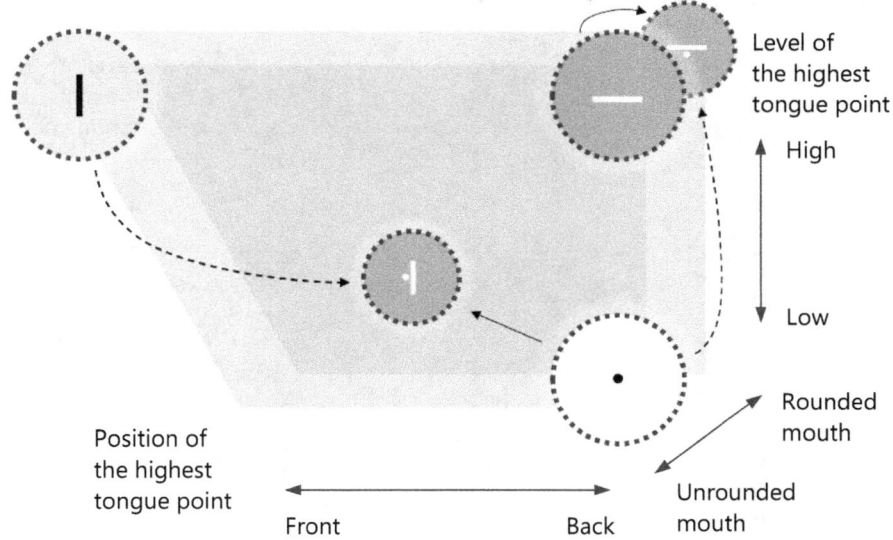

---

[38] *The manual* explains that ㅓ *is similar to* — *but with an open mouth* (ㅓ與—同 而口張), and *its form results from combining* · *with* ｜ (其形則·與｜合而成), also mentioning, *it embodies the action of the sky and the earth on the material world, completed as the human arrives* (亦取天地之用發於事物待人而成也). Being *similar to* —, as with ㅜ, denotes a sound attribute that is negative (refer to Figure I-10), and *with an open mouth* (口張구장) suggests lowering the tongue or moving it closer to the mouth front than when pronouncing — (refer to Footnote 34).

[39] Since · is first in the letter shape description, it is considered the principal of action. The letter's meaning, *awaiting the human to complete it*, leads to the translation · *moves forward to greet* ｜, *advancing slightly closer to* —. In the vowel quadrangle, *the movement of* · *toward* ｜, *which is closer to* — *than to* ㅏ, results in the sound of a mid-central vowel [ə] or a low-mid central unrounded vowel [ɜ].

These sounds are directly created by ᆞ. Now, let's compare how they are represented by letters in modern *Han'gŭl*. The following illustration (Figure II-10) considers —, ㅣ, ㅗ, ㅏ, ㅜ, and ㅓ, taking into account the standard Korean language and dialects and the rules applied when transcribing foreign languages into modern *Han'gŭl*.

Figure II-10. Matching with Modern Sounds

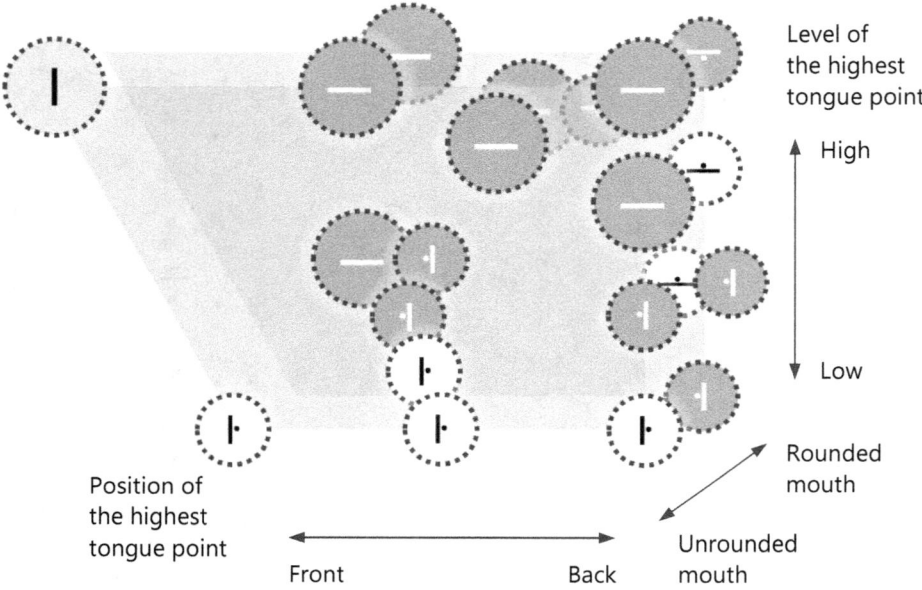

The bottom right corner that was assumed to be the place of ᆞ is occupied by ㅏ, and encircled by ㅓ. You can also see where ㅓ overlaps with ㅗ, ㅓ with —, and — with ㅜ. The —, thought to be at the top right, reaches down to the center, covering a broad area. Notably, the range of sounds marked by ㅓ appears extensive.

The · sound was not naturally unused; rather, it was unexpectedly prohibited by law despite active use. Since *Han'gŭl* allocates sounds generated by human speech organs to a limited number of alphabet letters, no sound can disappear or be lost even if the letter carrying it is no longer used, though its boundaries may blur. Consequently, another letter likely now represents the sound · was meant to depict. However, even so, drastically changing the usage of letters is challenging, and the modern *Han'gŭl* in use today must also be considered. Referring to the illustration above, let's properly tune up those sounds so that they can be used together with previous allocations, as follows:

Figure II-11. Fine-tuning with *The Sky* · [40]

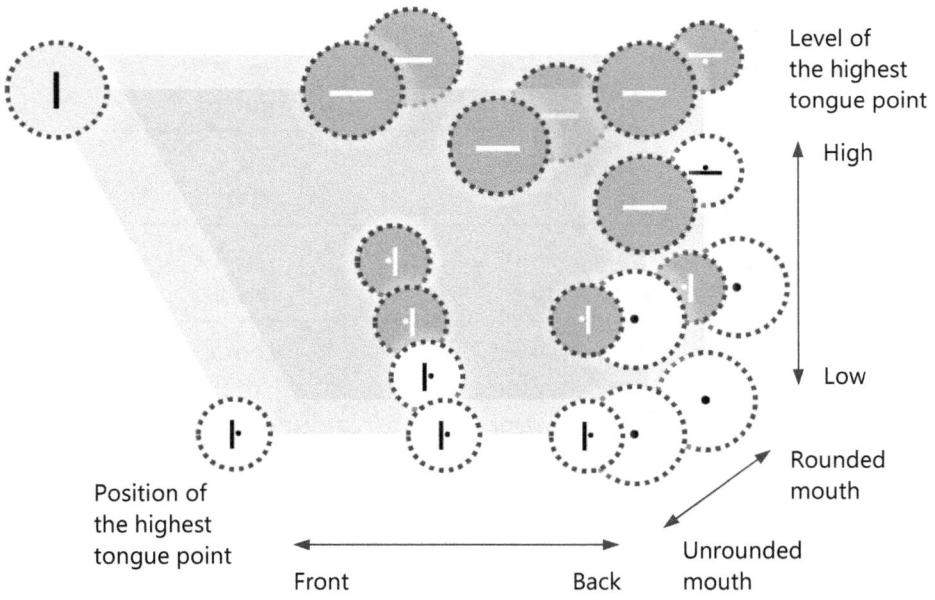

---

[40] Historical transformations have shown · changing to —, ㅓ, or ㅏ over the centuries. This suggests that · came in contact with all these letters. As a result, the range is broadened to include the low-mid back vowel, both unrounded [ʌ] and rounded [ɔ], for use in combination with ·.

Table II-1. Modern *Han'gŭl* vs. 15C *Han'gŭl* (revised)

Mid-sound Letter	Modern *Han'gŭl*	15C *Han'gŭl* (*revised*)
•	-	**awe**some hurry north start
—	hook push	hook push
ㅣ	free	free
ㅗ	north boat *oder*	boat *oder* (north)
ㅏ	cow start	cow (start)
ㅜ	boot food	boot food
ㅓ	about **awe**some hurry the	about the (**awe**some) (hurry)

Here is a recap of the differences based on the previous chapter's content, which organized examples of middle sounds in *Han'gŭl* by language:

Table II-2. 15C *Han'gŭl* Mid-Sounds (revised): ·, ⊥, ㅏ, ㅓ

Han'gŭl (Korean)	· (-)		⊥ ([o])		ㅏ ([ɑ], [ɐ], [ä])		ㅓ ([ʌ], [ɔ], [ə], [ɤ])	
Transcription into Korean	-		[o], [ɔ], [w]		[a], [ɑ]		[ʌ], [ə]	
15C *Han'gŭl* (revised)	[ɑ], [ɔ], [ʌ]		[o]		[ɐ], [ä], [a], ([ɑ])		[ə], [ɜ], ([ɔ], [ʌ]) *[ɤ]: —	
English	cop start hurry **a**wesome force north	[ɑ] [ɑ] [ʌ] [ɔ] [ɔ] [ɔ]	boat note force north	[o] [o(ʊ)] [ɔ] [ɔ]	cow gauss hire cop start	[a] [a] [a(ɪ)] [ɑ] [ɑ]	bird nurse about history serious the hurry **a**wesome	[ɜ] [ɜ] [ə] [ə] [ə] [ə] [ʌ] [ə]
French	glas homme notre rhum sort	[ɑ] [ɔ] [ɔ] [ɔ] [ɔ]	haut nôtre réseau sot	[o] [o] [o] [o]	patte femme glas	[a] [a] [a]	homme notre rhum sort	[ɔ] [ɔ] [ɔ] [ɔ]
German	kommen Stalken	[ɔ] [ɔ]	Boot oder	[o] [o]	das Speyer Staat	[a] [a] [a]	Beschlag Hose immer kommen Stalken	[ə] [ə] [ɐ] [ɔ] [ɔ]
Spanish	-		sol todo	[o] [o]	mal rata	[a] [a]	-	-
Russian	палка	[ɑ]	облако радио	[o] [o]	палка какой палка	[a] [ɐ] [a]	облако собирать	[ə] [ə]

In most languages, vowels typically have more ambiguous boundaries than consonants. There is more overlap and mixing than in cases like the *c* sounds in English *cut* and Spanish *casa*, distinguished as ㅋ and ㄲ.[41] Therefore, trying to strictly define the notation for middle sounds is impractical. Furthermore, if you must identify every sound's phonetic symbol whenever needed and then translate it into *Han'gŭl*, it will be very inconvenient. Therefore, when using those mid-sound letters, this level of approach is recommended, as follows:

A. ㅏ opens the mouth wider than ㆍ, and ㆍ opens the mouth wider than ㅗ.

B. ㅓ opens the mouth wider than ㅡ, and ㅡ opens the mouth wider than ㅜ.

C. ㅓ positions the tongue higher than ㅏ, and ㅜ positions the tongue higher than ㅗ (or slightly puckers the mouth).

These guidelines are all from *the manual*. If they seem unclear, feel free to use them as you see fit. You can always make changes later if people——who already know the basics of *Han'gŭl*——do not respond well to the sounds represented by your writing. Upon closer inspection, many sounds could be represented by ㆍ. Labeling those as ㅗ can seem too constricted, as ㅏ too open, and as ㅓ slightly constrained——there are ambiguous sounds that fit neither ㅗ, ㅏ, nor ㅓ. What could these be?

---

[41] Given the variability in vowel splits or mergers across different regions, the boundaries of middle sounds are expected to be more indistinct and unclear (e.g., trap-bath split, cot-caught merger, etc.).

EXAMPLES

Below is a comparison of names written using the 15th-century *Han'gŭl* · and their modern equivalents. Several other 15th-century letters are also used. Let's examine how the sounds differ.

Name	Modern *Han'gŭl*	15C *Han'gŭl*
Austin	오ㅅ띤	ㅇㅅ띤
Jacob	제이컵	제이컵
Jacob (*FR*)	쟈껍	자껍
Jacobo (*ES*)	하꼬보	하꼬ᄫᅩ
Jakob (*DE*)	야콥	야콥
Paul (*GA*)	퍼얼	풀
Paul (*RP*)	포올	ㅍ올
Paul (*FR*)	뽈	뽈
Robert	ㅇ뤄버ㅌ	ㄹ벌ㅌ
Thomas	타머ㅅ	투머ㅅ
Tom Cruise	탐 ㅋ루ㅅ	톰 ㅋ루ㅿ

§2. Rebuilding a Castle: ·ㅣ, ㅚ, ㅠ, ㅛㅑ, ㅠㅕ, ㅙ, ㅞ, !, and _ᴵ [42]

The 15ᵗʰ-century *Han'gŭl* middle sounds are differentiated first by eleven letters[43] and the various compound letters they form. Initially, the compounds shown in *the manual* are created with a latter- ㅣ , namely ·ㅣ, ㅓㅣ, ㅗㅣ, ㅐ, ㅜㅣ, ㅔ, ㅛㅣ, ㅐ, ㅠㅣ, and ㅖ, and four are made by combining letters of similar attributes, like so: ㅘ, ㅝ, ㅛㅑ, and ㅠㅕ. In addition, ㅙ, ㅞ, ㅙ, and ㅞ are formed with a latter- ㅣ , and separately, there is also ! and _ᴵ. Now, we reach a crucial question: since some letters are not used in modern *Han'gŭl*, how on earth are these crowded sounds supposed to be pronounced?

Today in Korea, there is a straightforward method for pronouncing these 15ᵗʰ-century *Han'gŭl* letters: sequentially. The method says, for instance, ㅐ was pronounced as, so to speak, ㅏ어 (i.e., ㅏ+ㅣ), and ㅔ as ㅓ어 (i.e., ㅓ+ㅣ) in the 15ᵗʰ century.[44] This allows all letters to be pronounced directly, making pronunciation both very easy and convenient.

---

[42] Naming these characters in line with other *Han'gŭl* middle sounds yields the following: 위, 외, 위, 야, 워, 왜, 웨, 오!, and 으ᴵ. The method of reading these characters is the focus of this chapter.

[43] *The manual* specifies that *there are eleven middle sounds* (中聲凡十一字): namely, ·, ㅡ, ㅣ, ㅗ, ㅏ, ㅜ, ㅓ, ㅛ, ㅑ, ㅠ, and ㅕ. It states that *all other middles are combinations of these*. The inclusion of ㅛ, ㅑ, ㅠ, and ㅕ among this *eleven* reflects a historical understanding of middle sounds at the time as distinct from the contemporary phonetic classification of monophthong and diphthong vowels.

[44] This is a 1940s hypothesis which posits that the *Han'gŭl* mid-letters ㅐ and ㅔ were originally pronounced as ㅏ어[aj] and ㅓ어[əj] in the 15ᵗʰ century, and that the vowel shortening (or fronting) to [ɛ] and [e] occurred later, respectively. Scholars who support this theory argue that the changes in ㅓ from [e] and [ə] to just [ə], and ㅔ from [əj] to [e], happened concurrently at some point between the 15ᵗʰ and 19ᵗʰ centuries. However, a Korean grammar book written by European missionaries in the late 19ᵗʰ century describes the sequential reading of ㅣ-based ligatures (see Footnotes 42 and 44 in Chapter III). This documentation suggests that these changes either rapidly occurred in the 20ᵗʰ century, or evolved from the comprehensive regional

However, recommending this approach to you here is inappropriate because, in modern *Han'gŭl*, letters such as ㅚ, ㅐ, ㅟ, ㅔ, ㅒ, and ㅖ are pronounced differently with it. As a result, it's challenging to specify how to pronounce letters like ㅙ or ㅞ. Should the sound for ㅚ be ㅗ+ㅣ or ㅣ+ㅗ? Moreover, using this method, ㅞ and ㅙ would become unusual and excessive combinations, forming *quadruple* or *quintuple* vowels like ㅣ우이어[jujə] or ㅣ우이어이[jujəj], which need to be pronounced at once. Is this really correct?

Further consideration generates even more questions. If ㅔ was pronounced as ㅓㅣ in the 15th century, then *Han'gŭl* at the time would not be able to distinguish the sound of *e*[e] in *dress* from *a*[ə] in *about*, though the sounds had long been notably differentiated in ancient and middle Chinese.[45] Given that *Han'gŭl* was also updated with consideration of Chinese tooth sounds, why weren't these sounds differentiated? Besides, using this method would mean that ㅛ should resemble the same sound as ㅗ. Why, then, add a dot to ㅗ, ㅏ, ㅜ, or ㅓ to create ㅛ, ㅑ, ㅠ, or ㅕ?

Just a list of examples of consecutive pronunciation would have offered a simple and straightforward explanation, but oddly, *the manual* specifically counts and presents the number of compound letters as exact numbers, such as *ten* or *fourteen*.[46] What meaning was intended by these numbers? In

---

phoneme system of 15th-century *Han'gŭl* into relatively simplified Korean phonemes over the centuries under sequential reading. Or possibly, they have been coexistent since their introduction.

[45] Although the interpretation by scholars* differs slightly due to periods and character types, there is an unchanged consensus that ancient and middle Chinese distinctly categorized front vowels [e] (or [ɛ], [æ]) and back vowels [ə] (or [ɔ]). These vowels are commonly found in *finals* (韻母운모), often involving a *medial* (介音개음) or *coda* (韻尾운미) [i] (or [j]), such as in the forms [ie], [ei], or [iei].

*Such as, *W. H. Baxter, L. Sagart, B. Karlgren,* 鄭張尚芳 (*Zhengzhang Shangfang*), 李方桂 (*Li Fang-Kuei*), 王力 (*Wang Li*), etc.

[46] *The manual* counts the number of letters six times. Initially, it acknowledges that *Han'gŭl* alphabet comprises 28 letters, with 17 as top and bottom sounds and 11 as middles. *The manual* also notes ten ligatures of one-letter mid-sounds with a latter-ㅣ,

addition, why weren't letters like ！ and ｣ included in the count? The reason for carefully presenting peculiar sounds, like those in ㅞ and ㅙ as letters is also unclear. If the method were just about sequential pronunciation, wouldn't examples like ㅗㅏ[ao] or ㅓㅜ[əʊ] have been more appropriate? While this method is easy and convenient, disappointingly, it fails to adequately explain various aspects of *the manual*.

Moreover, the linguistic environment around 15th-century Korea differed from this book's contemporary context. Languages like Mongolian, Sanskrit, and Chinese interacted with Korean at the time.[47] Today, this book includes languages such as English, French, German, Spanish, and Russian. This discrepancy shows why it's necessary to research a simple way of pronouncing various mid-letters without contradicting *the manual*. So, let's delve deeper into *the manual*.

The manual describes the sounds of ·, ㅡ, and ㅣ as based on tongue position, and the sounds of ㅗ, ㅏ, ㅜ, and ㅓ as based on mouth shape.[48] It goes on to explain that, ㅛ *starts with* ㅣ *and is the same as* ㅗ, which implies that the mouth shape is like ㅗ, and the tongue moves from ㅣ (to ㅗ).[49] Pronouncing ㅛ as described accurately yields the familiar sound of [jo] in *yogurt*. Similarly, the mouth shape of ㅑ is like ㅏ, ㅠ like ㅜ, and ㅕ like ㅓ, all beginning from the tongue's position at ㅣ.

---

four of two-letter mid-sounds with a latter- ㅣ, and explicitly states that there are 14 ligatures of mid-sounds using a latter- ㅣ. The combinations of ㅣ with · and ㅡ, represented by ！ and ｣, are not counted separately.

[47] Through diplomacy and trade, Manchu, Japanese, and many other languages would have been known, but Mongolian, Sanskrit, and Chinese were probably the only languages whose phonetic systems could be examined together in the creation of *Han'gŭl*.

[48] Refer to §1 and Footnotes 30 and 32–39.

[49] The original text states that ㅛ *is identical to* ㅗ *and arises from* ㅣ (ㅛ與ㅗ同而 起於ㅣ). Here, the underlined term 起기, which generally means arise, originate, and generate, translates as *starts (from* ㅣ).

Figure II-12. Combining with Former- | : ㅛ, ㅑ, ㅠ, ㅕ

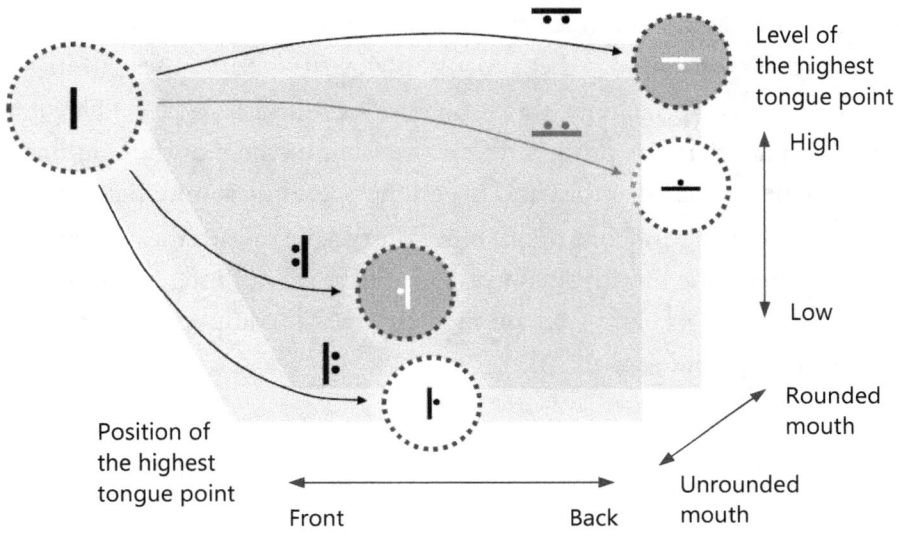

Compound Letter	Former	Latter	Mouth's Shape	Tongue's Position
ㅛ	|	ㅗ	ㅗ	Change from | to ㅗ
ㅑ	|	ㅏ	ㅏ	Change from | to ㅏ
ㅠ	|	ㅜ	ㅜ	Change from | to ㅜ
ㅕ	|	ㅓ	ㅓ	Change from | to ㅓ

Next, we will explore the compound letters with an added latter- | . Unlike ㅛ, ㅑ, ㅠ, and ㅕ, in these compounds, | attaches directly behind each letter, showing a different method of letter formation, and therefore, suggesting a different method of pronunciation. *The manual* also notes that *the sound of* | *is shallow,*[50] rendering it suitable for following various other sounds.

---

[50] The original reads: *(| makes) the tongue stretch and the sound shallow* (舌展聲淺而), *so it facilitates the mouth to open* (便於開口也). For the expression *the sound shallow*, refer to Footnote 30.

The manual repeatedly emphasizes the role of *the human* in speech production and the usage of ㅣ throughout the text.[51] It may be that ㅣ plays a more significant role or function in compound letters than just producing its own sound.[52] Let's focus on why *the manual* uses ㅣ in various compounds. Specifically, this is because its sound is *shallow*. This term *shallow* implies that it is produced near the front of the mouth. Could it be that ㅣ, when attached at the back, makes the preceding sound shallower? To create a shallower sound, one might move the tongue toward the mouth front or slightly open the mouth sideways. From this, we can infer the sounds of ·ㅣ, ㅡㅣ, ㅗㅣ, ㅐ, ㅜㅣ, and ㅔ among the *ten* ㅣ-compounds previously mentioned, as follows:

---

[51] *The manual* states that the character 人인, meaning *the human*, refers to both the letter ㅣ and the mid-sounds themselves. Important excerpts include: *Mid-sounds transmit what the top creates to the bottom for completion, a process akin to what the human acts* (中聲承初之生接終之成, 人之事也), ㅛ, ㅑ, ㅠ, *and* ㅕ *all encompass the human because humans are deemed the spirits capable of engaging in both celestial and terrestrial duties* (ㅛㅑㅠㅕ之皆兼乎人者 以人爲萬物之靈而能參兩儀也), *(In the way that* ㅣ *follows every sound,) one sees the human engaging and assisting in worldly matters, ensuring no place remains unconnected* (亦可見人之參贊開物而無所不通也), *(In the mid-sounds,)* ㅣ *is the most utilized, accompanying all fourteen sounds* (侵之爲用最居多, 於十四聲偏相隨), etc.

[52] The 15th century was a time when the remnants of the Mongolian language across Northeast Asia, as well as concerted efforts of Chinese language norms to shift away from it, were prominent. This period likely saw considerable changes in the Korean language, as well. *The manual* shows attempt to incorporate phonetic principles that reflect changes over time into *Han'gŭl*, extending beyond mere pronunciation documentation. The extensive current use of ㅣ in Korean, for subject marking particles or noun derivation suffixes, and its robust presence in all eras of Chinese as a coda [i], highlight the pivotal role of ㅣ in *Han'gŭl*. Even if the hypothesis of a so-called *Koreanic i-umlaut* developing from the 15th to 19th centuries is correct (refer to Footnote 44), the distinct use of ㅣ in *Han'gŭl* becomes even more significant. If we try to use the 15th-century *Han'gŭl* again now, we should focus not only on the sound of ㅣ but also on its functional or role-specific aspects.

Figure II-13. Blending with Latter- ㅣ : ·ㅣ, ㅡㅣ, ㅗㅣ, ㅐ, ㅜㅣ, ㅔ

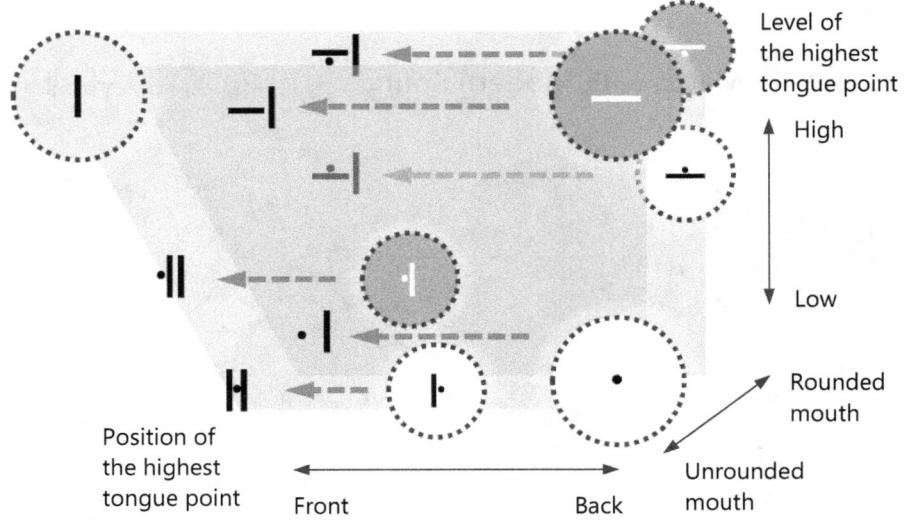

Compound Letter	Former	Latter	Mouth's Shape	Tongue's Position
·ㅣ	·	ㅣ	*default*	Move forward from ·
ㅡㅣ	ㅡ	ㅣ	*default*	Move forward from ㅡ
ㅗㅣ	ㅗ	ㅣ	ㅗ	Move forward from ㅗ
ㅐ	ㅏ	ㅣ	ㅏ	Move forward from ㅏ
ㅜㅣ	ㅜ	ㅣ	ㅜ	Move forward from ㅜ
ㅔ	ㅓ	ㅣ	ㅓ	Move forward from ㅓ

Excluding ·|, representations for other sounds in modern *Han'gŭl* generally appear within the expected range. However, since · and ·| are no longer used, ㅚ appears in their places and is adjusted for use alongside ·|.

Figure II-14. Match with Modern Sounds: ·|, ㅢ, ㅚ, ㅐ, ㅟ, ㅔ

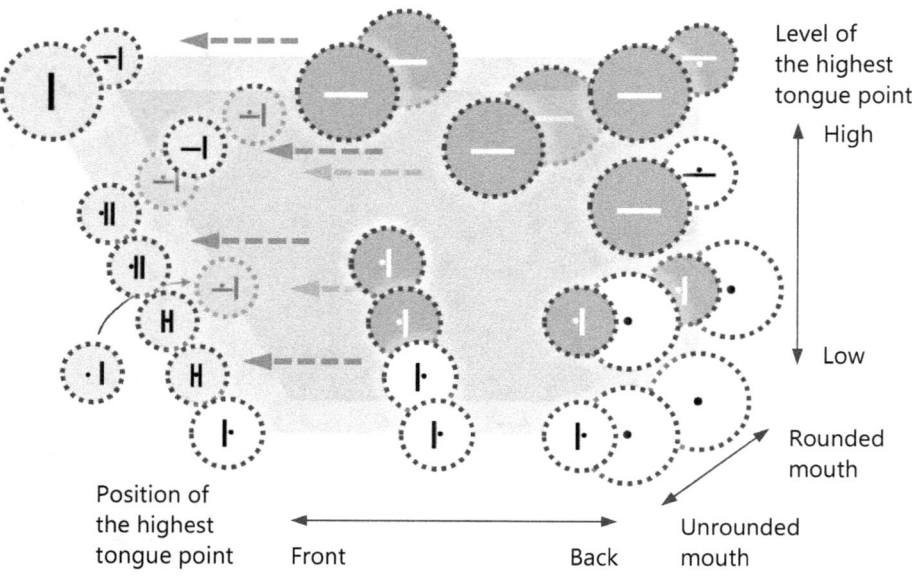

We have organized the monophthongs found in the 15th-century *Han'gŭl* mid-sounds, including *the sky* (·), which we've found again, and its compound (·|).

Figure II-15. 15C *Han'gŭl* Mid-Sounds (revised): Monophthong

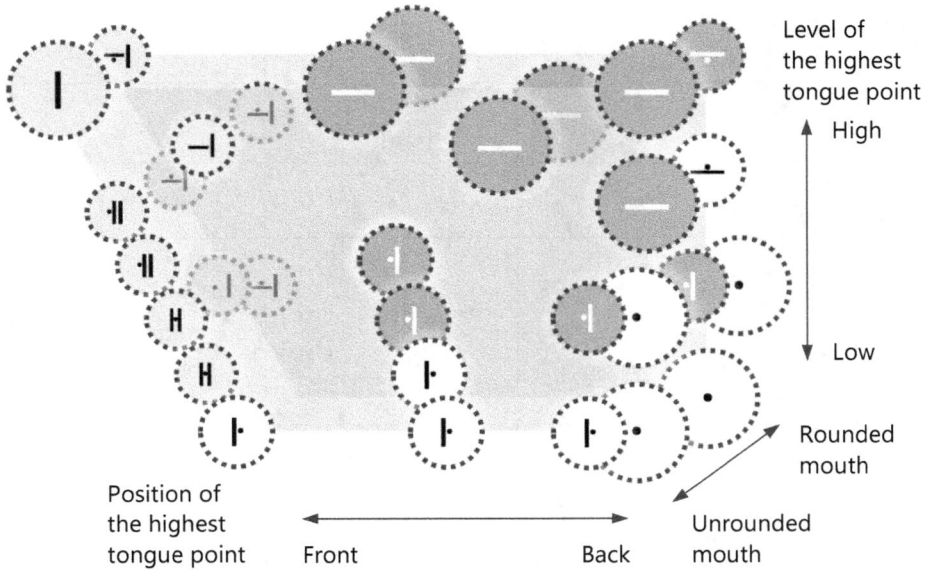

Mid-Sound Letter	Modern *Han'gŭl*	15C *Han'gŭl* (revised)
ㅚ	*ceux* *Köln* (**wea**pon)	*ceux* *(Köln)* (**wea**pon)
·ㅣ	-	*Köln*

Table II-3. 15C *Han'gŭl* Mid-Sounds (revised): ·|, ⏊, ᅦ

Han'gŭl (Korean)	·| (-)	⏊ ([ø], [ø], [we])	ᅦ ([e])
Transcription into Korean	-	[ø], [œ] *[we]: ⏊ᅦ	[e], [ɛ]
15C *Han'gŭl* (revised)	[œ]	[ø], [ø], [we], ([œ])	[e], [ɛ]
English	-	-	weapon [we] wedge [we]	dress [e] May [e] bake [e(ɪ)] bed [ɛ] pet [ɛ]
French	feuille [œ] jeune [œ] sœur [œ]	ceux [ø] jeûne [ø] feuille [œ]	été [e] fée [e] jeune [œ] sœur [œ]
German	Köln [œ] öffnen [œ]	Möhre [ø] schön [ø] Köln [œ] öffnen [œ]	Element [e]
Spanish	-	-	-	-	beso [e] guerra [e] pique [e]
Russian	-	-	-	-	жест [ɛ] этап [ɛ] этот [ɛ]

Now, let's examine the compound letters formed by adding | after the sounds ⏊, ᅣ, ㅠ, and ᅧ. For instance, ᅢ results from combining ᅣ and | (i.e., ᅣ + |). If | makes *the sound of* ᅣ shallower, it acts to make *the sound whose mouth shape is like* ᅣ *and whose tongue moves from* | *to* ᅡ (i.e., ᅣ) shallower. This ultimately leads to *the sound whose mouth shape is like* ᅡ *and whose tongue moves from* | *to* ᅢ, forming | + ᅢ. Similarly, ᅦ starts as ᅧ + | but becomes |· + ᅦ, and ⏊| is | + ⏊, while ㅠ| is | + ㅠ.

Figure II-16. Blending with Latter- |: ㅚ, ㅐ, ㅟ, ㅖ

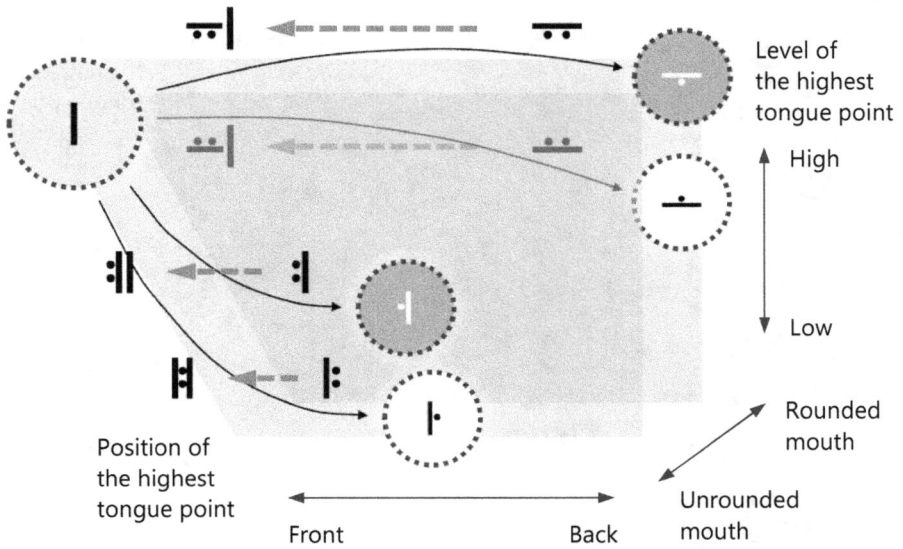

Compound Letter	Former	Latter	Mouth's Shape	Tongue's Position
ㅚ	ㅗ	ㅣ	ㅗ	Move forward from ㅗ
	ㅣ	ㅚ		Change from ㅣ to ㅚ
ㅐ	ㅏ	ㅣ	ㅏ	Move forward from ㅏ
	ㅣ	ㅐ		Change from ㅣ to ㅐ
ㅟ	ㅜ	ㅣ	ㅜ	Move forward from ㅜ
	ㅣ	ㅟ		Change from ㅣ to ㅟ
ㅖ	ㅕ	ㅣ	ㅕ	Move forward from ㅕ
	ㅣ	ㅖ		Change from ㅣ to ㅖ

Figure II-17. 15C *Han'gŭl* Mid-Sounds (revised): ㅚ, ㅒ, ㅟ, ㅖ

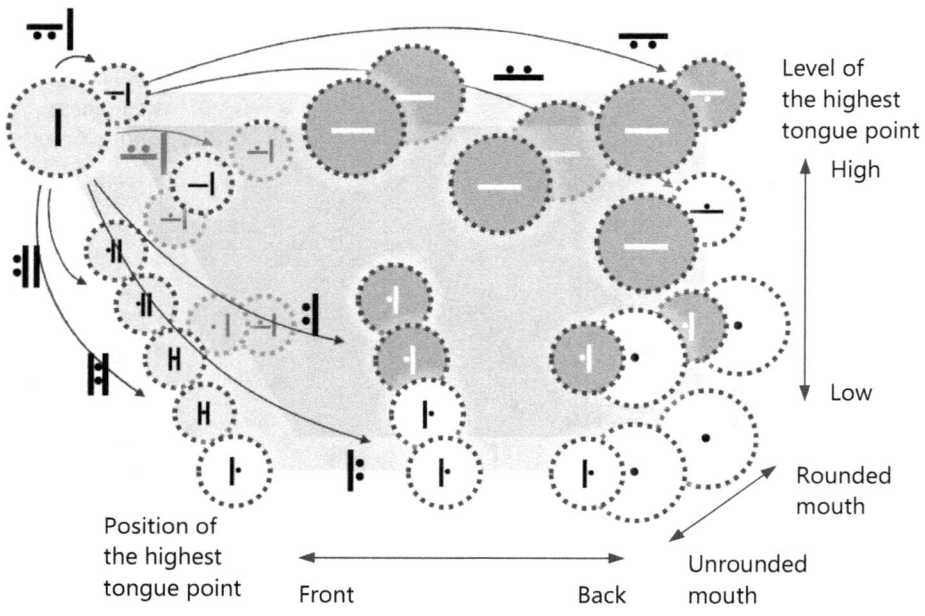

Let's also examine ㅘ and ㅝ formed by combining two, which share similar properties from ㅗ, ㅏ, ㅜ, or ㅓ, and ㅙ and ㅞ formed by combining two, which also share similar attributes from ㅛ, ㅑ, ㅠ, or ㅕ. These are sounds produced by changing the shape of the mouth. The sounds of ㅘ and ㅝ are straightforward. However, the sounds of ㅙ and ㅞ are created by combining ㅛ and ㅑ and ㅠ and ㅕ, respectively, though the ㅣ sound in ㅑ and ㅕ does not appear directly; instead, it makes the preceding ㅛ and ㅠ shallower before combining with ㅏ and ㅓ. This means they respectively become ㅚ+ㅏ and ㅟ+ㅓ.[53]

---

[53] Deconstructing ㅛ+ㅑ (= ㅣ+ㅗ+ㅣ+ㅏ) shows that the ㅛ+ㅑ combination, appearing as a w-glide [wa], is interrupted by ㅣ. This requires the tongue to move from ㅣ to ㅗ, return to ㅣ, and then proceed to ㅏ. Therefore, ㅙ simplifies this complex tongue movement within a single sound by merging ㅛ with a following ㅣ through vowel fronting, then combining with ㅏ to produce the ㅚ+ㅏ sound.

Figure II-18. 15C *Han'gŭl* Mid-Sounds (revised): ㅘ, ㅝ, ㆇ, ㆊ

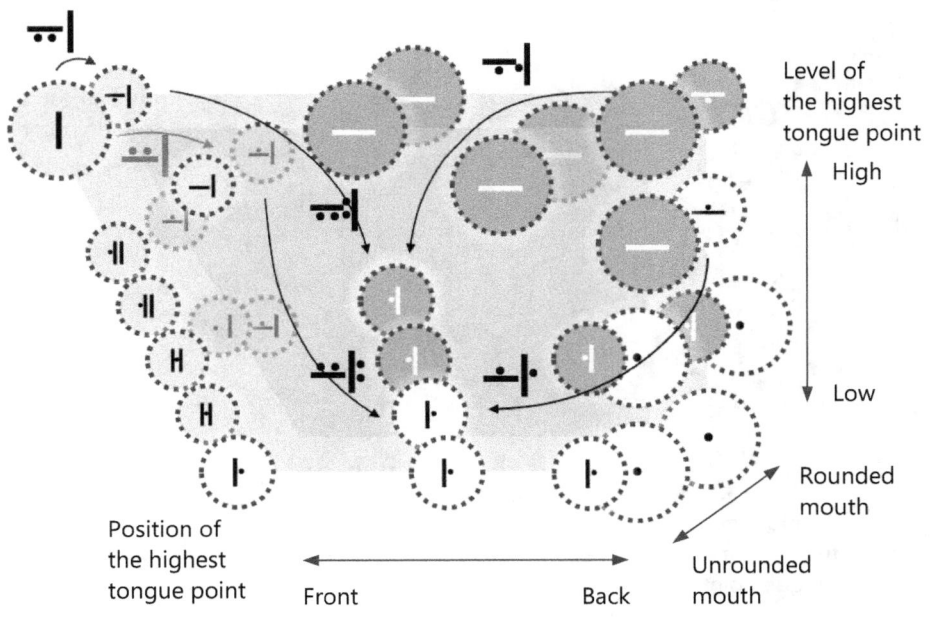

Compound Letter	Former	Latter	Mouth's Shape	Tongue's Position
ㅘ	ㅗ	ㅏ	ㅗ → ㅏ	Change from ㅗ to ㅏ
ㅝ	ㅜ	ㅓ	ㅜ → ㅓ	Change from ㅜ to ㅓ
ㆇ	ㅛ	ㅑ	ㅗ → ㅏ	*Not valid as a sound*
ㆇ	ㅛㅣ	ㅏ		Change from ㅛㅣ to ㅏ
ㆊ	ㅠ	ㆌ	ㅜ → ㅓ	*Not valid as a sound*
ㆊ	ㅠㅣ	ㅓ		Change from ㅠㅣ to ㅓ

Now, let's look at the letters formed by adding a latter- ㅣ to ㅘ, ㅝ, ㆇ, and ㆊ. The results, ㅙ, ㅞ, ㆈ, and ㆋ, all represent a *shallowing* of the latter sounds of ㅘ, ㅝ, ㆇ, and ㆊ. For ㅙ and ㅞ, the combination is straight-forward: ㅗ+ㅐ and ㅜ+ㅔ. The other two, ㆈ and ㆋ, as seen directly above, make ㅛㅣ+ㅏ (i.e., ㆇ) and ㅠㅣ+ㅓ (i.e., ㆊ) shallower, ultimately becoming ㅛㅣ+ㅐ and ㅠㅣ+ㅔ.

Figure II-19. 15C *Han'gŭl* Mid-Sounds (revised): ㅙ, ㅞ, ㆅ, ㆊ

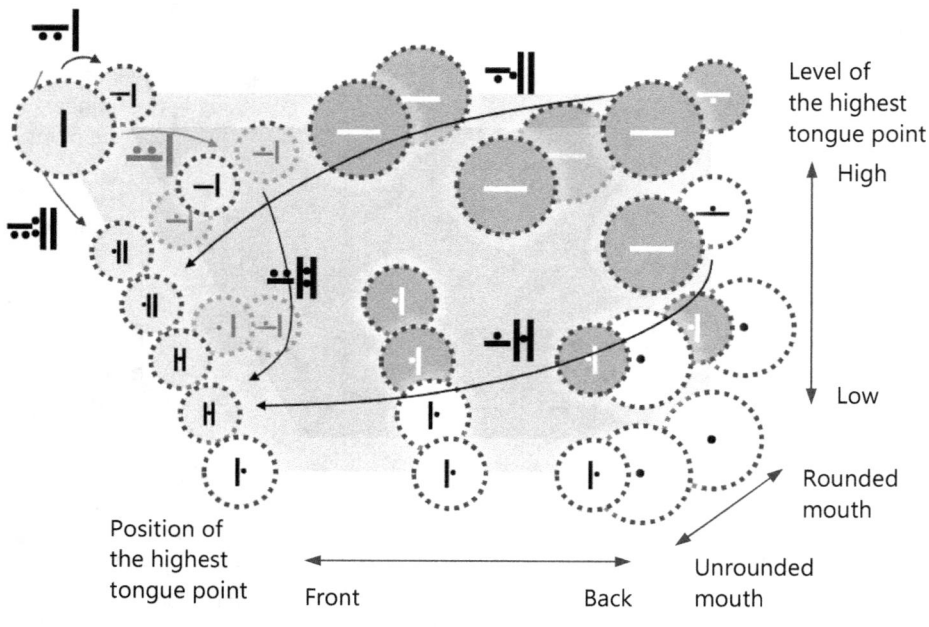

Compound Letter	Former	Latter	Mouth's Shape	Tongue's Position
ㅙ	ㅘ	ㅣ	ㅗ → ㅏ	Move forward from ㅘ
	ㅗ	ㅐ		Change from ㅗ to ㅐ
ㅞ	ㅝ	ㅣ	ㅜ → ㅓ	Move forward from ㅝ
	ㅜ	ㅔ		Change from ㅜ to ㅔ
ㆅ	ㅛ	ㅣ	ㅗ → ㅏ	Move forward from ㅛ
	ㅚ	ㅐ		Change from ㅚ to ㅐ
ㆊ	ㅠ	ㅣ	ㅜ → ㅓ	Move forward from ㅠ
	ㅟ	ㅔ		Change from ㅟ to ㅔ

The manual introduces two more sounds while describing how to write a character with combining letters——not while explaining the mid-sound letters themselves. After initially listing the horizontal mid-letters (i.e., •, —, ㅗ, ㅛ, ㅜ, and ㅠ) and the vertical ones (i.e., ㅣ, ㅏ, ㅑ, ㅓ, and ㅕ), it explains various notation methods and adds, *if you need to write a sound where* ㅣ *follows* • *or* —, *mark them respectively as* ㅣ *and* ⏌. In context, this seems to suggest a blending of all horizontal and vertical letters. For these two, i.e., ㅣ and ⏌, since ㅗ, ㅏ, ㅜ, and ㅓ do not appear to indicate the shape of the mouth, let's simply move the tongue in the default state as • or — to continuously produce the sound.

Figure II-20. 15C *Han'gŭl* Mid-Sounds (revised): ㅣ, ⏌

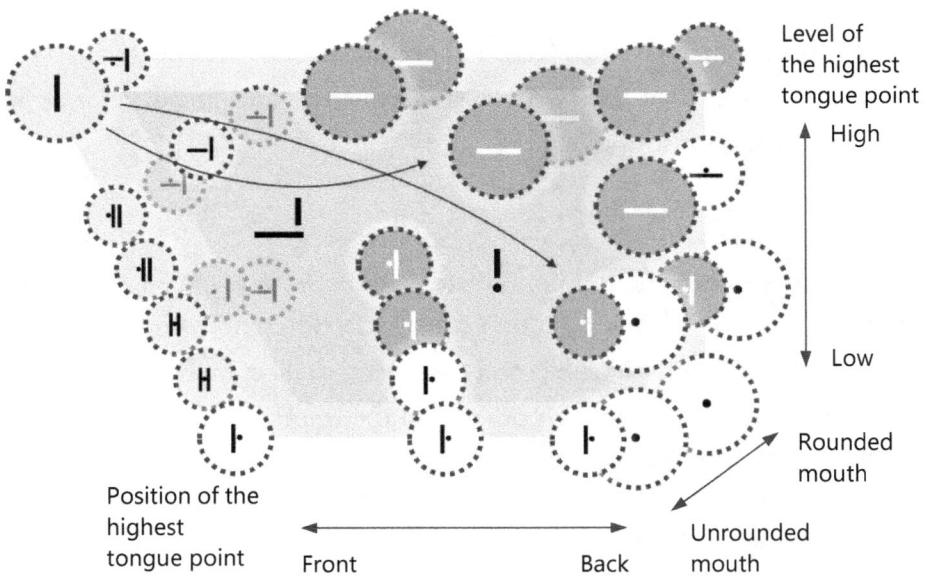

Compound Letter	Former	Latter	Mouth's Shape	Tongue's Position
ㅣ	ㅣ	•	*default*	Change from ㅣ to •
⏌	ㅣ	—	*default*	Change from ㅣ to —

Here's a summarized overview of the method discussed so far:

A.   The appearances of ㅗ, ㅏ, ㅜ, or ㅓ determine the shape of the mouth. When these appear together, the sound is produced by transitioning the mouth's shape as one read from top to bottom and left to right.

B.   Two dots accompanying ㅡ or ㅣ indicates that the tongue begins to move from the position of ㅣ.

C.   When a latter-ㅣ appears, it makes the preceding sound shallower (by either moving the tongue forward in the mouth or by slightly expanding the mouth sideways).

※   When vertical letters (e.g., ㅣ) precede horizontal ones (e.g., ·, ㅡ), they are written in sequence and produce a continuous sound (e.g., ㆎ, ㅢ).

Now let's look at the compound letters in *the manual* once again. Some letters, like ㅘ, ㅝ, ㅙ, and ㅞ, don't sound very different from consecutive pronunciation. Sounds like ㅟ and ㅠㅣ seem challenging to distinguish because they are so close to each other, and there are also triple vowels (i.e., triphthongs) that are likely to use other allophones more. Some groups seem like they will gradually lose their distinction from each other over time, or they may favor a single representative letter only.

Table II-4. 15C *Han'gŭl* Mid-Sounds (revised)

Sounds Classification	11 Alphabet Letters		Compound Letters			
	Letter	IPA	Letter	IPA	Allophone [e]	
Monophthong	•	[ɑ/ʌ/ɔ]	·ㅣ	[œ]		†
	―	[ɯ/ʊ]	ㅢ	[ɪ]	[ɯj]	†
	ㅣ	[i]				
	ㅗ	[o/ɔ]	ㅚ	[ø/ɤ]	[we]	†
	ㅏ	[a/ɑ]	ㅐ	[æ/ɛ]		†
	ㅜ	[u]	ㅟ	[y/ɤ]	[wi]	†
	ㅓ	[ə/ʌ/ɔ]	ㅔ	[e]		†
Diphthong	ㅛ	[jo]	ㅛㅣ	[jø]		†
	ㅑ	[ja/jɑ]	ㅒ	[jæ/jɛ]		†
	ㅠ	[ju]	ㅠㅣ	[jy]	[y:]	†
	ㅕ	[jə/jʌ/jɔ]	ㅖ	[je]		†
			ㅘ	[wa]		‡
			ㅝ	[wə/wɔ]		‡
			ㅙ	[wæ]		†
			ㅞ	[we]		†
			!	[jɑ]		
			ˌ|	[jɯ]		
Triphthong			ㅛㅑ	[jøa]	[wia]	‡
			ㅠㅕ	[jyə]	[wiə]	‡
			ㅛㅒ	[jøæ]	[wiæ]	†
			ㅠㅖ	[jye]	[wie]	†

† 14 ㅣ-compound letters specified in the manual.

‡ 4 compound letters without ㅣ specified in the manual.

(e) expected by author

Over the centuries, Koreans have developed over sixty identified letters that were used only temporarily and left behind. Historical records highlight their efforts to transcribe the sounds they envisioned into *Han'gŭl* letters. Without standard grammar or orthography, many likely wrote as they deemed best. In an era without national broadcasting, writers likely used personal preferences in their writings in the absence of a standard pronunciation guide. Since the king who invented *Han'gŭl* could not teach everyone personally for centuries, the appearance of irregularities, complexities, or diversities in later *Han'gŭl* writings was inevitable. What is crucial now is how we use these letters today.

Korean has consistently expressed numerous sounds through combinations of middle sound letters. *Han'gŭl* may have preserved many sounds from disappearing. How about you? Are there any sounds you know that could be represented using 15th-century *Han'gŭl* middle sound letters?

EXAMPLES   Below, names are transcribed using 15th-century *Han'gŭl* middle sound letters and compared with their modern representations. A few other previously examined 15th-century letters are also included. Let's explore how some of these sounds have transformed.

Name	Modern *Han'gŭl*	15C *Han'gŭl*
Lejeune (*FR*)	ㄹ쟌ㄴ	ㄹㄹ쥔ㄴ
Mathieu (*FR*)	마튜	마퇴
Vasseur (*FR*)	바쇠르/베서	봬씨ㅎ
Jörg (*DE*)	요ㅋ	외ㅋ/욀ㅋ
Jürgen (*DE*)	유ㄹ겐	외룽건
Krüger (*DE*)	ㅋ뤼거	ㅋ뤼거

3. 15ᵗʰ-Century Bottom Letters

Previously, we decided not to restrict the letters used for *Han'gŭl* bottom sounds. This means that any letter used for a top sound can also be used for a bottom sound. However, as explained, it is crucial to differentiate bottom sounds that stop the middle sounds from the top sounds of subsequent characters.[54] In addition, remember that pair letters are simply spoken sequentially for convenience.

QUIZ FOR FUN!

Ms. Elliott is preparing a game for the children to play in class. It's a two-player game where one child shows a nameplate with a name written in *Han'gŭl*, and the other tries to guess the original name on the back. The names are of famous people that everyone might know, mostly film stars, TV hosts, or singers, so she thinks it will be easy even for the kids to guess. But she wants to test you first. Look at the following nameplates and try to guess the original name——hopefully, you haven't forgotten that she doesn't like reactions that don't match her expectations. May a perfect score be with you![55]

---

[54] In 15ᵗʰ-century *Han'gŭl*, ᅙ (i.e., soft-ㅁ, refer to Footnote 2) at the bottom position was often pronounced as [w]. This action was more akin to continuing the sound of ㅜ than stopping the middle, leading over time to its replacement by ㅜ. Therefore, if transferring the [ɱ] sound from the bottom ᅙ to the top sound of the next character is desired, using ᅙ is acceptable. Moreover, the bottom ᅙ in the 15ᵗʰ century was primarily used to briefly stop the middle sound due to its characteristic of halting a sound near the throat. Since there was little necessity to distinguish such short middle sounds frequently, its usage began to decline. Therefore, if a brief interruption of the middle sound is needed without transferring any sound to the next top position, the bottom sound ᅙ could be useful.

[55] (1) Ed Sheeran, (2) Oprah Winfrey, (3) Tom Cruise, (4) Emma Watson, (5) Brie Larson, (6) Snoop Dogg, (7) Tom Holland, (8) Justin Bieber, (9) Meryl Streep, (10) Ariana Grande, (11) Morgan Freeman, (12) Kelly Clarkson.

No.	Name in the 15th-Century *Han'gŭl* on Nameplates	Original Name
(1)	헬 시런	
(2)	호ㅍ루 윈퓽릐	
(3)	톰 ㅋ루△	
(4)	헴마 와츤	
(5)	ㅂ릐 랄슨	
(6)	ㅅ늪 덕	
(7)	톰 홀랜ㄷ	
(8)	져ㅅ띤 비버	
(9)	메럴 ㅅ트륖	
(10)	우릐아나 ㄱ란데	
(11)	몰근 퓽릐먼	
(12)	켈리 클맑슨	

The Front of Nameplates

(1) 헬 시런

(2) 호ㅍ릏 윈퓽릐

(3) 톰 ㅋ루△

(4) 헴마 와츤

(5) ㅂ릐 랄슨

(6) ㅅ늪 덕

(7) 톰 홀랜ㄷ

(8) 셔ㅅ띤 비버

(9) 메럴 ㅅㅌ맆

(10) ᄋᆞ릐아나 ㄱ란데

(11) 몰근 퓽릐먼

(12) 켈리 클랔슨

4. Sounds That Are Difficult to Write in 15th-Century *Han'gŭl*

Several sounds that were challenging to denote in modern *Han'gŭl* can now be expressed using 15th-century *Han'gŭl*. Yet, *th* sounds frequently found in English and the rhotic [ʁ] sounds from French or German still present challenges. Moreover, the transcription of middle sounds remains less than ideal. Although the ability to notate many more sounds than when using modern *Han'gŭl* is advantageous, the necessity, for example, to consistently append the character 이 to accurately represent sounds of *y* in *my* or *i* in *bike* is not wholly satisfying. It is difficult to solve this problem using only *Han'gŭl*, created in the time and space we have experienced. Could there be a *Han'gŭl* somewhere out of this universe that has solved this problem? May we find hope in the *Multiverse* version of *Han'gŭl*, a collection of letters and notations that could have been used in different times and spaces? Let's take the final voyage of this book.

Multiverse *Han'gŭl*

1. Once Upon a Time Letters

In 2011, a letter written in 15th-century *Han'gŭl* (한글) by a soldier stationed on the northeastern border of Korea at the time was found. This letter, written in 1490, around 40 years after the creation of 한글, details a man's lament about not being able to visit home, despite passing nearby, and requests for several items needed at the border (Figure III-1).

An old 한글 letter was also unearthed during a real estate development project in 1998. It was written by a wife to her late husband; it was buried with the husband in 1586, while the wife was pregnant (Figure III-2).

Figure III-1. *Letter to My Wife*, 나신걸, 1490 [1]

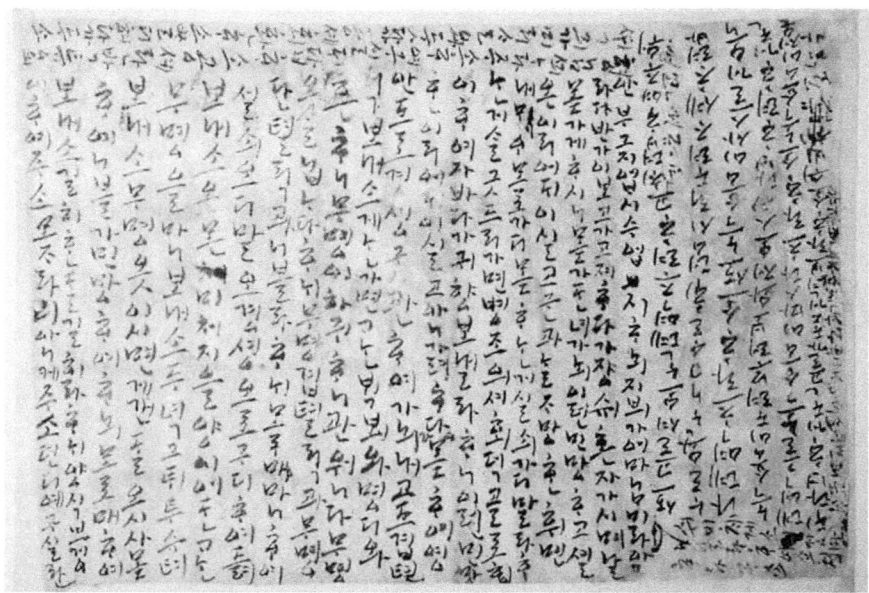

Figure III-2. *Letter to My Husband*, 원이엄마 (원's Mom), 1586 [2]

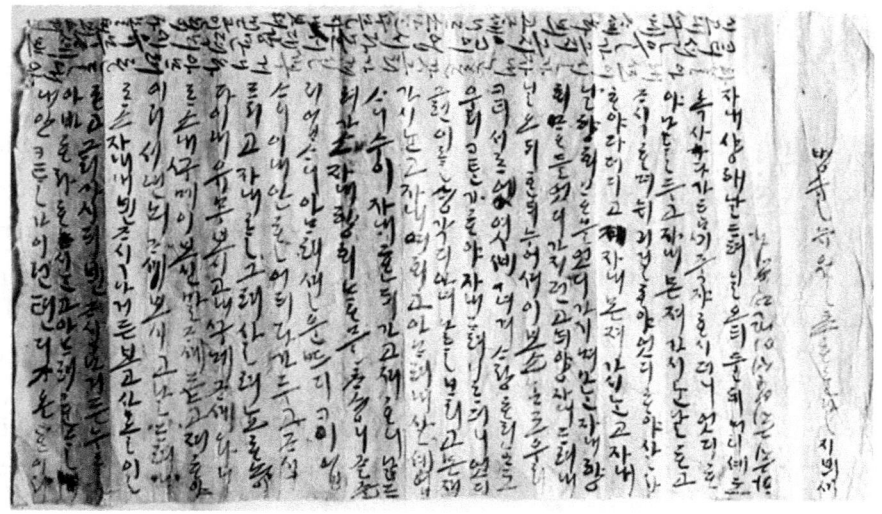

---

[1] Letter by 羅臣傑나신걸 (1461–1524). Housed at the *Daejeon* Municipal Museum.

[2] Tomb relics of 李應台이응태 (1556–1586). Housed at the *Andong* University Museum.

LETTER TO MY HUSBAND
by 원이엄마 *in 1586*

자내 샹해 날두려 닐오디 둘히 머리 셰도록 사다가 흠씌 죽쟈 흐시더니 You always told me that we should live and die together until our hair turns gray.

엇디흐야 나롤 두고 자내 몬져 가시는 Why then, have you gone first, leaving me behind?

날흐고 주식흐며 뉘긔 걸흐야 엇디흐야 살라 흐야 다 더디고 자내 몬져 가시는고 How are I and our baby supposed to live, relying on whom, after you've left us all behind?

자내 날 향히 무우믈 엇디 가지며 나는 자내 향히 무우믈 엇디 가지던고 How was your heart for me, and how was mine for you?

미양 자내두려 내 닐오디 흔디 누어셔 Always lying next to you,

이 보소 놈도 우리フ티 서루 에엿쎄 녀겨 스랑흐리 놈도 우리 フ툰가 흐야 I said, "Honey, do others cherish and love each other as we do? Are others like us?"

자내두려 니루더니 엇디 그런 이롤 싱각디 아녀 나롤 부리고 몬져 가시는고 Always told you so, but without reflecting on those days, how could you leave me behind and go away alone?

자내 여히고 아무려 내 살 셰 업스니 수이 자내 흔디 가고져 흐니 날 두려가소 I can't live without you, so I'm going to join you soon. Please, take me with you.

자내 향히 무우믈 추싱 니졸 줄리 업스니 아무려 셜운 쁘디 フ이 업스니 My heart toward you in this life is unforgettable, and my sorrow seems to never stop,

이 내 안홀 어디다가 두고 주식 두리고 자내롤 그려 살려뇨 흐노이다 Where should I put this heart on, and how could I live longing for you, with our child?

LETTER TO MY HUSBAND
by 원이엄마 *in 1586*

이 내 유무 보시고 내 쑤메 주셰 와 니ᄅ소
See this letter, come to my dream, and tell me everything

내 쑤메 이 보신 말 주셰 듣고져 ᄒ야 이리 서 년뇌
In my dream, I wish to hear what you would say seeing my letter, so I'm writing.

주셰 보시고 날두려 니ᄅ소
Please, take a closer look at this letter and tell me everything

자내 내 빈 주식 나거든 보고 사롤 일 ᄒ고
When the child in me is born, I would show you the baby

그리 가시디 빈 주식 나거든 누롤 아바 ᄒ라 ᄒ시ᄂ고
But you have just gone, and when the baby is born, who shall be called *papa*?

아무려 ᄒ둘 내 안 ᄀ툴가 이런 텬디 가슨 ᄒ이리
How can words ever show my heart, how heavenly and earthly sorrow.

(FROM THIS, IT CONTINUES IN THE UPPER MARGIN OF THE LETTER.)

하놀 아래 쏘 이실가 자내ᄂ ᄒ갓 그리 가 겨실 쑤거니와
Is there any sadness like this under heaven? But you may just be there alone.

아무려 ᄒ둘 내 안 ᄀ티 셜울가 No words can say my heart, my sorrow

그지그지 ᄀ이업서 다 몯 서 대강만 뎍뇌
It's endless, endless, endless—so I cannot write it all, but only a little.

이 유무 주셰 보시고 내 쑤메 주셰와 뵈고 주셰 니ᄅ소
See my letter closer, come to my dream closer, and tell me everything about you

나ᄂ 쑤믈 자내 보려 믿고 인뇌이다 몰래 뵈쇼셔
I believe I will see you in my dream, so let's meet without letting anyone know.

(FROM THIS, IT CONTINUES IN THE FRONT MARGIN OF THE LETTER.)

하 그지그지 업서 이만 젹뇌이다
It's endless, endless, so I write it down thus far.

한글 spread quickly across the country in the 15th century, significantly aided by the royal family and the nobles. King *Sejong* (세종)[3] was its most prominent advocate. After inventing 한글, he published an epic written in the script celebrating the nation's founding.[4] Following the death of his wife, the queen, in 1446, while praying for the repose of her soul, he directed his son to write a book about Buddha's life in 한글.[5] This book, the first 한글 commentary on Buddhist scriptures, was completed and 세종 personally added Buddhist hymns in 한글 to each section.[6] His son, who later became king himself, combined and republished this work with another Buddhist text.[7]

---

[3] 世宗세종, a.k.a. 세종대왕 (世宗大王; *Sejong the Great*), 1397–1450, ascended to the throne in 1418.

[4] 용비어천가 (龍飛御天歌; *Yongbieocheonga*; lit. *Songs of Dragons Flying to Heaven*, 1447) is an extensive epic that praises the foundation of the nation by likening six direct ancestors of 세종 to six dragons. Initially penned in 한글 in 1445, it was published with relevant history and explanations added by scholars in a traditional writing method. The 한글 poems contained in 용비어천가 are highly refined in expression and writing style and rich in flowery vocabulary with native Korean words, making it hard to believe that it is the first poem written with a newly created phonetic alphabet following thousands of years of using only ideograms (i.e., *Hanja*, refer to Footnote 12).

[5] 석보상절 (釋譜詳節; *Seokbosangjeol*, 1447) compiles various texts about Buddha's life into one book, translated into 한글. Currently, only 8 of the original 24 volumes are extant.* In contrast to 용비어천가 (refer to Footnote 4), where *Hanja*** lacks pronunciation markings, 석보상절 provides a 한글 pronunciation for each *Hanja*** character.

  *Book Nos. 6, 9, 13, 19, 20, 21, 23, and 24. **See Footnote 12.

[6] 월인천강지곡 (月印千江之曲; *Worincheongangjigok*; lit. *Songs of the Moon's Reflection on a Thousand Rivers*) is a Buddhist hymn book in 한글, authored by 세종 and complementing 석보상절 (refer to Footnote 5). The book is believed to have been published in 1447. Of the initial three volumes, only one, comprising 194 songs, survives, though estimates suggest there were originally about 580 songs. However, including the compositions in 월인석보 (refer to Footnote 7), 440 songs are presently extant. In contrast to 용비어천가 (refer to Footnote 4) and 석보상절, 월인천강지곡 primarily employs 한글, with meanings supplemented in *Hanja** when necessary.

  *See Footnote 12.

[7] 월인석보 (月印釋譜, 1459) serves as a compilation of 월인천강지곡 and 석보상절 (refer to Footnotes 5 and 6). This book's significant historical value is attributed to the

Figure III-3. 용비어천가, Chapter 2, 1447[8]

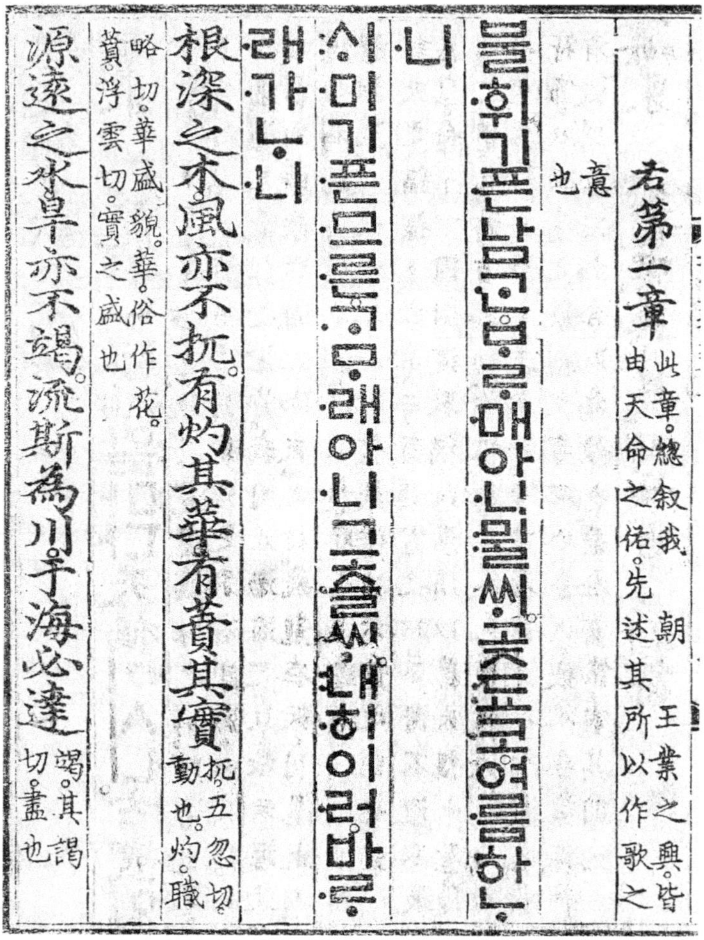
右第一章 此章總叙我朝王業之興皆由天命之佑先述其所以作歌之意也

불휘 기픈 남ᄀᆞᆫ ᄇᆞᄅᆞ매 아니 뮐ᄊᆡ 곶 됴코 여름 하ᄂᆞ니

ᄉᆡ미 기픈 므른 ᄀᆞᄆᆞ래 아니 그츨ᄊᆡ 내히 이러 바ᄅᆞ래 가ᄂᆞ니

根深之木風亦不扤有灼其華有蕡其實 扤五忽切動也灼職略切華盛貌華俗作花蕡浮雲切實之盛也

源遠之水旱亦不竭流斯爲川于海必達 竭其謁切盡也

loss of the other two. Both the original and the re-engraving editions are available, though some volumes are missing. Previously, 20 volumes were known to be extant;* however, in 2021, 28 volumes of a lithography edition were discovered, which are currently under study and verification.

*Missing Books: Nos. 3, 5, 6, 16, and 24.

[8] First edition, woodblock printing, held at the SNU *Kyujanggak* Institute for Korean Studies, Chapter 2 (refer to Footnote 4). The original no longer exists, and the cited version is a 16th-century reprint. 불휘기픈남ᄀᆞᆫ in modern language translates to 뿌리 깊은나무 (lit. *Deep Rooted Tree* or *Tree with Deep Roots*), and it is also the title of a

Figure III-4. 석보상절, Book 6, 1447 [9]

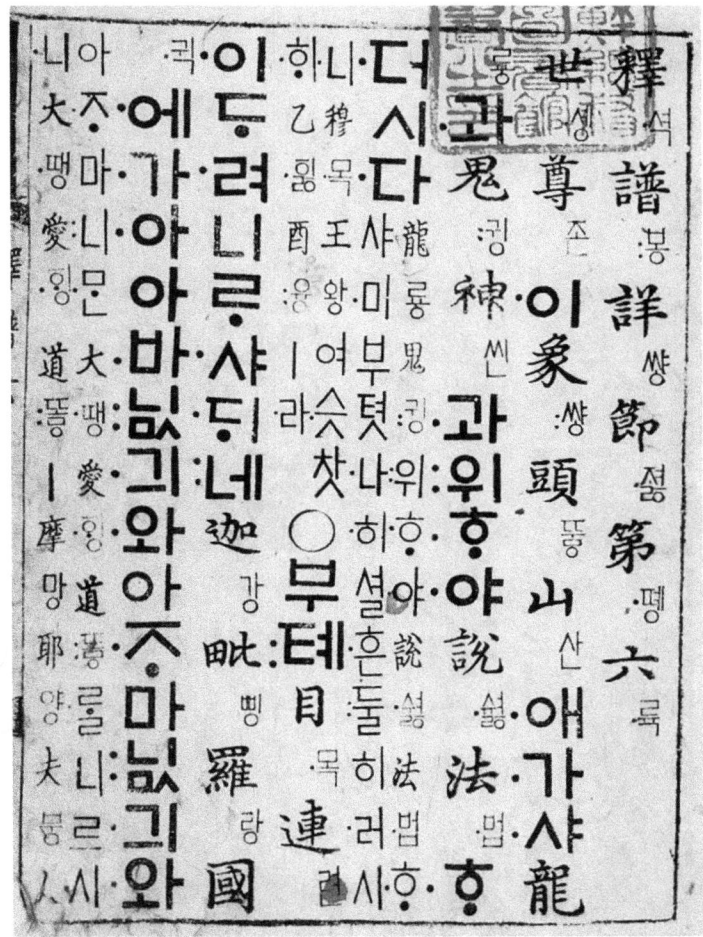

traditional historical drama about 세종's life (MBC, 1983) and a fusion period drama that reinterprets the creation of 한글 (SBS, 2011).

[9] First edition, copper movable type printing, housed at the National Library of Korea, p. 1 of Book 6 (refer to Footnote 5). The bottom sounds ㅇ and ㅸ are interpreted as [∅] and [w], respectively.

Figure III-5. 월인천강지곡, Book 1, 1447 [10]

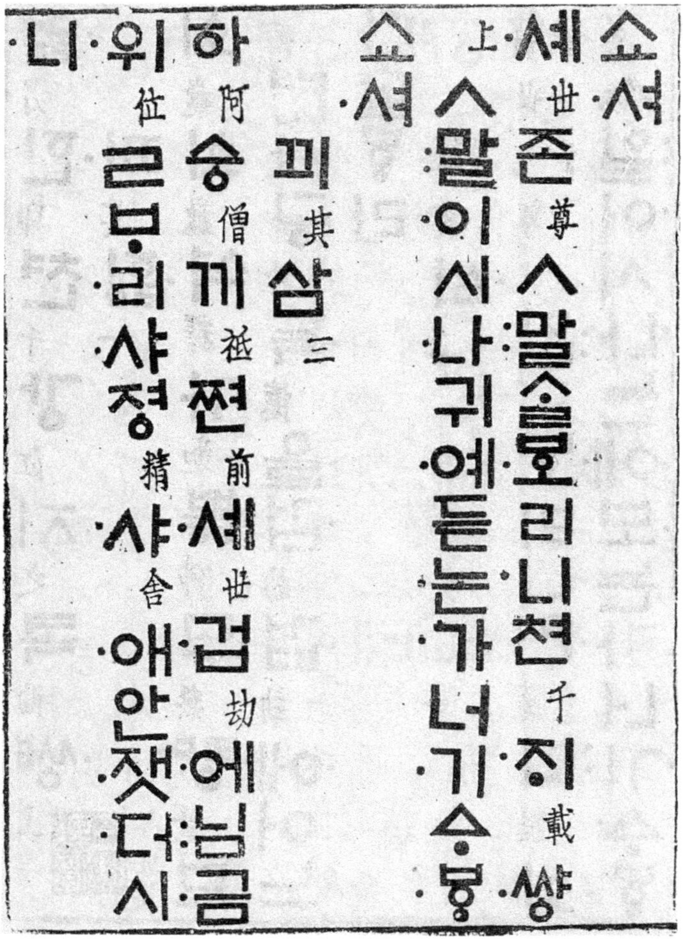

쇼·셔

·셰世존尊ㅅ :말ᄉᆞᆯᄫᅩ리·니 쳔千·ᄌᆡᆼ載·썅上

:말·이시·나 귀·예 듣논·가 너·기ᅀᆞ·ᄫᆞ쇼·셔

끠其삼三

하阿승僧끼祇쪈前·셰世·겁劫·에 님:금

·위位ㄹ ᄇᆞ·리·샤 졍精·샤舍·애 안·잿·더시·니

---

[10] First edition, copper movable type printing, stored at The Academy of Korean Study, p. 2 of Book 1 (refer to Footnote 6). The material referenced is the 1961 facsimile edition of the original. The standalone ㅅ functions as an adnominal case marker, and ㄹ as an object case marker, both generally read as bottom sounds (see Footnote 18 for further information).

Figure III-6. 월인석보, Book 21, 1459/1562 [11]

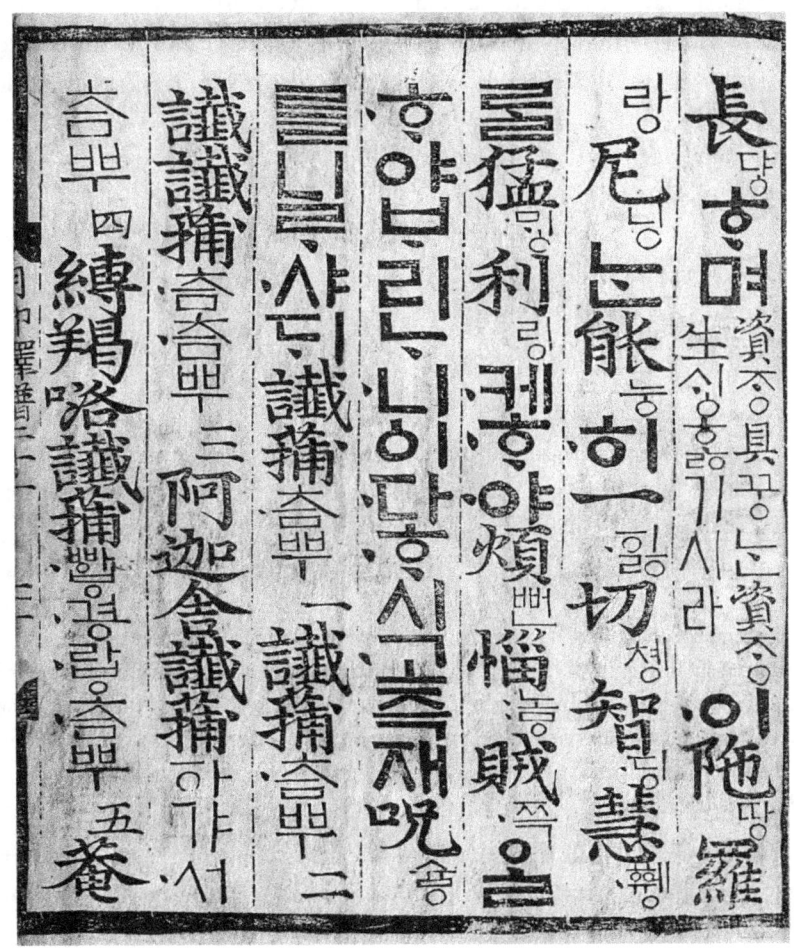

[11] Re-engraved in 1562, woodblock printing, housed at the National Library of Korea,
p. 139 of Book 21, part 1 (refer to Footnote 7). The re-engraving version is the only
surviving edition of Volume 21, featuring native Korean words, *Hanja** characters and
pronunciations (e.g., 長댱, 能능, 一힗, etc.), along with Sanskrit pronunciation notations (e.g., 훔뿌, 훔훔뿌, 빨경랄훔뿌, etc.).   *See Footnote 12.

Shortly after the creation of 한글, by royal decree, scholars collaborated to publish a dictionary of Korean standard pronunciations for *Hanja* characters,[12] [13] and they distributed a summarized version of *the manual*, translated into 한글.[14] Knowledge of 한글 was also included in examinations for selecting

---

[12] *Hanja* (漢字한자) is the modern Korean name for the East Asian ideographic system or its characters. Traditionally, Korea and China had referred to it as *Ja* (字자, lit. letter or character), *Mun* (文문, lit. writing), or *Kye* (契계, lit. engraved letter), but the Japanese practice of calling it *Kanji* (漢字; かんじ칸지, lit. letter from 漢한——the ancient dynasty in modern Chinese region during 202 BC–9 AD and 25–225 AD) seems to have influenced Korea since the 1930s. This writing system has been used in many East Asian countries throughout history, and the sounds of the same characters are different in each country. Although most characters share the same meaning and form, there are also exclusive uses of forms of the characters that are not compatible with each other or cannot be integrated into one. In this book, every *Hanja* sound written in *Han'gŭl* is in modern Korean.

[13] 동국정운 (東國正韻, 1448, refer to Footnote 15 in Chapter II) is a dictionary that organizes the standard pronunciations of 14,243 *Hanja* characters. This work was compiled shortly after the creation of 한글, following a royal directive involving two princes and nine scholars. This dictionary showcases the distinctive and innovative characteristics of 한글, which categorizes sounds into top, middle, and bottom segments, unlike traditional Chinese phonetics, which divides characters into initial and final sounds; which also uses the same phonetic letters for the top and bottom sounds; and which introduces the unique structure for the middle sounds letters, and so on.

[14] 훈민정음언해 (訓民正音諺解; *Hunminjeongeum Eonhae*, 1459) is a booklet translated with *the manual* into 한글. It is attached to 월인석보 and remains preserved to this day (refer to Footnote 7). Its structure and content clearly aim to simplify the distribution of 한글, likely created around the same time as *the manual* (estimated circa 1447). The existing 1459 edition also features additional descriptions of letters used for representing upper and lower tooth sounds in Chinese, as detailed in 사성통고 (refer to Footnote 8 in Chapter II, and see 1. §2 of Chapter II for further information).

officials,[15] and all children learned to read and write in 한글.[16] Within just one generation, the new script was thoroughly propagated throughout the whole society, filling every corner of Korean life alongside *Hanja*, the existing script. Numerous letters written in 한글 by the royal family over centuries illustrate who led this transformation. Given the societal structure of the time, this transformation with the spread of 한글 would not have been possible without the involvement of the palace and the nobles.

---

[15] 세종 introduced 한글 as a subject in the civil service examinations in December 1446, the same year he disseminated *the manual*. It thus became a mandatory subject in these exams. By the late 17th century, 한글 had established a broad societal base. In this regard, there is a record that 南九萬남구만 (*Nam Gu-man*, 1629–1711), the deputy prime minister, criticized the civil service examination system in a report to the king dated September 11, 1684. He expressed concerns that in rural areas, people focused solely on memorizing texts in 한글 to pass exams, resulting in officials who, despite passing, could not write even a single piece of letter in *Hanja* (refer to *the Annals*; 실록*).

> *朝鮮王朝實錄조선왕조실록; *Joseon wangjo sillok*; lit. *The Veritable Records of the Joseon Dynasty*, a.k.a. *The Annals of the Joseon Dynasty*; or just 실록, designated as National Treasure No. 151 of South Korea, housed at the SNU *Kyujanggak* Institute for Korean Studies. This comprehensive document chronicles major events from the reigns of 25 of the 27 kings of the 조선 dynasty (covering 472 years from 1392 to 1863) across approximately 50 million characters in 1,894 chapters and 888 books. All records were strictly composed posthumously, ensuring that neither the reigning king nor his immediate successors could view them. Future generations were also prohibited from making any alterations or deletions, preserving the independence and confidentiality of the historians.

[16] 한글 educational materials were mainly distributed in the form of thin brochures inserted at the beginning of various books. This approach significantly contributed to the elementary education of *Hanja*. In 1527, 최세진 (refer to Footnote 8 in Chapter II) authored 訓蒙字會훈몽자회, a *Hanja* textbook for children who had learned 한글 already. This work provided the meanings and pronunciations in 한글 for 3,360 characters of elementary *Hanja*, spread across three volumes with 1,120 characters each. Furthermore, 최세진's efforts to spread and educate about 한글 were supported by his publications of several books, including 번역노걸대 and 번역박통사 (both estimated to have been created before 1517, refer to Footnote 21) and 사성통해 (refer to Footnote 8 in Chapter II).

Figure III-7. 동국정운, Book 6, 1448 [17]

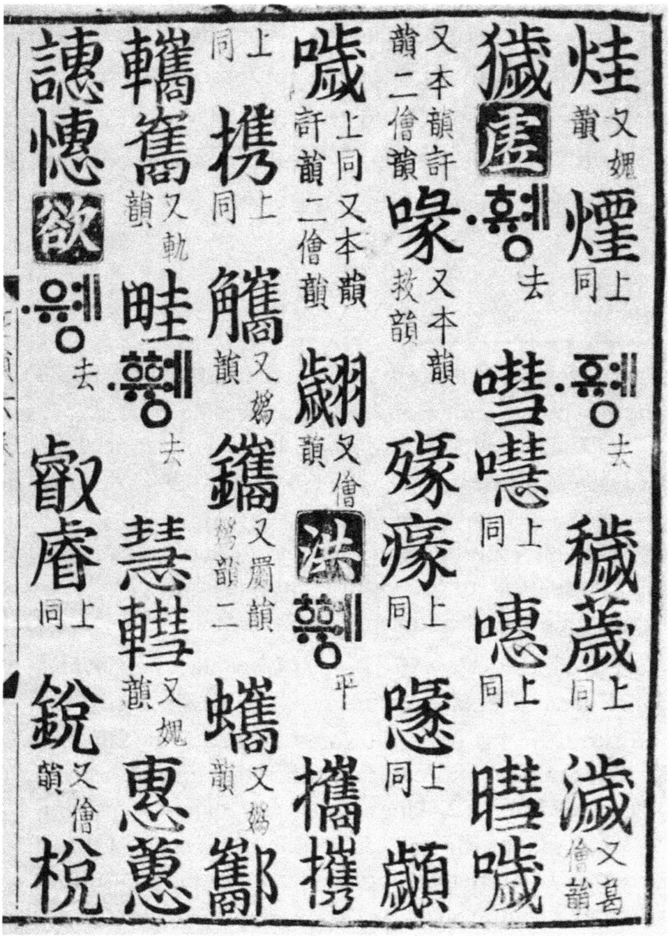

[17]　First edition, facsimile version of wood movable type printing, housed at the *Konkuk* University Museum, p. 19 of vol. 6 (refer to Footnote 13). The page clearly distinguishes the use of four throat sounds (i.e., ㅇ, ㆆ, ㆆ, and ㆅ) for the same middle sound letter ㆌ. The bottom sound ㅇ is noted as [∅].

Figure III-8. 훈민정음언해 (월인석보, Book 1), 1459[18]

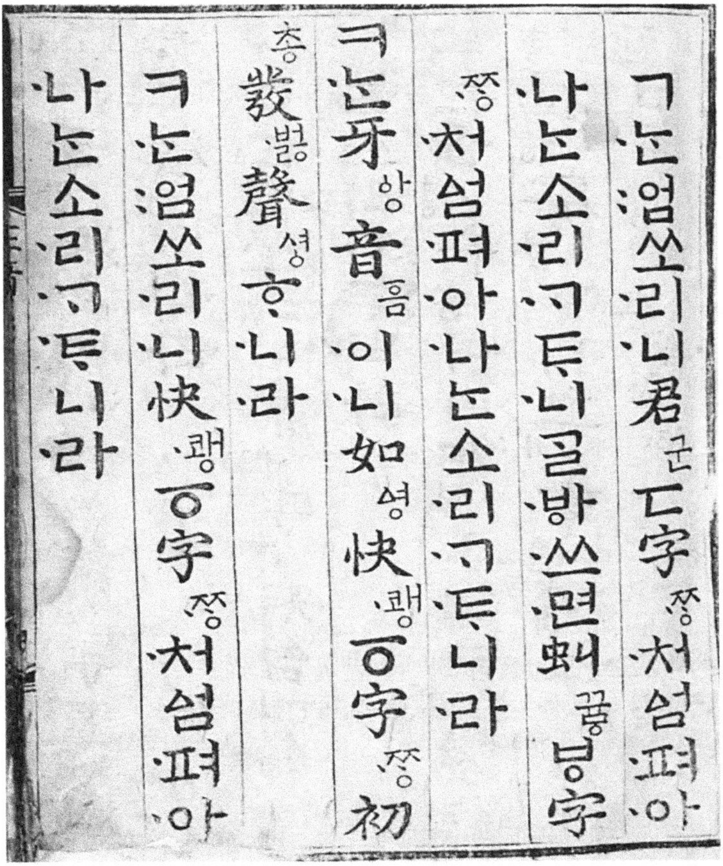
ㄱ·ᄂᆞᆫ :엄쏘·리·니 君군ㄷ字·쭝 ·처ᅀᅥᆷ·펴·아
·나·ᄂᆞᆫ 소·리·ᄀᆞ·ᄐᆞ·니 ·ᄀᆞᆯ·ᄫᅡ·쓰·면 虯뀽ᇢ字
·쭝 ·처ᅀᅥᆷ·펴·아 ·나·ᄂᆞᆫ 소·리·ᄀᆞ·ᄐᆞ니·라
ㅋ·ᄂᆞᆫ 牙앙音음·이·니 如ᅀᅧᆼ 快·쾡ㆆ字·쭝 初
총 發벓聲셩·ᄒᆞ·니·라
ㅋ·ᄂᆞᆫ :엄쏘·리·니 快·쾡ㆆ字·쭝 ·처ᅀᅥᆷ·펴·아
·나·ᄂᆞᆫ 소·리·ᄀᆞ·ᄐᆞ니·라

---

[18] 1459 edition, woodblock printing, housed at the *Sogang* University Loyola Library, p. 7 (refer to Footnote 14). The document uses different adnominal case markers for each bottom sound in *Hanja*. For example, the bottom sound ㄴ in 君군 is marked with ㄷ, the bottom sound ㅱ in 虯끃 with ㅸ, and the bottom sound ㅇ[∅] in 快쾡 with ㆆ. Adnominal case markers such as ㄷ, ㅸ, and ㆆ, as well as ㄱ, ㅂ, and ㅅ, appear throughout the book. This method is based on the guideline that *when Hanja and* 한글 *are used together, middle or bottom sounds can be added to the Hanja sound* (文與諺雜用則 有因字音 而補以中終聲者), exemplified by *Confucius* ㅣ *Lu*ㅅ *man* (lit. *Confucius is a man from Lu*;* 如孔子 ㅣ 魯ㅅ사ᄅᆞᆷ之類). This practice is rarely applied outside of **훈민정음언해, 용비어천가,** and **석보상절,** and often used partially (i.e., ㅣ, ㅅ, or ㄹ) or omitted entirely.   *Lu: 魯노, 1042–249 BC.

Figure III-9. 숙명신한첩, *From King to His Young Daughter*, 1652–1659 [19]

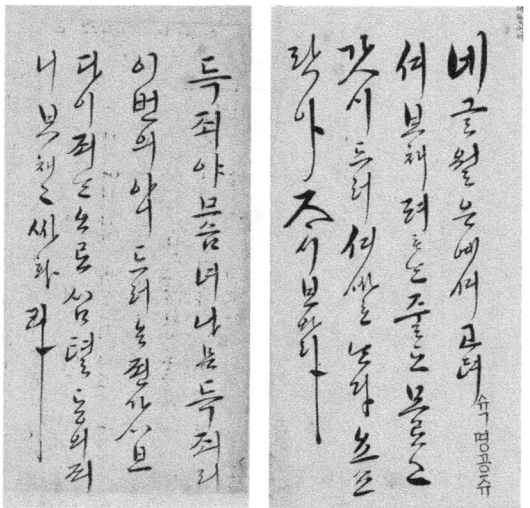

(LEFT)

득죄야 므슴 녀나믄 득죄리 이번의 아니 드러온 죈가 시브다
What other sin could there be? Not coming this time could be.

이 죄는 오로 심털동의 죄니 보채고 싸화라
This sin belongs entirely to 심철동,* so go ahead, scold and argue with him.

　*심철동: the childhood name of Princess 숙명's husband

(RIGHT)

네 글월은 예셔 고텨셔 보채려 ᄒ는 줄도 모로고
Unaware that I intended to revise and add to your writings here,

갓시 드러셔 싸호는다 요 쇼락아 ᄌ시 보와라
Have you already quarreled with him, you 쇼락.* Look closer.

　*쇼락: rash and charming little bird

---

[19] 숙명신한첩 (淑明宸翰帖; *Sukmyeong Shinhancheop*, 1652–1688), held at the *Cheongju* National Museum. Nos. 3 and 4. This compilation features letters from King 孝宗 효종 (1619–1659, ascended the throne in 1649) and his queen to their young married daughter, Princess 淑明숙명 (1640–1699), along with correspondence from other royal family members to her. The selected excerpts are brief notes from the king. Although the princess' responses are not included, limiting understanding of the full context, the notes vividly convey a father's concern for his young daughter who married so early. One note expresses his disappointment that she did not respond to a summons to the palace, while another shows his tender consolation after hearing about her marital quarrel.

Figure III-10. 정조한글어찰첩, *From Prince to His Aunt*, 1756–1758 [20]

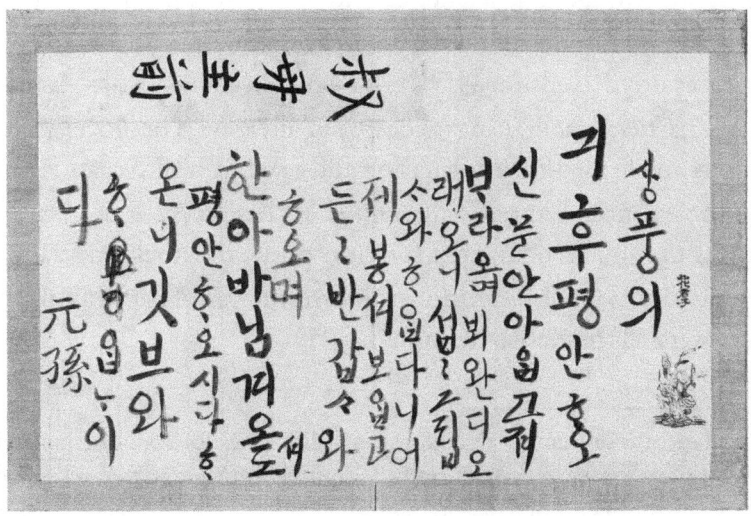

상풍의 긔후 평안ㅎ오신 문안 아옵고져 브라오며
Greetings to you, hoping you are healthy in both body and mind amid the autumn winds.

뵈완디 오래오니 섭~ 그립ᄉ와 ㅎ옵다니
Feeling slighted due to our prolonged separation,

어제 봉셔 보옵고 든~ 반갑ᄉ와 ㅎ오며
I was reassured and delighted to receive your letter yesterday.

한아바님겨오셔도 평안ㅎ오시다 ㅎ오니 깃브와 ㅎ옵ᄂ이다
And I am pleased to hear that grandfather is also doing well.

---

[20] 정조한글어찰첩 (正祖한글御札帖), preserved at the National *Hangeul* Museum, No. 3 consists of 14 한글 letters sent by 正祖정조 (1752–1800, ascended to the throne in 1776) to his aunt during his childhood. The cited letter is presumed to have been penned between 1755 and 1758 (ages 3 to 6), based on several lines of evidence from which to assume this: for one, the royal records in 1755 noted, *the young grandson could already read and write Hanja, much to the king's delight*; also, the prince referred to himself as 元孫원손 (i.e., Eldest Grandson) in the letter though his title became 世孫세손 (i.e., Eldest Son of Crown Prince) from 1759; finally evidence was provided by comparing his handwriting and used vocabulary with other letters he had written. The use of swung dashes (~) to abbreviate repeated characters in words (i.e. 섭섭→섭~, 든든→든~) is particularly noteworthy.

한글 proved especially useful in trade and diplomacy. Teaching materials for Mandarin, Mongolian, Manchu, and Japanese that incorporated 한글 pronunciations became essential for interpreters.[21] Envoys abroad communicated and reported back in 한글.[22] Beyond diplomacy, 한글 transcended social class barriers, facilitating widespread literacy. The government published books on life medical information and a public health manual in 한글,[23] allowing those unacquainted with *Hanja* to handle various contracts and transactions in 한글. Documents for land trade, livestock sales, inheritance property distribution, and petitions to government offices for aid or filing grievances were all frequently written in 한글.

---

[21] Historical records document that Korea established the Bureau of Interpreters (i.e., 司譯院사역원; *Sayŏgwŏn*) in the 13th century, though its origins date back to before the 10th century. Textbooks for practical foreign language instruction began appearing in the 14th century and became increasingly widespread (e.g., 老乞大노걸대, 朴通事박통사, etc.). These textbooks included 한글 pronunciations for several languages, such as Mandarin (e.g., 飜譯老乞大번역노걸대, 飜譯朴通事번역박통사, etc.), Mongolian (e.g., 蒙語老乞大몽어노걸대, 蒙語類解몽어유해, etc.), Manchu (e.g., 淸語老乞大청어노걸대, etc.), and Japanese (e.g., 捷解新語첩해신어, 隣語大方인어대방, etc.). Valued highly today, these texts not only detail contemporary pronunciations but also include commerce-related anecdotes, shedding light on the economic life of various regions.

[22] 실록 (see Footnote 15) cite three occasions in the 18th and 19th centuries (i.e., Nov. 14th, 1720; Mar. 6th, 1796; and Jan. 4th, 1796) when envoys abroad reported back to the king using 한글 documents. Since 실록 reflected selective records of significant matters only involving the king directly, these documents show that envoys frequently used 한글 for official communications in general. During the latter half of the 18th century, royal decrees also appeared in both *Hanja* and 한글, reflecting substantial public use of 한글 during this period (refer to Footnote 30).

[23] 향약집성방 (鄕藥集成方; *Hyangyak-jipseong-bang*, 1433) is a medical text from 세종's era, detailing approximately 10,700 treatments using Korean medicinal ingredients for over 950 diseases. Later, the government extracted and translated vital everyday medical information from this text into 한글 and distributed it (Sep. 20th, 1488; 실록; see Footnote 15). To address acute seasonal infectious diseases, specialized books such as 辟瘟方벽온방 (*Byeok-on-bang*, estimated early 15th century) were either supplemented with explanations in 한글 or fully translated and published repeatedly (e.g. 簡易辟瘟方간이벽온방 in 1515, 諺解辟瘟方언해벽온방 in 1518, 疸瘧易解方달학이해방 in

Figure III-11. 첩해신어, 1676 [24]

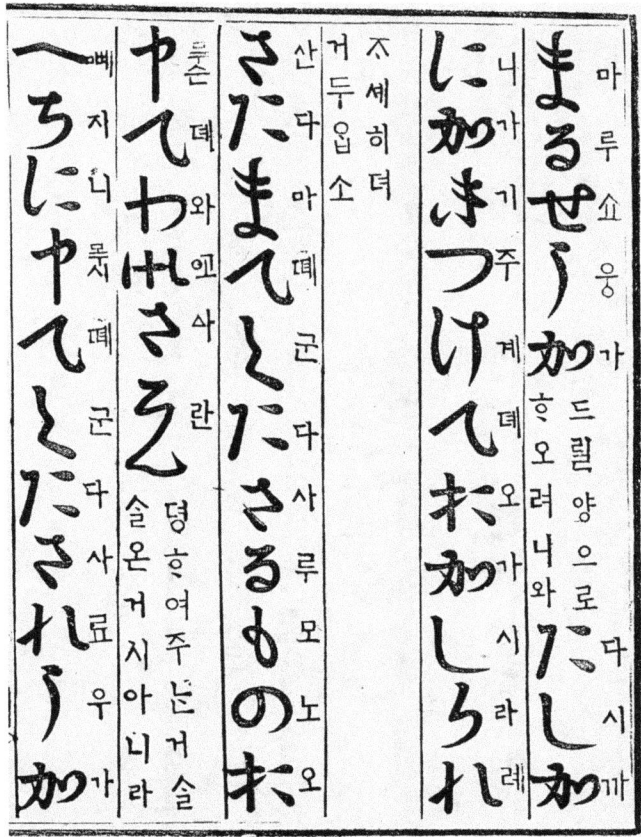

1550, 辟疫新方**벽역신방** in 1613, 辟瘟新方**벽온신방** in 1653, etc.). In addition, sum-
maries relating to severe outbreaks were urgently distributed as needed (Jan. 23rd, 1525;
Nov. 17th, 1724; 실록).

[24] **첩해신어**捷解新語, copper movable type printing, preserved at SNU's *Kyujanggak*
Institute for Korean Studies, p. 49 of Book 1 (refer to Footnote 21). 康遇聖**강우성**
(1581–?) compiled this Japanese language textbook in 1618, later revising and supple-
menting it himself, and the government published it in 1676, also producing the
typeset. After he was taken to Japan as a war prisoner in 1593, **강우성** served under
Tokugawa Ieyasu (德川 家康, 1543–1616), joined in *the Battle of Sekigahara* (関ヶ原の
戦い, Oct. 21st, 1600), and returned to Korea in 1601. He later became an interpreter
and assisted envoys on multiple missions to Japan (in 1617, 1624–25, and 1636–37),

Figure III-12. 청어노걸대, 1765 [25]

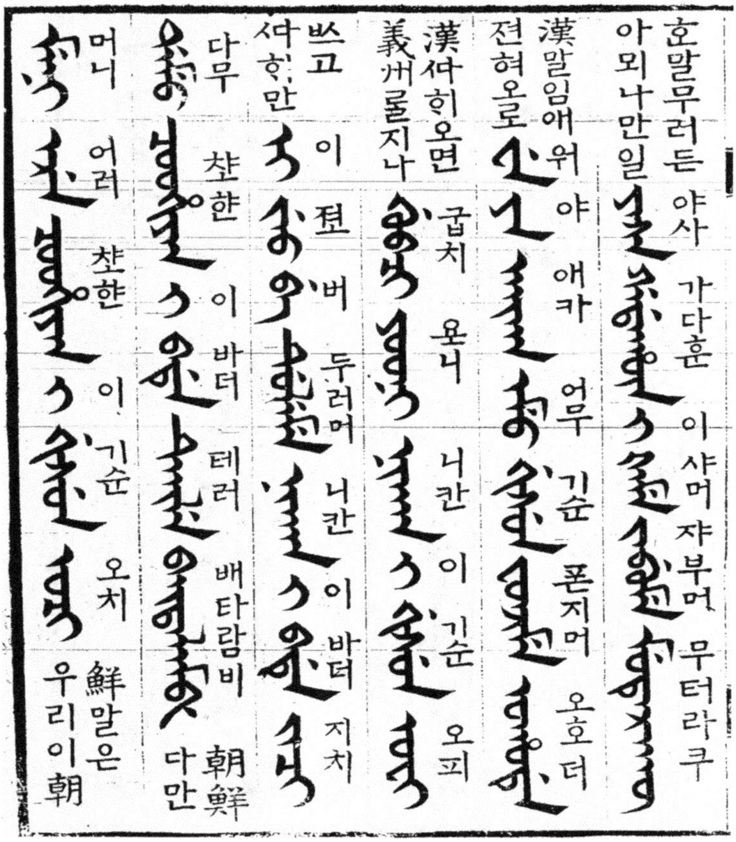

completing 첩해신어. His expertise in the Japanese language was noted for its alignment with the colloquial *Kansai* dialect of that era. The cited page features varied representations of the same character sound (i.e., old notation of 申, modern sound もうす[mousu]) as 모슨 or 모시,* and employs 어 to distinctly denote the unique [ŋg] sound in contemporary Japanese, represented by 오.

   *Other sections of the book also use notations like 모 and 무수.

[25] 청어노걸대 (淸語老乞大, a 1765 facsimile edition——microfilm, 1982*), stored at the National Library of Korea, p. 13 of Book 1 (refer to Footnote 21). Originally published by movable type printing in 1703, the surviving copy is a woodblock edition republished in 1765 by 金振夏김진하 (?–?), who revised the Manchu pronunciation notations. He later compiled several Manchu textbooks for children (e.g., 三譯總解

Figure III-13. 몽어노걸대, 1790 [26]

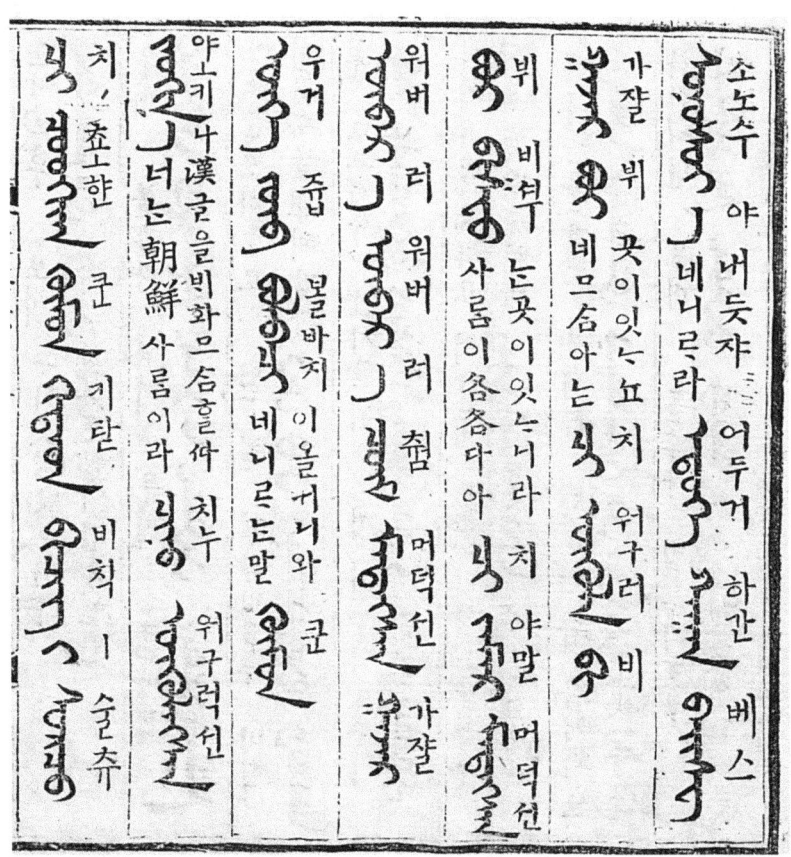

삼역총해 in 1774, 新譯小兒論신역소아론 in 1777, and 八歲兒팔세아 in 1777), making significant contributions to the teaching and study of Manchu. The cited page displays characters such as 묘, 젼, 챤, and throughout the book, various mid-sound ligatures like 빗, 럇, 쟌, 과, 튀, 갇, 도, or 훤 appear in diverse forms.

*The original is housed at INALCO, the British Library, and *Komazawa* University Library (駒澤大学図書館).

[26] 몽어노걸대 (蒙語老乞大, estimated 1790 edition), woodblock printing, housed at SNU's *Kyujanggak* Institute for Korean Studies, p. 12 of Book 1 (refer to Footnote 21). Scholars believe this to be an expanded version published either in 1766 or 1790, compiled anew in 1741 after previous Mongolian language textbooks were lost during consecutive wars. The page in the text displays various middle sound ligatures, such as

Figure III-14. 초계정씨단자, 1689 [27]

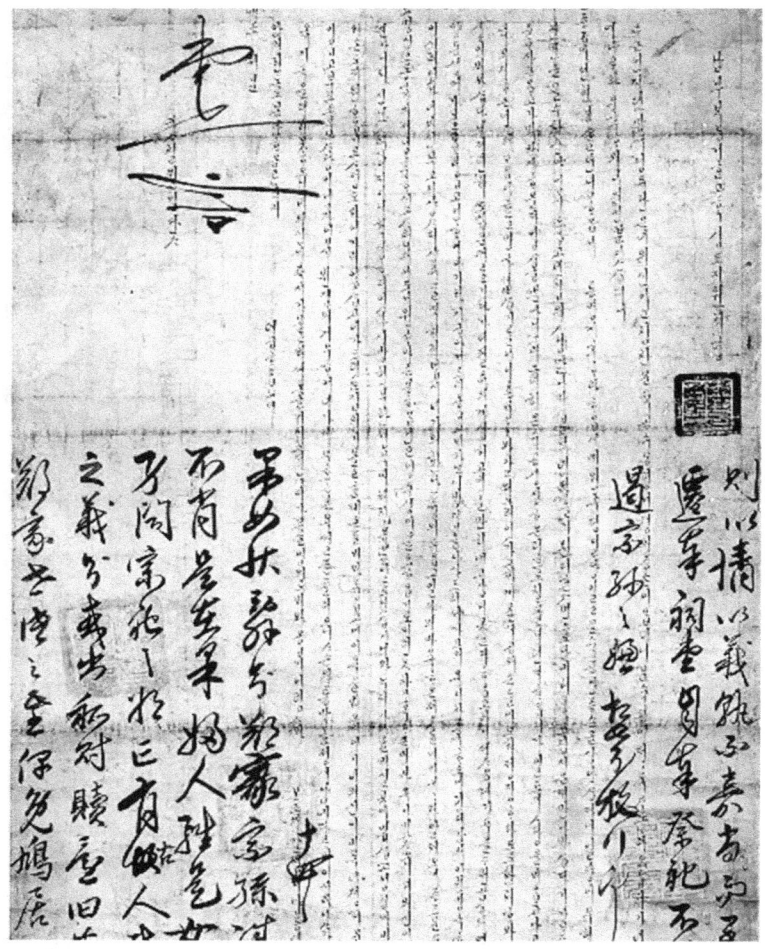

혐, 쵼 (or 쵸ㅗ), 얀, and 셩 (or 셔ㅜ), alongside characters like 확, 샨, 각, and 롣 throughout the book. The text also incorporates grammatical morphemes like ㅣ and ㅅ (refer to Footnote 18) and presents characters without top sounds, such as ㅜ, ㅜ, and ㄷ, showcasing the flexibility of 한글 usage.

[27] In 1689, 草溪초계 鄭氏정씨,* the wife of 趙持元조지원, submitted a 單字단자 to the national government, known as 초계정씨단자. Now it is preserved at the National Museum of Korea. 단자 is a type of petition or complaint presented to a government office, where judgments are written, sealed, and returned to the petitioner for retention

At the end of the 16th century, when the nation was embroiled in war, the king disseminated messages in 한글 to all people, regardless of their social status or class.[28] In 1668, the first book showcasing various aspects of Korea, including *easy writing*, was published in the Netherlands.[29] By the 18th century, royal decrees were issued in both *Hanja* and 한글.[30] Long-form novels

---

as an official document. The document in text narrates the plight of the only married daughter seeking inheritance rights after the family's foster son mishandles the family property and shrine. This 한글 단자, submitted directly to the central government instead of a local office, possesses considerable historical value.

　*lit. Mrs. 鄭정 from 草溪초계 area; Korean women maintain their family name even after marriage.

[28] 빅셩의게 니루는 글, or 백성에게 이르는 글 in modern Korean, lit. *a message to the people*, a.k.a. 宣祖國文諭書선조국문유서, preserved at the *Gimhae Hangeul* Museum, dates to September 1593. This 한글 document contains 宣祖선조's (1552–1608, ascended the throne in 1567) proclamation made during the war stating that those forced to assist the enemy would not face punishment, and those achieving military feats would receive significant rewards. The descendants of 權卓권탁 (1544–1593), who kept this document in his clothes and infiltrated enemy lines to rescue approximately 100 prisoners, have safe-guarded it to the present day.

[29] Commonly known as *Hamel's Journal*, this publication originated from Dutch sailor *Hendrik Hamel* (1630–1692), who sought to claim unpaid wages for the thirteen years (1653–1666) he was detained in Korea. He compiled his experiences into a report for the Dutch East India Company, which was published in 1668. The journal was later translated into French in 1670, German in 1672, and English in 1705, gaining broad recognition across Europe. The book's commentary on 한글 is notable:

> *It is very easy to learn and one is able to write everything. One can write down names one has never heard before, easier and better than in the other ways (of writing).* (Hendrik Hamel, *Hamel's Journal and a description of the kingdom of Korea 1653–1666*, trans. *Jean-Paul Buys*, 2011: p. 71)

[30] Documentation from the 15th century shows that kings consistently utilized 한글 in managing political affairs (e.g., July 13th, 1483; July 5th, 1485; Dec. 29th, 1519; Mar. 25th, 1646; Apr. 24th, 1689; Dec. 5th, 1752; etc., 실록; see Footnote 15). By the 17th century, local government offices extensively used 한글 documents (Sep. 27th 1694, 실록), and 18th century records confirm that royal proclamations were issued in both *Hanja* and 한글 (June 3rd, 1771, 실록) following the era of 선조 (refer to Footnote 28).

in 한글, created and consumed by women, became popular.[31] 한글 versions of the Christian Faith Catechism and the Bible were also published.[32] Finally, foreign missionaries started to write books in 한글.

---

[31] 한글 novels evolved from the 16th century onward, beginning with titles such as 薛公瓚傳설공찬전 and 洪吉童傳홍길동전 and progressing in the 17th and 18th centuries to works like 九雲夢구운몽 and 玉樓夢옥루몽. Originally, these novels were adaptations from *Hanja* into 한글, but eventually, authors began creating original 한글 novels. By the 18th century, the writing of 한글 novels had become well-established. The popularity of epic novels written by women rose among royal and upper-class ladies. Book rental shops (a.k.a. 貰冊家세책가) flourished, distributing works such as 玩月會盟宴완월회맹연, 玉鴛再合奇緣옥원재합기연 (a.k.a. 玉鴛重會宴옥원중회연), and 明珠寶月聘명주보월빙, which predominantly fell within the romance genre.

[32] Christianity, first introduced to Korea as *Western Learning* (a.k.a. 西學서학), began gaining followers in the mid-18th century through the initiative of local believers, well before missionaries set foot in the country. Due to the prolonged tradition of circulating religious texts as manuscripts, pinpointing the exact publication dates and authors for these materials proves difficult. The oldest known 한글 catechism, written by the Catholic believer 丁若鍾정약종 (1760–1801), is titled 쥬교요지 (主教要旨, a.k.a. 주교요지, late 18th century). The first 한글 Bible, 예수성교 누가복음전서 (the Gospel of Luke, 1882), was translated collaboratively by Scottish Presbyterian missionaries *John Ross* (1842–1915) and *John Macintyre* (1837–1905), along with Korean translators.

Figure III-15. 완월회맹연, Mid-18th Century [33]

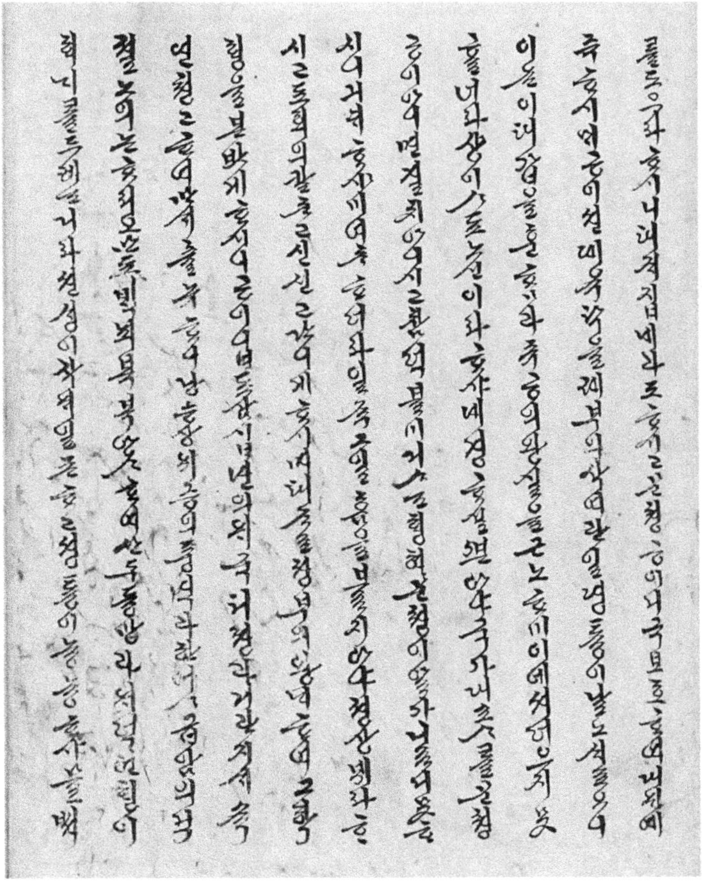

---

[33] 완월회맹연 (玩月會盟宴, lit. *A Gathering at* 玩月완월 *to Pledge Mutual Promises*; 완월 means *full moon* and also refers to the name of a house in the story), estimated to have been handwritten in the mid-18th century, resides at The Academy of Korean Study, p. 2 of Book 1 (refer to Footnote 31). This narrative, believed to be from the early 18th century, describes individuals at a summerhouse called, 완월대, who pledge marriage ties for their yet-to-be-born children over drinks. The story follows their children, who despite various challenges, eventually meet each other and live happily together, seemingly destined by fate. Spanning approximately 70 pages per volume across 180 volumes, the story appears to be a product of collaborative writing. The narrative inspired numerous fan-written sequels, and as a popular novel, it was often meticulously transcribed by royal court ladies for the royal library, where queens and princesses frequently read it. The mentioned edition here is one such copy.

Figure III-16. 홍길동전, Around 1850 [34]

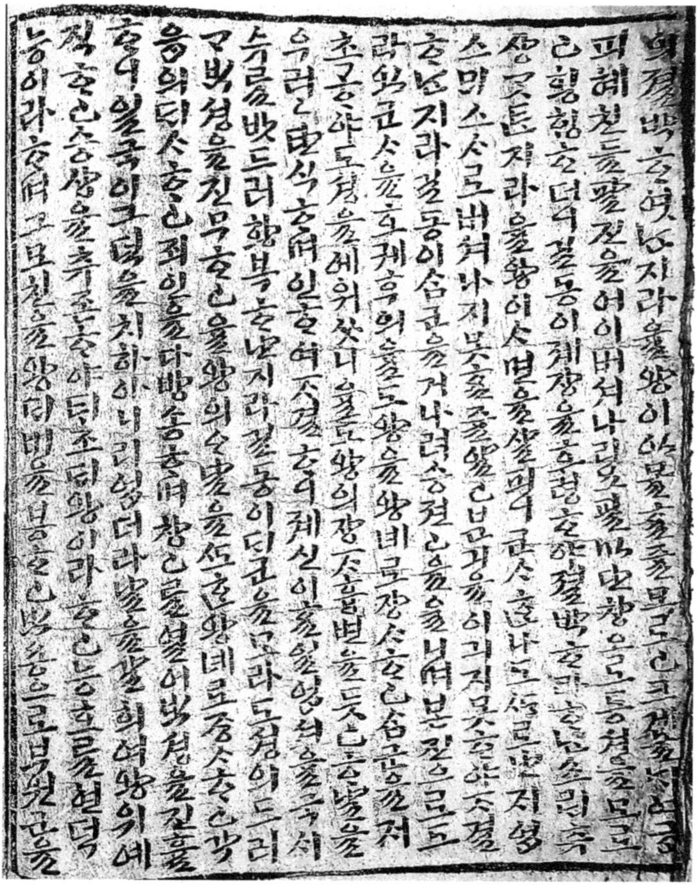

---

[34] 홍길동전 (洪吉童傳, lit. Tales of 홍길동) is housed at *Ojukheon & Gangneung* Municipal Museum, p. 60 (refer to Footnote 31). Attributed to 許筠허균 (*Heo Gyun*, 1569–1618) and dates from the late 16th or early 17th century. Though the original is lost, this novel has survived in various editions, leading to ongoing discussions about its authorship, dating, and original content. The plot follows 홍길동, born an illegitimate son, who leaves his home to overcome numerous challenges through his innate talents and mystical martial arts, ultimately rising to prominence. The novel, a celebrated fantasy, critiques societal issues such as class discrimination and government corruption. The cited edition is a woodblock print from the *Jeonju* city, a prominent publishing center after Seoul since the late 19th century, discovered near 허균's hometown in *Gangneung* in 1997.

Figure III-17. 예수성교 누가복음전서, J. Ross, 1882 [35]

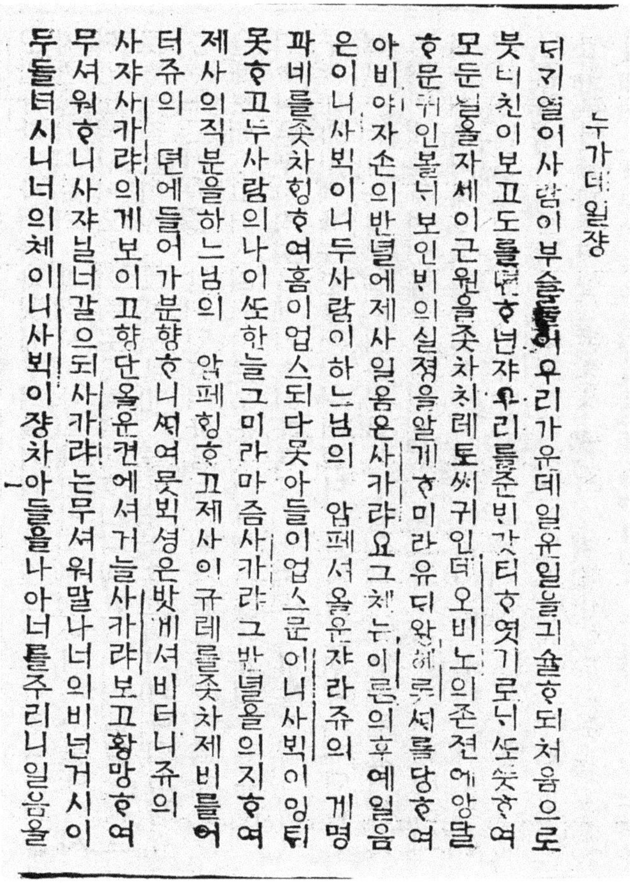

[35] 예수셩교젼셔 (a.k.a. 예수성교전서), stored at the Korean Bible Society, p. 1 (refer to Footnote 32). This book was translated into 한글 over a period between 1877 and 1887. The translation was a collaborative effort led by *John Ross, John Macintyre,* and Koreans 이응찬, 백홍준, 김진기, 서상훈, 이성하, and 이익세. The Gospel of Luke (i.e., 누가복음젼셔) was initially published in March 1882, followed by the Gospel of John (i.e., 요안늬복음젼셔) two months later. The Korean contributors first translated from the Mandarin Bible; *Ross* and *Macintyre* then refined these translations, consulting both English and Greek Bibles. This effort marked the first translation of many biblical terms into Korean. (e.g., *God* rendered as 하느님 or 하나님, instead of the earlier term 텬쥬 transliterated from the Mandarin 天主.)

Figure III-18. 주교요지, 정약종, 1897 [36]

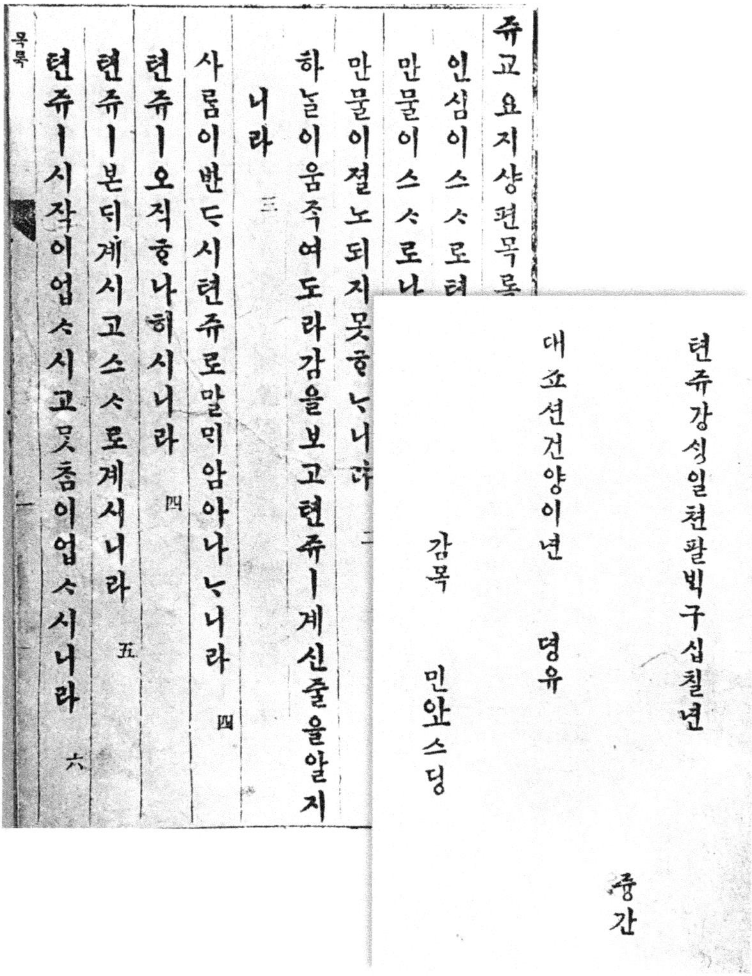

---

[36] Housed at the National Folk Museum of Korea (refer to Footnote 32). This book has significantly contributed to the rise in voluntary Catholic converts in Korea since the late 18th century by elating Catholic doctrines through Neo-Confucian concepts. The edition cited is a printed version released about a century after the original, with the publication year noted in the *anno Domini* system (i.e., 텬쥬강싱; AD, 일쳔팔빅 구십칠년; 1897). The subject marker ｜ is employed to emphasize 텬쥬 (God), and the censor, French priest *Gustave Mutel* (1854–1933, a.k.a. 閔德孝·민덕효), is referred to by his Korean last name, 민, and the French pronunciation of his baptismal name, *St. Augustine*, in 한글: 앗스딩.

In 1869, French priest *S. Féron* firstly introduced horizontal writing to 한글 words publishing a French–Korean dictionary.[37] Scottish missionary *J. Ross*, in 1877, published a Korean language primer, applying both horizontal writing and word spacing together to 한글 sentences for the first time.[38] French bishop *F. Ridel* published a French–Korean dictionary and a Korean grammar book[39] around 1880, and English missionary *H. Underwood* published

---

[37] Stanislas Féron,* *Dictionnaire Français-Coréen*, 1869. This is the earliest surviving French-Korean dictionary, stemming from the prolonged efforts of French missionaries, starting in the early 19th century, to create dictionaries translating French, Chinese, Korean, and Latin. After enduring severe religious persecution in Korea between 1866 and 1871, which led to numerous fatalities and the destruction of various materials, Father *Féron* escaped the country. By 1869, in *Shanghai*, he had compiled and transcribed a manuscript containing over 10,000 words. This manuscript is now maintained by The Research Foundation of Korean Church History.

   *French priest, 1827–1903. After experiencing persecution, he realized that extraordinary measures were necessary to open Korea's doors. In 1868, he orchestrated an unsuccessful attempt with German *Ernst Oppert* (1832–1903) to excavate the tomb of the king's grandfather. He later continued his missionary work in India.

[38] John Ross,* *Corean Primer*, 1877. Before the release of this book, European understanding of the Korean language and 한글 was quite limited, based primarily on a few pages by the German physician *P. F. B. von Siebold* (1796–1866), only including brief mentions of the languages and scripts of Japan's neighboring countries in an 1832 work published in the Netherlands;** French linguist *Léon de Rosny* (1837–1914) later systematized *Siebold*'s descriptions in a scholarly work published in 1864.*** Rev. *Ross*'s publication marked the first comprehensive European effort to compile the Korean language and 한글, learned directly from Koreans, notably focusing on the northwestern dialects of the language.

   *Scottish missionary, 1842–1915, refer to Footnotes 32 and 35. **Philipp Franz Balthasar von Siebold, *Nippon: Archiv zur Beschreibung von Japan*, 1897: p. 315–318. ***Léon de Rosny, *Aperçu de la langue coréenne*, Imprimerie Impériale, 1864.

[39] Félix-Clair Ridel,* *Grammaire Coréenne*, 1881. This book stands as the first grammar of the Korean language, authored by Fr. *Ridel* and published in *Yokohama* in 1881. He compiled the work based on the efforts of French missionaries, notably bishop *Antoine Daveluy* (1818–1866), Fr. *Michel Petitnicolas* (1828–1866), and Fr. *Jean Pourthié* (1830–1866), who perished during the wave of religious persecution in Korea in 1866. Released under the names of missionaries from the *Paris Foreign Missions Society*. The book is historically significant as the first thorough exploration of the Korean language's grammar, focusing on the Seoul dialect.

a Korean–English dictionary in 1890. American missionary *H. Hulbert* published a world geography textbook in 한글 in 1889.[40] In 1892, he also contributed an essay, *The Korean Alphabet*, to an English-language magazine published by his fellow missionaries in Korea, introducing the background and characteristics of 한글 to English-speaking readers.[41]

---

*French priest, 1830–1884. Following the 1866 religious persecutions in Korea, he escaped and led a French fleet from *Tianjin* to assault *Ganghwa* island (江華島 강화도, located 50km west of Seoul). Following years of evasion, he was captured in 1878 and deported to Manchuria. Later, he moved to Japan, where he went on to publish a Korean dictionary and grammar books.

[40] 수민필지 (士民必知; *Saminpilji*, lit. *What Nobles and Commoners Must Know*, a.k.a. 사민필지), authored by Homer B. Hulbert,* 1889. This publication stands as the first 한글 textbook crafted by a foreigner for Koreans. It begins by discussing the solar system surrounding the earth and extends to the geography, culture, industries, and military capabilities of various nations.

*American Methodist missionary, 1863–1949. Following his appointment as an English teacher at Korea's premier Western-style royal school in 1886 (i.e., 育英 公院육영공원), he developed a profound interest in 한글. He took a leading role in academic research, orthographic reform, and the publication of newspapers and magazines, seeking to elevate 한글's profile globally (refer to Footnote 41). A staunch advocate for Korean sovereignty and a critic of Japanese policies, he was ultimately expelled by Japanese authorities. His dedication to the Korean independence movement persisted until his death in 1949, a week after his return to Korea following a 40-year absence. His role as a royal secret envoy is depicted in the TV drama 미스터션샤인 (*Mr. Sunshine*, tvN, 2018).

[41] *The Korean Repository* initially appeared in 1892 under the aegis of American Methodist missionaries *Franklin Ohlinger* and his spouse. It was later revitalized by *Henry Appenzeller* (1858–1902), *George Jones* (1867–1919), and Prof. *Hulbert* (refer to Footnote 40) between 1895 and 1899. *Hulbert*'s contributions began in January and March 1892 with an article titled *The Korean Alphabet*. After joining the publication team in 1895, he regularly penned articles exploring Korean politics, society, history, language, and art. He later launched and edited the monthly English publication *The Korea Review*, beginning in 1901 and continuing for six years. In 1903, he presented the paper *The Korean Language* at the American Smithsonian Association's annual meeting, and thereafter, he continued to promote Korean culture through his books *The History of Korea* in 1905 and *The Passing of Korea* in 1906. He also authored a history book of Korea in 한글 (i.e., 대한력ᄉ, 1908), maintaining his commitment to literary projects

Figure III-19. *Corean Primer*, J. Ross, 1877 [42]

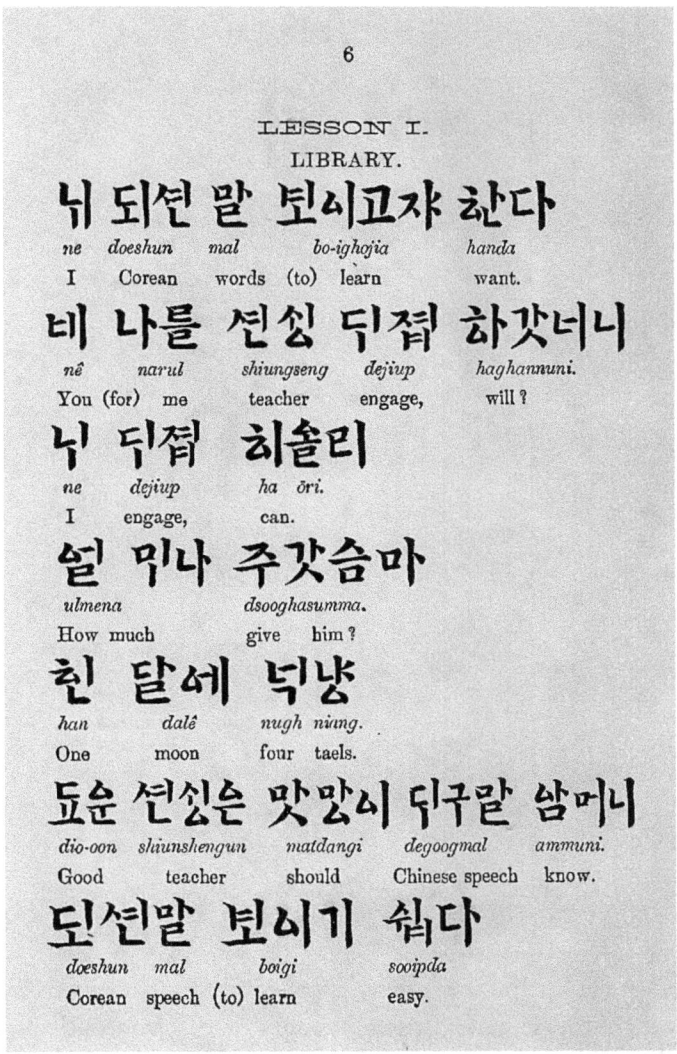

for the Korean people.

[42] Shanghai: American Presbyterian Mission Press, 1877: p. 6 (refer to Footnote 38). This page outlines the application of 한글 for writing Korean, with corresponding pronunciations presented in italicized Roman letters and meanings given in regular font below. The legend introduces the inclusion of ｜ in ｜-compounds as bottom letters (refer to Footnote 44). The publication features numerous deviations from

Figure III-20. *Dictionnaire Coréen-Français*, F. Ridel, 1880[43]

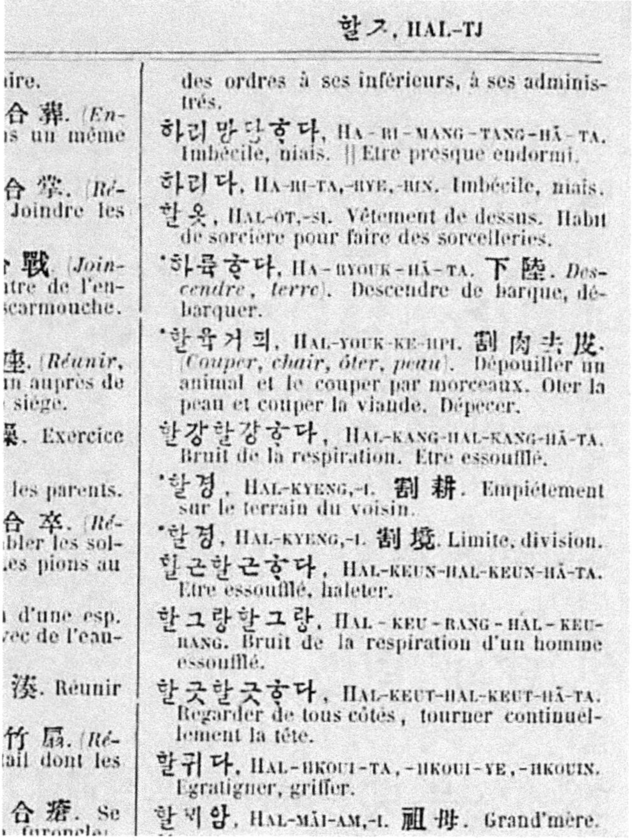

할ᄌ, HAL-TJ

des ordres à ses inférieurs, à ses administrés.

하리망당ᄒᆞ다, HA-RI-MANG-TANG-HĂ-TA. Imbécile, niais. || Etre presque endormi.

하리다, HA-RI-TA,-RYE,-RIN. Imbécile, niais.

할옷, HAL-OT,-SI. Vêtement de dessus. Habit de sorcière pour faire des sorcelleries.

*하륙ᄒᆞ다, HA-RYOUK-HĂ-TA. 下陸. (Descendre, terre). Descendre de barque, débarquer.

*할육거피, HAL-YOUK-KE-HPI. 割肉去皮. (Couper, chair, ôter, peau). Dépouiller un animal et le couper par morceaux. Oter la peau et couper la viande. Dépecer.

할강할강ᄒᆞ다, HAL-KANG-HAL-KANG-HĂ-TA. Bruit de la respiration. Etre essoufflé.

*할경, HAL-KYENG,-I. 割耕. Empiétement sur le terrain du voisin.

*할경, HAL-KYENG,-I. 割境. Limite, division.

할근할근ᄒᆞ다, HAL-KEUN-HAL-KEUN-HĂ-TA. Etre essoufflé, haleter.

할그랑할그랑, HAL-KEU-RANG-HAL-KEU-RANG. Bruit de la respiration d'un homme essoufflé.

할긋할긋ᄒᆞ다, HAL-KEUT-HAL-KEUT-HĂ-TA. Regarder de tous côtés, tourner continuellement la tête.

할퀴다, HAL-HKOUI-TA,-HKOUI-YE,-HKOUIN. Egratigner, griffer.

할미암, HAL-MĂI-AM,-I. 祖母. Grand'mère.

traditional 한글 usage, such as the representation of the sound for 뒤 as *dooi* (p. 15 of the book). Furthermore, several misrepresentations of ㆍ, erroneously marked as ㅣ (e.g., 닉, 딕, 믹, etc.), are observed. In addition, the book seems to introduce a variety of new glyph types, including 빅 (*beg*, p. 11), 이가 (*ingga*, p. 13), 완 (*wan*, p. 15), 므 (*mo*, p. 16), and 늬 (*nungi*, p. 49).

[43] F. Ridel, *Dictionnaire Coréen-Français* (한불ᄌᆞ뎐韓佛字典, a.k.a. 한불자전), Yokohama: *C. Lévy, Imprimeur-Libraire*, 1880: p. 80 (refer to Footnote 39). Compiled by French missionaries after years of direct interaction with Koreans, this dictionary comprises approximately 29,000 entries. This specific page groups various Korean terms for *grandfather*, such as 할아뵈양, 할아베, 할아버니, and 할아비, and also displays numerous native Korean words, including 할강할강ᄒᆞ다 and 할그랑할그랑.

Figure III-21. *Grammaire Coréenne*, F. Ridel, 1881 [44]

DE L'ADJECTIF.			
CONJUGAISON DES ADJECTIFS VERBAUX.			
et INDICATIF PRÉSENT	소랑스럽다 .	SĂ-RANG-SEU-REP-TA	*être aimable d'être aimé.*
? VERBAL PASSÉ	소랑스러딈 .	SĂ-RANG-SEU-RE-OUE. . . .	*étant aimable.*
LATIF PASSÉ *ou* ADJECTIF	소랑스러온 .	SĂ-RANG-SEU-RE-ON.	*aimable.*
T DE L'INDICATIF	소랑스럽더니 . .	SĂ-RANG-SEU-REP-TE-NI . . .	*était aimable.*
DE CONDITION	소랑스럽더면 . .	SĂ-RANG-SEU-REP-TE-MYEN . . .	*s'il était aimabl*
FUTUR	소랑스럽겟다. .	SĂ-RANG-SEU-REP-KEIT-TA . . .	*il sera aimable.*
IMPARFAIT	소랑스럽겟더니	SĂ-RANG-SEU-REP-KEIT-TE-NI. . .	*il serait aimabl*
CONDITIONNEL	소랑스럽겟더면	SĂ-RANG-SEU-REP-KEIT-TE-MYEN.	*« s'il serait aima*
ÉSENT (réponse : supérieur)	소랑스럽쉬다. .	SĂ-RANG-SEU-REP-SOI-TA . . .	*il est aimable.*
ÉS. (à un égal, le et réponse)	소랑스럽지 .	SĂ-RANG-SEU-REP-TJI	*est-il aimable ? aimable.*
ÉS. (à un égal)	소랑스럽쇼 . .	SĂ-RANG-SEU-REP-SYO.	*id.*
RÉS. (id., plus espect.)	소랑스럽지오. .	SĂ-RANG-SEU-REP-TJI-O	*id.*
ADVERBE	소랑스럽게 . .	SĂ-RANG-SEU-REP-KEI.	*aimablement.*
et INDICATIF NÉGATIFS	소랑스럽잔타. .	SĂ-RANG-SEU-REP-TJAN-HTA. . . .	*il n'est pas aim*
'INDICATIF PRÉSENT			—
ERBAL ABSTRAIT	소랑스러온이	SĂ-RANG-SEU-RE-	*« le être aimabl*

---

[44] Yokohama: Imprimerie de L. Lévy et S. Salabelle: p. 35, *Conjugation of verbal adjectives* (refer to Footnote 39). This page provides explanations for various conjugations of the Korean adjective 사랑스럽다 (i.e., lovable, adorable, endearing). The book consistently presents Korean text in 한글, pronunciations in uppercase letters, and meanings in italicized text. It includes detailed explanations of vocabulary and grammar, complemented by step-by-step practice exercises for translating Korean. Notably, like *Corean Primer* (refer to Footnotes 38 and 42), this publication largely aids in understanding the Korean pronunciation encountered by the authors at that time, particularly through its introduction of various ㅣ-compound letters and their pronunciations, listed in the preface (p. xxii).

Figure III-22. 사민필지, H. Hulbert, 1889[45]

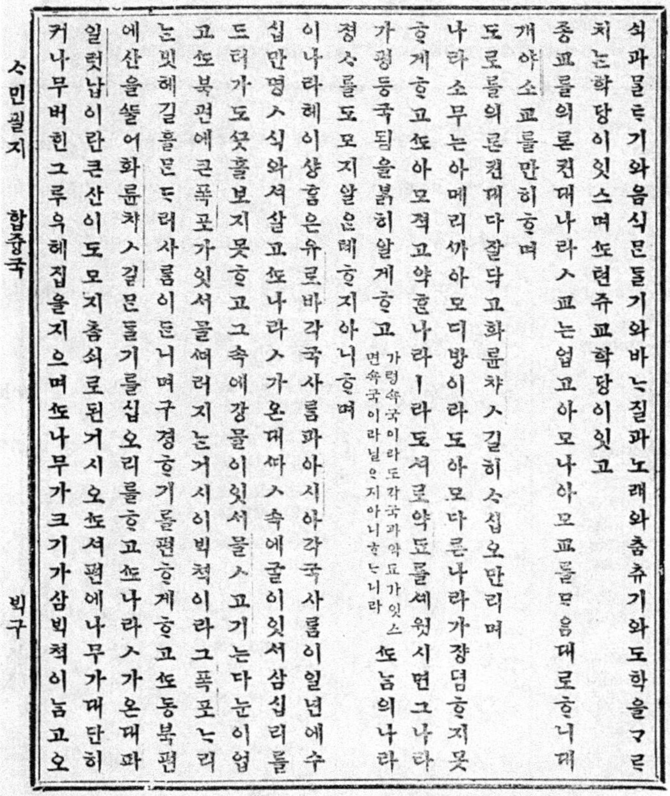

식과믈ᄃᆞ기와음식믄돌기와바ᄂᆞ질과노래와춤츄기와도학을ᄀᆞᄅᆞ
치ᄂᆞᆫ학당이잇스며ᄯᅩ련쥬교학당이잇고
종교를의론컨대나라ᄉᆞ교ᄂᆞᆫ업고아모나아모교를ᄆᆞ음대로ᄒᆞᄂᆞ니대
개야소교를만히ᄒᆞ며
도로를의론컨대다잘닥고화륜챠ᄉᆞ길히ᄉᆞ십오만리며
나라소무ᄂᆞᆫ아메리ᄭᅡ아모디방이라도아모다른나라가쟝뎜ᄒᆞ지못
ᄒᆞ게ᄒᆞ고ᄯᅩ아모젹고약ᄒᆞᆫ나라ㅣ라도셔로약됴를세웟시면그나라
가평등국됨을ᄇᆞᆰ히알게ᄒᆞ고 가령속국이라도각국과약됴가잇스면속국이라닐ᄋᆞ지아니ᄒᆞᄂᆞ니라 ᄯᅩ놈의나라
졍ᄉᆞ를도모지알은톄ᄒᆞ지아니ᄒᆞ며
이나라헤이샹ᄒᆞᆫ은유로바각국사ᄅᆞᆷ과아시아각국사ᄅᆞᆷ이일년에수
십만명ᄉᆞ식와셔살고ᄯᅩ나라ᄉᆞ가온대ᄯᅡᄉᆞ속에굴이잇서삼십리를
드더가도ᄭᅳᆺ흘보지못ᄒᆞ고그속에강물이잇서믈ᄉᆞ고기ᄂᆞᆫ다눈이업
고ᄯᅩ북편에큰폭포가잇서믈ᄊᆡ려지ᄂᆞᆫ거시이빅쳑이라그폭포ᄂᆞ리
ᄂᆞᆫ빗헤길흘ᄆᆞᆫᄃᆞ러사ᄅᆞᆷ이ᄃᆞᆫ니며구경ᄒᆞ기를편ᄒᆞ게ᄒᆞ고ᄯᅩ동북편
에산을ᄯᅮᆯ어화륜챠ᄉᆞ길ᄆᆞᆫᄃᆞᆯ기를십오리를ᄒᆞ고ᄯᅩ나라ᄉᆞ가온대파
일럿납이란큰산이도모지춤쇠로된거시오ᄯᅩ셔편에나무가대단히
커나무버힌그루우헤집을지으며ᄯᅩ나무가크기가삼빅쳑이놈고오

ᄉᆞ민필지 합즁국 빅구

[45] Held at the National *Hangeul* Museum, p. 109 (refer to Footnote 40). In the cited page, the author discusses his homeland, the United States, and highlights its diplomatic philosophy: *(The U.S.) unequivocally shows that any nation, no matter its size or strength, becomes equal upon entering into agreements* (in the right 7th column, from 아모젹고약ᄒᆞᆫ until ᄇᆞᆰ히알게ᄒᆞ고). Following the Japanese forceful annexation of Korea's sovereignty (a.k.a. *Eulsa* Unwilling Treaty, 1905), he visited Washington D.C. in October 1905 as a royal envoy, based on the Treaty of 1882 (a.k.a. *Shufeldt* Treaty), to request U.S. intervention. However, the president (*Theodore Roosevelt*, 1858–1919, term 1901–1909), who had already signed a secret agreement with Japan (i.e., *Taft-Katsura* Memorandum, July 29th, 1905), didn't even meet him. This refusal led him to transition from a scholar and missionary into a critic of American foreign policy and an advocate for Korean independence, evolving into a journalist and international activist (See Dec 13th, 1905; May 16th, 1908; Dec 6th, 1914; Dec 12th, 1915; May 5th, 1916; Aug 15th & 17th, 1919 in *The New York Times*, and Aug 18th, 1919, Vol. 58, Part 4, 3924–3926 in *the US Congressional Record – Senate*).

By 1894, 한글 was designated as the primary script for creating official government documents. [46] Korean-authored English textbooks in 한글 began to emerge. [47] Although the Japanese occupation halted or altered government-led changes, within the community, 한글 deeply entrenched itself as *Korea's own*. A surge of Korean poetry and novels written in 한글 followed. Colonial government scholars and nationalist scholars alike studied the Korean language and 한글, competing to create textbooks and dictionaries. During the Pacific War, nationalists' efforts to compile a Korean dictionary in 한글 became a perilous hide-and-seek game with the colonial government, risking lives. Many were imprisoned, their work confiscated. However, in September 1945, a stack of manuscript pages for a Korean dictionary in 한글 was miraculously found in a corner of Seoul Station's warehouse. [48] It became the touchstone for using the Korean language in modern Korea and is preserved to this day.

---

[46] On November 21, 1894, the Korean government officially proclaimed 한글 the primary official script of the country (국문國文; lit. the national written language). This declaration mandated that all governmental laws and decrees initially be drafted in 한글, with translations into *Hanja* or combinations thereof, permitted as needed.

[47] Originally, 兒學編아학편 was a children's *Hanja* textbook developed by 丁若鏞 정약용 (1762–1836) in the early 19th century, intended to supplement 최세진's 훈몽 자회 (refer to Footnote 16). This textbook provided meanings and sounds for 2,000 *Hanja* characters in 한글. In 1908, 池錫永지석영 (1855–1935), working with 田龍圭 전용규 (?–?), republished the work, enriching the content with Mandarin pronunciations, corresponding Japanese and English terms with the same meanings, and their pronunciations, all annotated in 한글.

[48] Prof. *Hulbert* (refer to Footnotes 40, 41, and 45) served as a mentor to 주시경 (周時經; *Ju Si-gyeong*, 1876–1914) who founded 국어연구학회 (lit. the Korean Language Research Society) and began compiling the first 한글 Korean dictionary, titled 말모이, in 1911. Unfortunately, 주시경's life ended before he could finish this monumental undertaking. His disciples, despite changing their organizational name several times, continued his work, resuming the dictionary compilation in 1929 and obtaining publication approval by 1940. In 1942, just as the manuscript was about to be sent to the printing house, the colonial government suddenly arrested dozens of the group's members, declaring them anti-state, and confiscated all documents. Fortunately, on September 8, 1945, after Korea's liberation, a dramatic discovery was made in a storage

Figure III-23. 아학편, 지석영, 1908 [49]

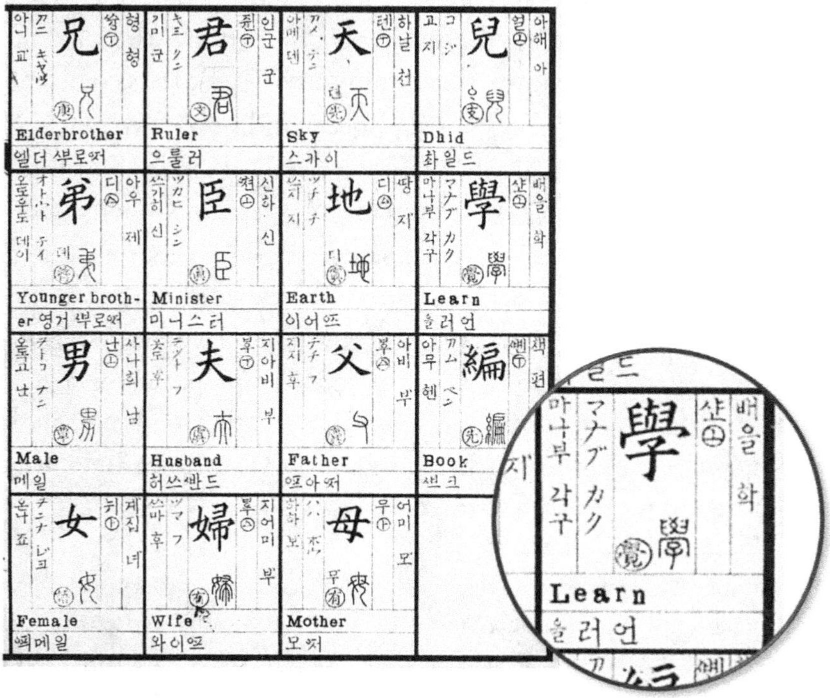

area of Seoul Station, 17 volumes comprising 5,448 pages of the manuscript were found, allowing publication efforts to restart. On October 9, 1957, 한글학회 (*Korean Language Society*, lit. 한글 Academic Society) published the dictionary, titled 큰사전 (lit. The Dictionary Unabridged). It spans six volumes and includes 3,804 pages with 164,125 entries. The story behind this project inspired the film 말모이 (*MAL-MO-E – The Secret Mission*, 2019).

[49] Stone-print edition, privately owned, with a digital copy provided by the National *Hangeul* Museum, p. 1 (refer to Footnote 47). Each character on this page is annotated from right to left, detailing its meaning and pronunciation, Mandarin pronunciation, *Hanja* and indexing information, Japanese words in *Kana*, Japanese pronunciations (i.e., 訓読み*Kun'yomi*, 音読み*On'yomi*), and the corresponding English words in Roman script with their 한글 pronunciations underneath. This page notably uses characters such as 쥔, 샨, 뗜, 쎈, and 붚 for Mandarin pronunciations. In addition, the transcription method used for English sounds into 한글, where the word-initial *l* sound is represented as 을ㄹ, *r* as 으ㄹ, *th* as �, and *f* as ᄑ, offers a fascinating glimpse into linguistic adaptation.

Figure III-24. 깁더조선말본, 김두봉, 1922 [50]

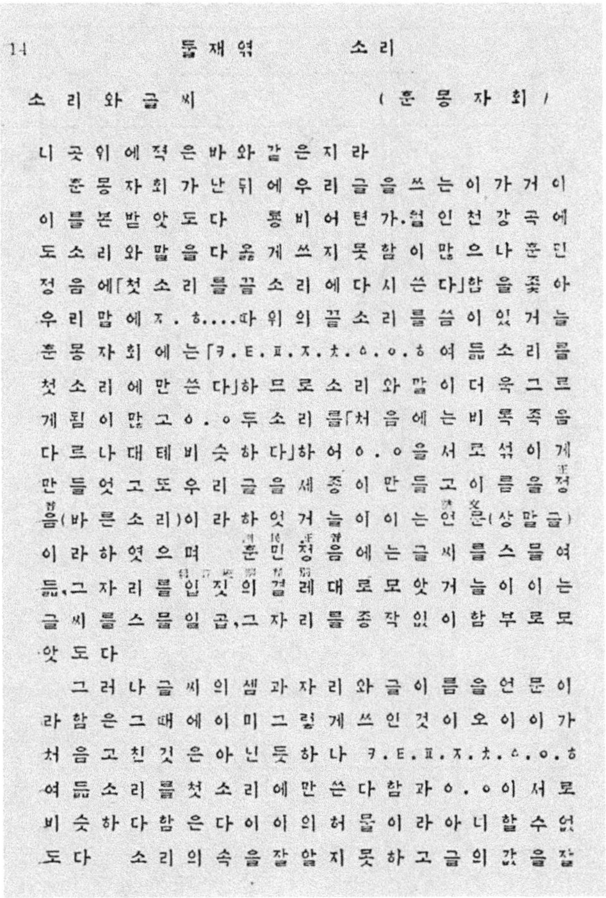

14 둘재엮 소리

소리와글씨 (훈몽자회)

니곳위에적은바와같은지라

훈몽자회가난뒤에우리글을쓰는이가거이
이를본받앗도다 룡비어텬가.월인천강곡에
도소리와말을다옳게쓰지못함이많으나훈민
정음에「첫소리를끝소리에다시쓴다」함을좇아
우리말에ㅈ.ㅎ....따위의끝소리를씀이있거늘
훈몽자회에는「ㅋ.ㅌ.ㅍ.ㅈ.ㅊ.ㅿ.ㅇ.ㅎ여듧소리를
첫소리에만쓴다」하므로소리와말이더욱그르
게됨이많고ㆁ.ㅇ두소리를「처음에는비록좀
다르나대테비슷하다」하어ㆁ.ㅇ을서로섞이게
만들엇고또우리글을세종이만들고이름을정
음(바른소리)이라하엿거늘이이는언문(상말글)
이라하엿으며 훈민정음에는글씨를스믈여
듧,그자리를입짓의결례대로모앗거늘이이는
글씨를스믈일곱,그자리를종작없이함부로모
앗도다

그러나글씨의셈과자리와글이름을언문이
라함은그때에이미그렇게쓰인것이오이이가
처음고친것은아닌듯하나 ㅋ.ㅌ.ㅍ.ㅈ.ㅊ.ㅿ.ㅇ.ㅎ
여듧소리를첫소리에만쓴다함과ㆁ.ㅇ이서로
비슷하다함은다이이의허물이라아니할수없
도다 소리의속을잘알지못하고글의값을잘

[50] 김두봉 (金枓奉; *Kim Tu-bong*, 1889–?), 깁더조선말본, 2nd ed, 滙東書館회동서관, 1934, held at the National *Hangeul* Museum, p. 14. This publication is a reprint of the expanded 1922 edition of the original 조선말본 (1916) by 김두봉, who was a co-creator of 말모이 and celebrated as the best pupil of 주시경 (refer to Foot-note 48). This work expands on 주시경's 국어문법 (lit. Korean Language Grammar, 1910) and 말의 소리 (lit. Sounds of Speaking, 1914), by elucidating the phonetic principles of 한글 and the grammatical system of the Korean language. In the referenced passage, 김두봉 criticizes 최세진's approach in 훈몽자회 (refer to Footnote 16) for arbitrarily limiting the use of certain letters for top and bottom sounds and for reducing 세종's original 28 alphabet letters to 27 (excluding ㆆ). He suggests that the change shows a

Figure III-25. 서시 Manuscript, 윤동주, 1941 [51]

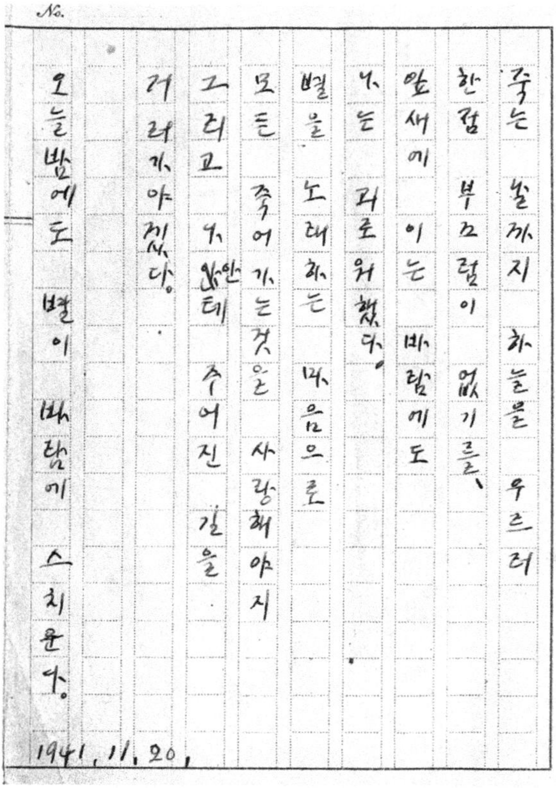

No.

죽는 날까지 하늘을 우르러
한 점 부끄럼이 없기를,
잎새에 이는 바람에도
나는 괴로워했다,
별을 노래하는 마음으로
모든 죽어가는 것은 사랑해야지
그리고 나안테 주어진 길을
거러가야겠다.
오늘 밤에도 별이 바람에 스치운다.

1941. 11. 20.

---

lack of understanding of 한글's principles. Further, on page 2, he critiques the direct adoption of foreign academic systems and terminology as akin to *choosing a mountain path beside a paved road* (i.e., 길을두고뫼로감), and he states that his book aims to *disturb the brief ease of a few* (i.e., scholars) *to alleviate the prolonged difficulty of many.*

[51] 윤동주 (尹東柱; *Yun Dong-ju*, 1917–1945), among his handwritten manuscripts, 서시 (序詩, lit. Prelude), preserved at the *Yun Dong-ju* Memorial Hall in *Yonsei* University. Born in *Gando* (間島간도), he studied in *Pyongyang* and *Seoul*, and became a student poet. In 1942, he enrolled at *Doshisha* University (同志社도시샤) in Kyoto, Japan, but was arrested as a thought criminal in 1943. After one year and seven months, he died in *Fukuoka* Prison. Reports indicate that 윤동주 studied Korean and 한글 under 최현배 (refer to Footnote 52), a disciple of 주시경, in Seoul, and held 최현배 in high esteem, profoundly influenced by his teachings. In 1948, to commemorate the poet's early death, a collection of his 31 posthumous poems, titled 하늘과 바람과 별과 시

Figure III-26. 큰사전, 한글학회, 1957 [52]

(lit. Sky and Wind and Stars and Poetry), was published. In 2016, his life story was adapted into the film 동주 (*DONGJU: The Portrait of A Poet*).

[52] 을유문화사, Seoul, Book 6, p. 3335 (refer to Footnote 48). 큰사전 was accomplished through a great collaboration of scholars, including 이극로 (李克魯; *Yi Kuk-no*, 1893–1978), 최현배 (崔鉉培; *Choe Hyeon-bae*, 1894–1970), 이희승 (李熙昇; *Lee Hee-seung*, 1896–1989), and 정인승 (鄭寅承, 1897–1986). Over nearly 30 years, they

2. 한글 From the Multiverse

Over the centuries, 한글 has seen various characters emerge and orthographic standards evolve. Some attempts were completely unrelated to the content of *the manual*, let alone the concepts and principles of 한글. Still, there have also been many attempts to make 한글 more extensible, good enough to be able to adopt even today. One might imagine such versions of 한글 widely used in another universe.

However, importing any kind of letter from random multiverse without limitation is not appropriate. 한글 was designed to be easy to learn and use without knowledge of complex social agreements. Preserving this original intent requires maintaining the basic framework that divides the appearance of the vocal organs and the nature of sound into 28 alphabet letters. Moreover, overturning or ignoring the established letter-sound relationships of 한글 would be problematic. If one had to learn different letter-sound relationships for each language used, it would contradict the original purpose of 한글. So, what letters would be suitable to import?

---

compiled this unabridged dictionary, which includes the standard language, dialects, Sino-Korean words, loanwords, idiomatic expressions, technical terms, archaic words, and proper nouns. Regrettably, as noted on the cited page, the dictionary sometimes lacks several native Korean words previously collected by missionaries, such as 할강할강ᄒ다 or 할그랑할그랑 (refer to Footnote 43).

§1. New Soft Letters: ㅌ, ㄸ

You have explored both modern and 15th-century 한글, yet you may still find certain sounds lacking, such as the *th* sound or the rhotic consonants common in French and German. These are rare in Korean and languages geographically near Korea.

Firstly, the *th* sound incorporates features of tooth sounds and tongue sounds simultaneously. Instead of blocking and releasing air, the tongue moves between the upper and lower front teeth to create a space that lets the breath escape. There is a sound produced using a pretty similar method: *the soft lip sound*, unlike those that require opening the lips, is produced by releasing air through a small gap between the lips, with ㅇ added beneath the lip sound letter. What if ㅇ is placed beneath ㄷ, and the tongue detaches from the upper gum while releasing breath? This action would place the tongue in a similar position to when the *th* sound in *this* or *then* is produced, closely mimicking a [ð] sound. Similarly, adding an ㅇ under ㄸ and attempting to produce a sound would place the tongue near the position where the *th* sound in *thin* or *thumb* is made, something close to a [θ] sound (Figure III-27).

Had 세종 considered English pronunciations while creating 한글, how might he have represented *th* sounds? Perhaps *the manual* would have described a *soft tongue sound*. What if we adopted the newly envisioned soft-ㄷ (i.e., ㅌ) and soft-ㄸ (i.e., ㄸ), already used in other universes, for *th* sounds?

Below, we compare names written with *th* sounds using Multiverse 한글's ㆆ and ㄸㆆ to their modern counterparts. We also use some 15th-century 한글 letters to examine how the sounds have transformed.

Name	Modern *Han'gŭl*	15C *Han'gŭl*
Anthony (*GA*)	앤뜨니	핸뜡니
Elizabeth	을리ㅈ베ㅆ	을리ㅿ베뜡
Heather	헤더	헤뎌
Matthew (*GA*)	매띠유	매뜡
Thatcher (*RP*)	땦쳐	땣쳐
Timothy	티모씨	티머뜡

Figure III-27. Multiverse 한글 Tongue Sounds: ㆆ, ㄸㆆ

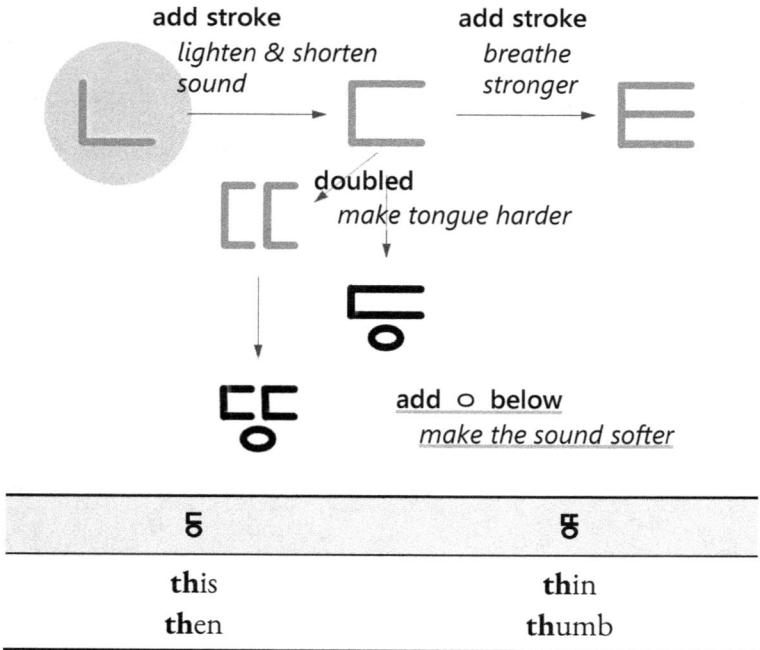

ㆆ	ㄸㆆ
this	**th**in
then	**th**umb

§2. New Pair and Double Letters: ㄱㄹ, ㄱㅎ, ㅎㄱ, ㄱㅎ, ㄹㄹ, and More

The use of pair letters has been versatile over centuries, simplifying the notation of complex sounds. We will begin by notating French and German rhotic consonants using pair letters.[53] These sounds blend elements of ㄱ, ㄹ, and ㅎ, resembling a *cocktail* that mixes a ㄱ-*base* with a ㄹ- or ㅎ-*liquor* and can be paired as shown: ㄱㄹ, ㄱㅎ, and ㅎㄱ. Similarly, [x] or [χ], found in German *Buch* or *Dach* or Spanish *jardin* or *traje*, can be notated by ㄱㅎ paired with ㅋ and ㅎ. Nevertheless, careful attention must be given to ensure that these symbols accurately reflect the actual sounds produced, as phonetic symbols or spellings may vary significantly across languages.

Double letters, which overlay the same letter to create a *thicker and stronger flavor*, can also be used more flexibly than before.[54] For example, the use of ㄹㄹ would be appropriate to emphasize the *l* sound, and for the resonance of *n* or *m* sounds, ㄴㄴ and ㅁㅁ would be helpful. Pairing with double letters is also feasible. For instance, the word *stop* could be written as ㅅ땁, ㅅ뚑, or even 쏩——using a pair letter with ㅅ and ㄸ. It is crucial, however, that these notations are easy for others to distinguish and interpret. Overloading a character with too many letters can hinder reading and make it difficult to convey the sound effectively. If emphasizing simultaneous pronunciation is unnecessary, splitting the word into multiple characters might be more effective.

---

[53] This sound might be described as a soft molar sound (i.e., ᴣ, ᴣ), but this description does not adequately capture the nuanced differences between the rhotic sounds of French and German, prompting an approach as a pair letter. In situations where similar sounds appear in adjacent languages or dialects without a mixture of ㄹ and ㅎ, or where the sequence of ㄱ and ㅎ is unclear, it could also be represented as soft-ㄱ (i.e., ᴣ) or soft-ㅋ (i.e., ᴣ).

[54] The letter ㅇ, as described in *the manual, does not intertwine* (refer to Footnote 23 of Chapter II), so it was not used for making a double letter. Yet, considering the previous analysis of ㅇ's sound value and the definition of a double letter (refer to

Now let's summarize all the preceding 한글 top-sound letters we've seen so far. Based on 17 alphabet letters, 11 double letters were introduced, and 9 soft letters were provided by combining ㅇ below the alphabet letters. To mark various tooth sounds, six more modified letters and four double letters were also added. Pair letters have too many cases, so they are not organized here separately; you can just use them freely. Let's use ㄲ, ㅎ, or ㅎ for indicating the French or German rhotic, and we'll use ㆅ for expressing the German or Spanish sounds mentioned above.

EXAMPLES

Below are comparisons between names written using various pair and double letters from Multiverse 한글 with their contemporary 한글 equivalents. We also include some 15th-century 한글 characters. Let's explore how the sounds change.

Name	Modern *Han'gŭl*	15C *Han'gŭl*
Aaron (*FR*)	아ㅎ곤	아ᅙᆫ
Gabriel (*FR*)	갸ㅂㅎ기|엘ㄹ	기!ㅂ히|엘ㄹ
Gabriele (*DE*)	가브ㄱ리엘러	가ㅂ끼엘러
Alejandro (*ES*)	알렉한ㄷ로	할레ᆑ한ㄷ로
Jesús (*ES*)	헤수ㅅ	꼐수ㅅ
Louise (*FR*)	ㄹ루이ㅈ	루이ㅿ
Nina (*FR/ES*)	니나/늬나	니나
Marco (*ES*)	마ㄹ꼬	빠룽꼬
Raphaël (*FR*)	ㄱ하빠엘ㄹ	갸하빠엘ㄹ
Raphael (*DE*)	ㄱ라파엘	까퐈엘

Footnotes 7 and 92 of Chapter I), one could argue that in scenarios like lifting a heavy object or groaning in pain while holding one's breath, the sound could be notated as a double-ㆆ (i.e., ㆅ).

Table III-1. 한글 Top Sounds (revised)

Sound Category	17 Alphabet Letters*		Double letters		Soft letters	
	Letter	IPA	Letter	IPA	Letter	IPA
Molar Sounds	ㄱ	[g/g̊/ɣ]	ㄲ	[k]	ㄱ̅**	[ʀ/ʁ]
	ㅋ	[kʰ/k]			ㅋ̅**	[x/χ]
	ㆁ	[ŋ]				
Tongue Sounds	ㄴ	[n]	ㅐ	[ñ]		
	ㄷ	[d/d̥]	ㄸ	[t]	ㆆ	[ð]
					ㅤ	[θ]
	ㅌ	[tʰ/t]				
	ㄹ	[ɾ/l]	ㅉ	[l]	ㅀ	[ɾ/ɹ/r]
Lip Sounds	ㅁ	[m]	ㅁㅁ	[m̃]	ㅱ	[ŋ]
	ㅂ	[b/b̥]	ㅃ	[p]	ㅸ	[v]
					ㅹ	
	ㅍ	[pʰ/p]			ㆄ	[f]
Tooth Sounds	ㅿ	[z]				
	ㅅ	[ʂ]	ㅆ	[ʂ]		
	ㅈ	[d͡ʐ/d͡ʑ̊]	ㅉ	[t͡ɕ]		
	ㅊ	[t͡ɕʰ]				
	ㅅ	[s]	ㅆ	[ʂ]		
	ㅅ	[ʃ]	ㅆ	[ʃ]		
	ㅈ	[d͡z]	ㅉ	[d͡z]		
	ㅈ	[d͡ʒ]	ㅉ	[d͡ʒ]		
	ㅊ	[t͡s]				
	ㅊ	[t͡ʃ]				
Throat Sounds	ㅇ	[∅]	ㅇㅇ	이 + ㅇ		
	ㆆ	[ʔ]	ㆆㆆ***	[ʔ]		
	ㅎ	[h]	ㆅ	[ʔh]		

*Chinese tooth sound letters in 한글 are considered to be notations, not alphabet
**Refer to Footnote 53.   ***Refer to Footnote 54.

§3. New Notations for Consecutive Middle Sounds

The persistent issues with 15th-century 한글 middle sounds primarily arise from complications with adjacent vowels. For instance, representing the sound [aɪ], as used in ***my*** or ***bike***, with two characters, ㅏ이, is cumbersome and forces an unnatural division of a single sound into two characters. This challenge similarly affects sounds such as the [oʊ] in ***home*** or ***go*** and the [eɪ] in ***cake*** or ***game***. Furthermore, the [u̯a] sound in French words like ***coi*** or ***roi***, which differs distinctly from the English [wa], feels insufficiently captured by ㅜ아.

This longstanding concern has garnered attempts to address it for centuries. These attempts have involved trying to fit multiple sounds within the structural framework of 한글. Documented examples that have been mentioned earlier include ㅗㅣ[ɪo], ㅗㅏ[ao], ㅜㅏ[aʊ], ㅗㅑ[jao], ㅗㅕ[jɔo], and ㅜㅕ[jɔʊ],[55] written using approaches akin to ㅗㅣ. In addition, the configurations ᆉ[u̯a] and ᆎ[ju̯a] (or [ɥa]) have been rendered using a method similar to ㅘ. Even more extended formations, such as ㅗㅗ[o:], ㅛㅗ[jo:], ㅡㅗ[ɯo], ㅗㅜ[oʊ], and ㅜㅜ[u:], have broadened the scope of expression beyond the boundary that seemed to exist, although *the manual* did not explicitly denote such a line.[56]

Nonetheless, several sounds remain difficult to convey with a single character, particularly the sequences involving upright middle sounds (i.e., ㅣ, ㅏ, ㅑ, ㅓ, and ㅕ), such as [aɪ], [eɪ], [ɔɪ], [ɪɚ], or [ɛɚ]. Despite historical discussions suggesting that ㅐ might have been used for [aɪ] in some previous era, it is not applicable today because of the current usage of [æ] for the letter ㅐ. Furthermore, there appears to be no viable solution for [eɪ] and [ɔɪ] beyond employing ㅔ이 and ㅓ이.

55 Refer to Footnotes 24, 25, 26, 36, 42, and 49.

56 All letters mentioned are utilized for denoting pronunciations in languages such as Mongolian, Manchu, Japanese, or Mandarin, rather than in Korean.

Reflection on these issues invites interest in the 한글 glyphs detailed in missionary *J. Ross*'s 1877 publication.[57] Reexamining the striking examples throughout his book may provide a fresh understanding and new perspective on these linguistic challenges. Let's take a look.

Table III-2. 한글 Glyphs in *Corean Primer* [58]

Type	Glyph and Pronunciation*
A | or ·?	누 뇌 늬 듸 믜 싱 흐 *na ne ne de me seng ha*
B *Middle at Bottom*	왔슴 밍 빅 완 첫 민 월에 *wassum meng beg wan tset men worê* 된 잉 뷀 *doen eng bail*
C *Over-shorten*	다이가지 능 *dainggaji nungi*
D *Wrong, But Possible*	뀌 픔 목욕 나슨 섭 탸 구 굴이 *ge ghom mogyog gusun sup da goo goori* 돈 듀 푸 푱 꺛치 *do doo poo dioong gótchi*

*Transliterated by *J. Ross*

---

[57] Refer to Fig. III-19, Footnoes 38 and 42.

[58] Pages in the book, *Corean Primer*, from which each glyph is excerpted include: (Type A) *na*, p. 2; *ne/ne/de/me/seng*, p. 6; *ha*, p. 36. (Type B) *wassum*, p. 7; *meng*, p. 10; *beg*, p. 11; *wan*, p. 15; *tset*, p. 16; *men*, p. 21; *worê*, p. 29; *doen*, p. 47; *eng*, p. 66; *bail*, p. 74. (Type C) *dainggaji*, p. 13; *nungi*, p. 49. (Type D) *ge*, p. 11; *ghom*, p. 13; *mogyog*, p. 18; *gusun*, p. 19; *sup*, p. 24; *da*, p. 26; *goo*, p. 28; *goori*, p. 30; *do*, p. 58; *doo*, p. 65; *poo/dioong*, p. 66; *gótchi*, p. 86.

Firstly, these cases are all examples of incorrect notations. Type A incorrectly represents ・ as ｜, while Type B changes the reading order by placing bottom sound letters next to middle sound letters, diverging from the traditional method.[59] Type C loads too many sounds into ㅇ, making the sound difficult to guess without Romanized phonetic notation, and Type D resembles drawing more than writing; it is even drawn incorrectly.

Rev. *Ross* published this 한글 text when both 한글 and the Korean language were largely unrecognized in Western societies. He met Koreans in person and learned Korean abroad to ensure accuracy.[60] Considering whether indirect translations of biblical terms through Mandarin into Korean would convey the original meanings, he carefully selected appropriate Korean words by himself, reflecting this commitment.[61] The errors in this book were corrected in a revised edition released five years later and seem to just be minor oversights.[62] In other words, these errors (or simple mistakes) are never

---

[59] Typically, 한글 characters should be read from left to right, starting with the top portion and then moving to the bottom. However, for Type B, the left column is read from top to bottom first, followed by the right column in the same order to accurately produce the sounds as indicated by the Romanized pronunciation.

[60] In 1876, Rev. *Ross* met the trader 李應贊이응찬 (*Yi Ungch'an*) and his associates at *Corean Gate* (高麗門고려문),* located in Manchuria. Subsequently, he learned Korean from 이응찬 in *Moukden* (i.e., *Shenyang*) and began writing his *Corean Primer* (refer to Footnotes 35 and 38).**

*This site is about 50 km northwest of the current North Korean border, near *Fengcheng* in modern China. The original structure was destroyed during the *Cultural Revolution* in 1966, and in 1995, the Chinese government erected a stele named *Bianmen Zhen* (邊門鎭변문진), with *Corean* removed.

**John Ross, *The Christian Dawn in Korea*, The Missionary Review of the World, New 3(4), 1890: p. 241–248; James H. Grayson, *The Legacy of John Ross*, International Bulletin of Missionary Research, 23(4), 1999: p. 167–172.

[61] John Ross, *Corean New Testament*, The Chinese Recorder and Missionary Journal, 14(6), 1883: p. 491–497.

[62] John Ross, *Korean speech with grammar and vocabulary*, 1882. This book is an expanded edition based on Ross's *Corean Primer*, with refined examples and enhanced grammar and vocabulary. Although errors in glyphs from the previous version have been corrected, the preface still incorrectly includes ｜ with the bottom sounds (i.e., ㄱ, ㄴ, ㄷ, ㄹ, ㅁ, ㅂ, ㅅ, ㅇ, and ｜).

insincere, and appear in this book only. This observation raises questions about why this book, in particular, contains such frequent mistakes.

Notably, this book was the first to apply horizontal writing and word spacing to 한글, particularly for colloquial sentences. Like many East Asian scripts, 한글 was traditionally written vertically, creating character boundaries above and below, with margins on the sides (Figure III-28). In contrast, horizontal writing results in character boundaries on the left and right, altering the spatial function and role of the characters. This shift between two different writing methods can make character layouts, once smooth and convenient, seem awkward and cumbersome. This effect is reciprocal; trying to write English sentences vertically illustrates this point clearly.

Moreover, during the 19ᵗʰ century, when Rev. *Ross* wrote this book, 한글 was primarily a script centered around calligraphy and handwriting, similar to *Hanja*. This detail is crucial: in the past, Korea was a leader in printing technology, yet it did not continue developing innovations in book publishing like Europe's *Gutenberg*.[63] Handwriting typically involves irregular character sizes and may blur the boundaries between characters, allowing for a high degree of compositional freedom. While initially standardized in the 15ᵗʰ century, 한글 has evolved over the centuries, increasing in flexibility and artistic value while gradually reducing its beautiful clarity and efficiency (Table III-3).

---

[63] To be precise, Korea's foremost achievement was in *type founding technology*. The country holds the oldest extant book printed with metal movable type from the 14ᵗʰ century,* and records indicate the use of metal type as far back as the 11ᵗʰ and 12ᵗʰ centuries. In addition, in the 15ᵗʰ century, under national auspices, Korea continued to develop new font types such as 癸未字계미자 in 1403, 庚子字경자자 in 1420, and 甲寅字갑인자 in 1434, producing 3,000 to 4,000 types daily and 100,000 to 200,000 types for each font. However, the printing method remained reliant on manual rubbing, limiting production to only 40 pages per mold per day by the end of the 15ᵗʰ century (cf. Around 1450, *Gutenberg*'s press was capable of printing 2 to 10 sheets per minute). Due to the high costs of metal types, Korea gradually returned to woodblock and manuscript-based methods. Only in the late 19ᵗʰ century did it adopt Western printing presses (1882), lagging China (1876) and Japan (1870).

*直指心體要節직지심체요절, a.k.a. *Jikji* (直指직지), 1377, housed at the *Bibliothèque nationale de France* (a.k.a. BnF).

Figure III-28. Vertical Writing of Various East Asian Scripts [64]

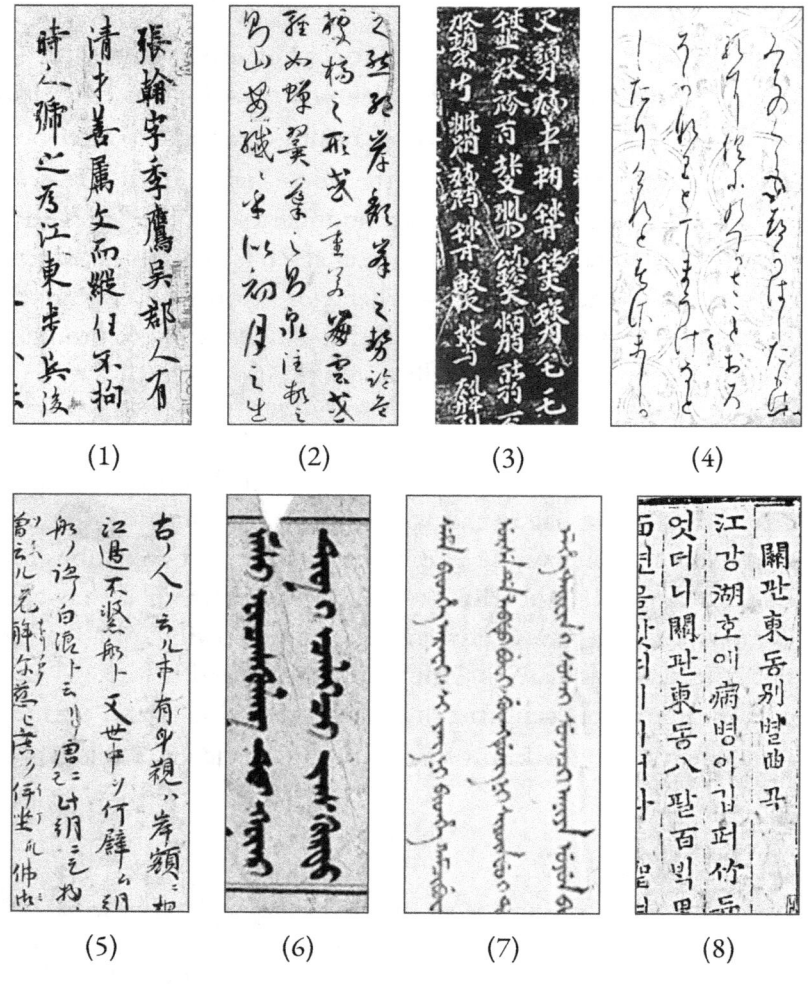

(1)   (2)   (3)   (4)

(5)   (6)   (7)   (8)

---

[64] (1) 張翰帖장한첩, 歐陽詢 (*Ouyang Xun*, 557–641), Regular Sinitic, 6–7C. (2) 書普서보; lit. Treatise on Calligraphy, 孫過庭 (*Sun Guoting*, 646–691), Cursive Sinitic, 7C. (3) 宣懿皇后哀冊文선의황후애책문; lit. Sad Poems of Empress *Xuanyi*, Khitan script, 11C. (4) 古今和歌集 (こきんわかしゅう; *Kokin Wakashū*), Hiragana, 12C. (5) 三寶繪詞 (さんぼうえことば; *Sanbōe Kotoba*), Katakana, 1273. (6) Altan Tobchi (a.k.a. 黃金史; lit. The Golden History), *Lubsandanzan*, Mongolian script, 1651. (7) Open letter from Emperor *Kangxi* to Pope *Clement XI*, Manchu alphabet, 1716, (8) 松江歌辭송강가사; lit. Poems and Songs of *Songgang**, *Seongju* ed., *Hanja* and 한글, 1747.   *Art name of 鄭澈정철 (*Jeong Cheol*, 1536–1594).

Table III-3. Changes in 한글 Typeface Over Time [65]

Period	한글 Glyphs in History
1446 ~ 1447	(a) (b) (c) (d) — historical glyphs
1459 ~ 16C	(e) (f) — historical glyphs
17~18C	(g) (h) (i) (j) / (k) (l) (m) (n) — historical glyphs
19C	(o) (p) (q) — historical glyphs

✒ : *hand-written*

---

[65] (a) 훈민정음해례 (i.e. *the manual*), 1446. (b) 용비어천가, 1447. (c) 석보상절, 1447. (d) 월인천강지곡, 1447. (e) 월인석보, 1459. (f) King 선조's letter, 1603. (g) 첩해신어, 1676. (h) 청어노걸대, 1765. (i) 몽어노걸대, 1766 or 1790. (j) 송강가사, 1768 (refer to Footnote 63). (k) King 효종's letter, 1652–1653. (l) Princess 숙명's letter, 1652–1659. (m) 완월회맹연, 18C. (n) 옥원중회연, 18C. (o) 구운몽, 19C re-engraved ed., 1914. (p) 홍길동전, 19C re-engraved ed., 1916. (q) Queen 孝定효정's (*Hyojeong*, 1831–1903) letter, 1868–1883.

Despite these changes, the fundamental structure of the characters has remained largely unchanged. Consider why, in 한글, the opening sound is positioned at the top of the glyph, and the closing sound, which halts the relaying sound, is located at the bottom. Furthermore, why do we read 한글 from the top left to the right, then continue at the bottom in the same direction? This design closely ties to the original creation of 한글 alongside *Hanja* for vertical writing. This robust framework ensures that even significant changes do not easily disrupt the structure. However, when Rev. *Ross* adopted 한글 sentences for horizontal writing alongside English, numerous errors emerged.

Upon examination of 한글 texts from the 17th and 18th centuries, how two vertically written characters merge becomes evident. Table III-3., section (i), illustrates how ㅛㅗ in 쵸ㅗ햔 could be abbreviated as 퓨 in 룧둥. Entries in section (h), such as 요 and 됴, are examples of such abbreviations. Likewise, in section (i), whether 슈 constitutes one or two characters (i.e., 셔ㅜ) is irrelevant in a vertical writing context. The same applies to ligatures containing various mid-sound letters, such as 뫂, 젺, 챦, or 샨. Conversely, 귀 and 쥾 in (h) show side-attached compounds, suggesting that in the original design of 나, 쌰, 뎌, and 쮜, ㅏ would have been attached next to ㅜ or ㅠ.

In Table III-2., if 늬 (*nungi*) in Type C is written vertically, ㅣ will be written below 능.[66] In vertical writing, there is no need to decide whether the written form of *dainggaji* is 다ㅇ가지, 다ᄋᄀ지, or 당가지.[67] In addition, from as far back as the 15th century, Koreans already started using a *fashionabe* stroke rather than a dot to represent the mid-sound ·. By the 19th century, broad variations of · had appeared in prints——as well as in hand-written

---

[66] In the expanded edition, *Korean Speech* (1882, refer to Footnote 62), 늬 (i.e., *can*) is updated to 능히.

[67] 당가지 is a northwestern dialect term for *cayenne*. If transcribed solely by sound, variations such as 다잉가지 (*dainggaji*) or even 다응가지 could also be plausible, depending on the speaker.

materials——where the letter sometimes even resembled ㅜ or ㄱ.[68] Moreover, it was extremely common for ㅣ to be placed alone under the preceding character when it was used as a nominative particle. It shouldn't be surprising, then, that a beginning Korean learner might assume that 누', 두', and 무' were correct glyphs. Thus, the letter that was supposed to be written as ᄂᆡ (*ne*) in Type A was represented as 뉘 or 누', and those representing *meng*, *beg*, and *eng* in Type B could also be written as such.[69]

Let's go back to our initial goal. We are searching for a multiverse where the English word *my* will be transliterated as a single 한글 glyph instead of as 마이. In one 15th-century universe, king 세종 is creating a 한글, which, right from the beginning, can be written horizontally alongside English. However, if his world is too different from ours, it might be challenging to adopt its script for us. We'll try again——let's look somewhere else that is more like our universe. In another place, the other 세종 is trying to incorporate English pronunciation and horizontal writing, while he is creating the 15th-century 한글 that we know. He is adding some notes to *the manual*, similar to the case of ! and ⊥, suggesting that we *write this way in such instances*. Which style will this glyph take to represent *my*? It is likely to become the vertically represented 마ㅣ, combined as a single character. As there is already another letter that takes a horizontal combination style (i.e., ㅐ) to represent a different sound (i.e., [æ]), we only have one option here. The glyph that Rev. *Ross* accidentally left behind in our world must, after all, have been included in *the manual* and widely used in that universe.

---

[68] Shown in the middle row of (o) in Table III-3. is 밧ᄌᆞ와. Here, ㆍ almost looks like ㅜ or ㄱ in a slanted form. It is intriguing that such a fashionable glyph style was engraved in woodblock printing. In (q), one can see 열ᄒᆞᄃᆡ, 통확ᄒᆞ며, and ᄉᆞ연이만 in order from the left row. Since it is a handwritten manuscript, you can observe more freedom in the form of the glyphs. But of course, there are still instances where ㆍ is written relatively straight as in (p).

[69] Not all errors can be explained this way. The letter for *ge* in Type D appears to be an error made during the editing process in trying to choose between ᄀᆡ and 게. Additionally, an incorrect addition or omission of a stroke seen in other cases of Type D was surely a mistake made by beginners who were not familiar with 한글.

Table III-4. 한글 Mid-Sounds : New Notations' Examples[70]

English	Vertical Writing	한글: Old & New	English	Vertical Writing	한글: Old & New
pie [aɪ]	파 ㅣ	파이 파ㅣ	f**i**ve [aɪ]	ᅗᅡ ㅣ ㅸ	ᅗᅡ이ㅸ ᅗᅡㅣㅸ
pr**i**ce [aɪ]	ㅍ ᄛᅡ ㅣ ㅅ	ㅍᄛᅡ이ㅅ ㅍᄛᅡㅣㅅ	b**i**nd [aɪ]	바 ㅣ ㄴㄷ	바인ㄷ 바ㅣㄴㄷ/바ㅣㄴㄷ
m**ou**th [aʊ]	마 ㅜ ㄸㅇ	마우ㄸㅇ 마ㅜㄸㅇ	h**ow** [aʊ]	하 ㅜ	하우 하ㅜ
f**a**ce [eɪ]	ᅗᅦ ㅣ ㅅ	ᅗᅦ이ㅅ ᅗᅦㅣㅅ	m**a**ke [eɪ]	메 ㅣ ㅋ	메이ㅋ 메ㅣㅋ
sm**o**ke [oʊ]	ㅅ 모 ㅜ ㅋ	ㅅ모우ㅋ ㅅ모ㅜㅋ	g**oa**t [oʊ]	고 ㅜ ㅌ	고우ㅌ 고ㅜㅌ
n**oi**se [ɔɪ]	노 ㅣ ㅿ	노이ㅿ 노ㅣㅿ	ch**oi**ce [ɔɪ]	쵸 ㅣ ㅅ	쵸이ㅅ 쵸ㅣㅅ
b**ear** [ɛɚ]	베 ㅓ ᄛ	베얼 베ㅓᄛ	y**ear** [ɪɚ]	이 ㅓ ᄛ	이얼 이ㅓᄛ
tour [ʊɚ]	투 ㅓ ᄛ	투얼	f**ire** [aɪɚ]	ᅗᅡ ㅣ ㅓ ᄛ	ᅗᅡ이얼 ᅗᅡㅓᄛ/ᅗᅡㅣㅓᄛ

[70] Due to differing linguistic standards, determining whether these characters represent diphthongs or *hiatuses* is challenging. They are also not associated with the criteria for syllable division. However, these characters differ from most listed in Table II-4 (excluding ! and _!) because they are read consecutively. Where there is a significant tendency to distinguish two consecutive sounds, it would be advisable to write them as separate characters (e.g., French onset glides).

Now, we have one more way to represent 한글 mid-letters. A small variation has been introduced to the criteria for distinguishing glyphs and constructing them. It is most important that they are easy enough to read, even without explicit directions on how to pronounce them. In other words, on seeing the written characters, one should be able to read them simply by knowing how previously known letters are pronounced in a character. Even if additional tips or guides are needed, the characters should be easy enough for even a child to pick up quickly. This of course means that they should not deviate greatly from the content of *the manual*.[71] How about the characters in Table III-4.? Do they meet the mentioned criteria? Are they convenient and easy to use?

You don't always have to use these characters to represent such sounds. For example, it's still okay to write ㅏ이, ㅖ이, or ㅣ어. If you want to emphasize that a sound should be pronounced in one go, you can write it in one character. If you want to pronounce it more leisurely, or distinguish the following vowel from the preceding one, or if it doesn't really matter to you, or for any other reasons, you can split the sound into two characters. As long as someone who knows the sounds of 한글 letters can read it as it is written, it is acceptable.

---

[71] In a strict sense, this does not match the explanation in *the manual*; *vertical mid-letters* (ㅣ ㅏ ㅑ ㅓ ㅕ) *are written to the right of the top sounds* (縱者在初聲之右 ㅣ ㅏ ㅑ ㅓ ㅕ 是也). From another perspective, however, it is equivalent to combining two characters into one rather than attaching another letter to a character, which somewhat reflects the variation seen in the 17th and 18th centuries. The use of the bottom letter next to the second mid-letter also reflects the characteristics of a horizontal writing system, where it is difficult to have a lengthy vertical representation. Thus, rather than a deviation from *the manual*, this can be considered a step beyond the tacit boundaries or customs implied by *the manual* as 한글 gets exposure to English, French, and so on.

QUIZ FOR FUN!

Maybe you should have said you couldn't do it in the first place. Ms. Elliott seems to take this for granted now. But somehow, you seem to enjoy doing it too. She left you with the nameplates, asking you to write their original names on the back, along with a reminder that class is about to start. Good luck![72]

No.	Name in Multiverse *Han'gŭl* on Nameplates	Original Name
(1)	키아누 릐ᄫ人	
(2)	텔럴 ㅅ위퐁ㅌ	
(3)	비얀쎄	
(4)	롸벌ㅌ 닪니 주늲	
(5)	ㅂ륃니 ㅅ쀓人	
(6)	쌘ㄷ릏 부로ㅋ	
(7)	뢴날도 디카ㅍ휜	
(8)	말ㅋ 릏퐁룿	
(9)	빌리 핱뤠人	
(10)	썰리ᄂ 곰메△	
(11)	볠 ㄱ륃ㅅ人	
(12)	제니펄 룿페△	

---

[72] (1) Keanu Reeves, (2) Taylor Swift, (3) Beyoncé, (4) Robert Downey Jr., (5) Britney Spears, (6) Sandra Bullock, (7) Leonardo DiCaprio, (8) Mark Ruffalo, (9) Billie Eilish, (10) Selena Gomez, (11) Bear Grylls, (12) Jennifer Lopez.

The Front of Nameplates

(1) 키아누 리븡ㅅ

(2) 텔럴 ㅅ위픙ㅌ

(3) 비얀쎄

(4) 랴벌ㅌ 닥니 주닗

(5) ㅂ맅니 ㅅ삡ㅅ

(6) 쌘ㄷ릉 부로ㅋ

(7) 뢴날도 디카ㅍ힌

(8) 맑ㅋ 릉 퐁롴

(9) 빌리 학뢔ㅅ

(10) 썰리ㄴ 곰메△

(11) 벨릥 ㄱ릷ㅅ

(12) 제니펄 롶페△

3. Writing Names in 한글

The 203 names covered in this book are brought together below, where we compare how they sound (1) in the modern 한글 refined in the 20th century, and (2) a combination of 15th-century 한글 and Multiverse 한글, referred to here as '한글 (revised).' Of course, the table below does not provide definitive answers, as the appropriate representation may vary depending on the sound you or the name's owner wishes to convey. If you want to represent a different sound, feel free to write the name differently. Consider both the attractiveness and the clarity of the character's shape to enhance its appearance. It is recommended that you try handwriting first for characters that are initially difficult to type on a computer. The goal is to *write as spoken* and *read as written*. Now, it's your turn.

What's your name?

Table III-5. Writing Names in 한글: Examples

Name (alphabetic)	Modern 한글	한글 (revised)
Aaron (*FR*)	아ㅎ곤	아흰
Adam (*FR*)	아담/앋동	아람/핟동
Alejandro (*ES*)	알렉한ㄷ로	할레꺈ㄷ로
Alma	얼마 (*EN*)/ 알마 (*ES*)	올마 (*EN*)/ 할마 (*ES*)
Angelika (*DE*)	앙겔리카	앙게쀠카
Ann	앤	핸
Anthony	앤ㄸ니/앤ㅌ니	핸똥니/핸ㅌ니
Antoine (*FR*)	앙ㄸ완	훙ㄸ완
Antonio (*ES*)	안또니오	안또늿
Ariana Grande	아리아나 그란데	으릭아나 ㄱ란데
Ashley	애슐리	해슬리
Ashton	애슈튼/애쉬튼	해ㅅ튼
Austin	오ㅅ띤	후ㅅ띤
Barbara	바-ㅂ라	바-ㅂ햐/밣ㅂ햐
Bear Grylls	베어-ㄹ ㄱ륄ㅅ	뻴 ㄱ륄ㅅ
Becket	베킽(ㅌ)/벡킽(ㅌ)	배큍(ㅌ)/백큍(ㅌ)
Betty	베티	배흰
Beyoncé	비얀쎄	비얀쎄
Billie Eilish	빌리 아일리쉬	빌리 햐쀄ㅅ
Blaze	블레이즈	블렊ㅿ
Brandon	ㅂ랜든	ㅂ핸든
Brian	ㅂ라이은	ㅂ햐인/ㅂ햑은
Brie Larson	브뤼 라-ㄹ슨	ㅂ릭 랄슨
Britney Spears	ㅂ릳니 ㅅ삐어ㅅ	ㅂ릳니 ㅅ쀑ㅅ
Camille (*FR*)	꺄미	꺄믿
Carla (*ES*)	까를라	까롤라/까롱꽈
Carmen (*ES*)	까ㄹ멘	까롱 멘

Name (alphabetic)	Modern 한글	한글 (revised)
Catherine Deneuve	꺄뜨린 드눠브	꺄뜨힌 드눠븡
Charles	챠-르ㅅ/챨ㅅ	챨ㅅ
Chiwetel Ejiofor	츄어텔 엣지오포	취어탤 엣진풀
Christa (*DE*)	ㅋ리ㅅ타	ㅋ릐ㅅ타
Christopher	ㅋ리ㅅ따퍼	ㅋ릐ㅅ뜨퍼
Churchill	처-췰/처-ㄹ췰	처-칠/철칠/쳐-칠/쳘칠
Cliff	클리ㅍ	ㅋ뤠ㅍ
Daisy	데이즤	뎅ㅅㅣ
Daniel	대니을 (*EN*)/ 다니엘 (*DE*)	대닐 (*EN*)/ 다니엘/다닒ㄹ (*DE*)
Daniela (*ES*)	다니엘라	다닐라/다닊라
David (*FR*)	다뷔ㄷ	다븨ㄷ
Dieter (*DE*)	디터	딪터
Djimon Hounsou	쟈이몬 헌쑤 (*EN*)/ 지몽 운쑤 (*FR*)	쟈몬 헌쑤 (*EN*)/ 진몽 운쑤 (*FR*)
Donald	다널ㄷ/도늘ㄷ	드늘ㄷ
Douglas	덕을러ㅅ/더글러ㅅ	더ㄱ뤄ㅅ/덕뤄ㅅ
Dustin Nguyen (Nguyễn Xuân Trí)	더ㅅ띤 응우인 (응우인 쓰언찌)	더ㅅ띤 우인 (우인 쒼찌)
Ed Sheeran	엗 쉬런	헫 시헌
Edwin	엗윈/에ㄷ윈	핻윈/해ㄷ윈
Elizabeth	을리ㅈ베ㅆ	ㅇ릐ㅅ베뚱
Eloise	엘로위ㅅ	앨뤄이ㅅ
Elton	엘튼	핼흔
Emma Watson	엠마 왓쓴	헴마 와츤
Faye	페이/풰이	퍡
Frank	ㅍ랭ㅋ	퓽랭ㅋ
Gabin (*FR*)	갸방	긫붕
Gabriel (*FR*)	갸ㅂㅎ기엘ㄹ	긫ㅂ히엘ㄹ

Name (alphabetic)	Modern 한글	한글 (revised)
Gabriele (*DE*)	가브ㄱ리엘러	가ㅂᄀ리옐러/가ㅂᄀ리엘
George	죠-ㄹ쥐	조-ㅈ/조ᄛᅳㅈ/조ᄛㅈ
Grace	ㄱ뤠이ㅆ	ㄱᄛᅦᅵㅆ
Gregory	ㄱ레ㄱ뤼	ㄱᄛᅦㄱᄛᅵ
Günter (*DE*)	군터/귄터	
Gustav (*DE*)	구ㅅ타ㅂ	구ㅅ타ㆄ
Haddad (حداد)	핟다ㄷ	ᅘᅡᆮ다ㄷ
Haile Gebrselassie (ኃይሌ ገብረ ሥላሴ)	헤일 게ㅂㄹ쓸라씨에	헤일 게ᄫᆯ쓸라쒸
Halsey	할씨	ᄒᆞᆯ씨/ᄒᆢᆯ씨
Hampton	햄튼/햄ㅍ튼	
Hashim (هاشم)	하쉼	하심
Hazel	헤이즐	헤ᅵ슬
Heather	헤더	헤ᄹᅥ
Henri (*FR*)	앙뤼	ᅙᅩᆼᄛᅵ
Henry	헨뤼	헨ᄛᅵ
Hildegard (*DE*)	힐더가-ㄷ	힐더갈ㄷ
Holmes	홈ㅈ	ᄒᆞᆷㅿ/훔ㅿ/ᄒᆢᆷㅿ
Hudson	헏슨	
Hugo	휴고 (*EN*)/ 위고 (*FR*)/ 후고 (*DE*)/ 우고 (*ES*)	휴고 (*EN*)/ 위고 (*FR*)/ 후고 (*DE*)/ 후고 (*ES*)
Jack	재-ㅋ	재-ㅋ/잭
Jacob	제이컵 (*EN*)/ 쟈껍 (*FR*)	제ᅵ컵 (*EN*)/ 자ᄁᆞᆸ (*FR*)
Jacob Wallenberg	요콥 발렌베리	외콥 발른배ᄛᅵ
Jacobo (*ES*)	하꼬보	ㅋ하꼬보
Jakob (*DE*)	야콥	야ᄏᆞᆸ
Jade (*FR*)	쟈ㄷ	자ㄷ/쟈ㄷ

Name (alphabetic)	Modern 한글	한글 (revised)
Jason	제이슨	젝슨
Jeffrey	졔프뤼	제퓽릐
Jennifer	졔니퍼	제니퍼/제니펄
Jennifer Lopez	졔니퍼 로우페ㅈ	제니펄 롭페△
Jessica	제씌까 (*EN*)/ 예씨까/흐씨까 (*ES*)	제씨까 (*EN*)/ 예씨까/ㅎ씨까 (*ES*)
Jesús (*ES*)	헤수ㅅ	ㄲ혜수ㅅ
Jimmy	쥐미	지미
Joe	죠/죠우	조/쥭/쟉/죠/쭄/졐
John	좐/줜 (*EN*)/ 죤 (*FR*)/ 욘/존 (*Swe.*)	즌 (*EN*)/ 촌 (*FR*)/ 욘/존 (*Swe.*)
Jonas Gahr Støre	요나ㅅ 가ㄹ ㅅ뚸러	읜나ㅅ 가릉 ㅅ뙤르
Jorge (*ES*)	호르헤	ㄲ호룽ㄲ혜
Jörg (*DE*)	요ㅋ	외ㅋ/욀ㅋ
José (*ES*)	호세	ㄲ호세
Joseph	죠우세ㅍ/죠우제ㅍ (*EN*)/ 요제ㅍ (*DE*)	죾세퓽/젃세퓽 (*EN*)/ 요세퓽 (*DE*)
Joshua	쟈슈아	자슈/자수아
Julia (*DE*)	율리아	윌릳
Justin Bieber	져ㅅ띤 비버	져ㅅ띤 비버
Jürgen (*DE*)	유ㄹ겐	외릉건
Keanu Reeves	키아누 리브ㅅ	키아누 튁ㅂㅇㅅ
Kelly Clarkson	켈리 클락슨	켈리 클랅슨
Kevin	케븐	케븐
Kimberly	킴벌리	킴벌릐
Kingston	킹ㅅ뜬	킹ㅅ뜬
Krüger (*DE*)	ㅋ뤼거	ㅋ뤼거
Kylian Mbappé Lottin	킬리언 음밮페 로땅	킬릔 음뵾페 로뚱
Langley	랭리	랭릐

Name (alphabetic)	Modern 한글	한글 (revised)
Larry	ㄹ래ㅇ뤼/ㄹ래-뤼	래륑/쨰륑
Lejeune (*FR*)	ㄹ쟌ㄴ	ㄹㄹ진ㄴ
Léon (*FR*)	레옹/리옹	
Leonardo DiCaprio	리오나ㄹ도 디카프리오	뤤낟도 디카프륑
Linda	ㄹ린더	륀두/롄두
Livingston	리빙ㅅ떤	뤼빙ㅅ떤
Louis	루위 (*FR*)/ 루에ㅅ (*DE*)	
Louise (*FR*)	ㄹ루이ㅈ	룾이ㅿ
Lucas	루꺼ㅅ/루커ㅅ (*EN*)/ 류꺄 (FR)/ 루카ㅅ (*DE*)	
Lucia (*ES*)	루씨아	룾띄아
Madison	매디슨	매륑슨
Maël (*FR*)	매엘	매엘/맬
Marceau (*FR*)	막ㅎ쑤	마ㄲㅎ쒀
Marco (*ES*)	마ㄹ꼬	마룽꼬/빠룽꼬
Marcos (*ES*)	마ㄹ꼬ㅅ	마룽꼬ㅅ/빠룽꼬ㅅ
Mark Ruffalo	마ㅋ 러플로우	맕ㅋ 류풍룾
Martina (*ES*)	마ㄹ띠나	마룽띠나/빠룽띠나
Mathieu (*FR*)	마튜	마퇴
Matthew	매띠유/매튜	매뜌
Meryl Streep	메럴 ㅅ트륍	메럴 ㅅ트륖
Michael (*ES*)	미까엘/마이끌	미까엘/맠끌
Millie	밀리/믤리	
Morgan Freeman	모-ㄹ근 프뤼먼	몰근 풍릐먼
Muhammad (محمد)	무함마ㄷ	무함마ㄷ
Naguib Mahfouz (نجيب محفوظ)	나지ㅂ 마푸ㅅ	누지ㅂ 맗푸ㅿ/ 누지ㅂ 마ㅎㅎ푸ㅿ
Nancy	낸씨	낸씨
Nash	내쉬	내ㅅ

Name (alphabetic)	Modern 한글	한글 (revised)
Nina (*FR/ES*)	니나/느나	니나/느나/띠나
Nathan (*FR*)	나떵	
Nicolás (*ES*)	닉꼴라(ㅅ)/니꼴라(ㅅ)	
Olivia	올리비어	ㅇ뤄뷕
Oprah Winfrey	오프라 윈프뤼	호프루 윈풍릐
Pablo (*ES*)	빠블로	빠ㅂ로
Patricia	퍼트뤼샤 (*EN*)/ 파트리찌아 (*DE*)/ 빠뜨리띠아 (*ES*)	펄릐샤/퍼트릐샤 (*EN*)/ 팥릐칩/파트릐칩 (*DE*)/ 빠뜨릐뛸 (*ES*)
Patrick	패ㅊ륍/패ㅊ뤼크	패ㅊ릭/패ㅊ릐ㅋ
Paul	퍼얼/포올 (*EN*)/ 뽈 (*FR*)/ 빠울 (*ES*)	풀/푸올 (*EN*)/ 뽈 (*FR*)/ 빠울 (*ES*)
Peter	피러	피러
Pippa	핖파	핖푸
Ramsay	ㅇ램즈	램시/램싀
Raphael (*DE*)	ㄱ라파엘	까퐈엘
Raphaël (*FR*)	ㄱ하빠엘(ㄹ)	꺄하빠엘(ㄹ)
Rebecca	뤄베카	러배카/러백카
Richard	뤼쳐ㄷ	릐철ㄷ/릐쳘ㄷ
Rob	ㅇ랍	룹/루ㅂ
Robert	라버-ㅌ/뤄버ㅌ	루벌ㅌ
Robert Downey Jr.	라버-ㅌ 다우니 주니어	햐벌ㅌ 닦니 주닢
Rodrigo (*ES*)	ㅇ로ㄷ리고	로ㄷ릐고
Rosie	ㅇ로우즈	로싀/루싀
Roy	뤄이/ㅇ로이	루/럭
Ryan	롸이언	롹언/하윈
Sacha	싸샤 (*EN*)/ 쌋샤 (*FR*)/ 싸챠 (*ES*)	싸샤 (*EN*)/ 쌋샤 (*FR*)/ 싸샤/싸챠/쌋챠 (*ES*)
Sandra Bullock	샌ㄷ라 불록	쌘ㄷ루 부로ㅋ

Name (alphabetic)	Modern 한글	한글 (revised)
Samantha	써맨타	써맨뚜
Sean	셔ㄴ	서ㄴ/셔ㄴ
Selena Gomez	썰리나 고우메ㅈ	썰리ㄴ 곰메△
Snoop Dogg	ㅅ늪 덕	
Sofía (*ES*)	쏘피아	쏘퓌야/쏘퓍ㅣ아/쏘퓌잍
Steven	ㅅ띠븐 (*EN*)/ 슈띠븐 (*DE*)	ㅅ띠븐 (*EN*)/ ㅅ띠븐 (*DE*)
Susanne (*DE*)	수잔ㄴ	수잔ㄴ
Taylor Swift	테일러 ㅅ위ㅍㅌ	텔럴 ㅅ위퓽ㅌ
Thatcher	땥쳐	땟처
Thomas	타머ㅅ/토머ㅅ (*EN*)/ 토마 (*FR*)	투머ㅅ (*EN*)/ 토마 (*FR*)
Timothy	티모씨	티머띠
Tom Cruise	탐 ㅋ루ㅅ	톰 ㅋ루△
Tom Holland	톰 홀랜ㄷ	
Upton	업튼	헙튼
Valentina (*ES*)	발렌띠나	봘렌띠나
Vasseur (*FR*)	바쇠르/베서	배씨ㅎ
Veronica Ngo (Ngô Thanh Vân)	버뤄니카 응오 (응오 타잉반)	버로니카 오 (오 탕봔)
Victoria	빅토리아	빅토퉑
Vincent	빈쓴ㅌ	빈쓴ㅌ
Washinton	워쉥튼	워싱튼
Webster	웹ㅅ터-ㄹ	웹ㅅ떨
William	윌리음	윌륌
Александра	알릭싼ㄷ라/ 알릭싼ㄷㄹ라	할릭싼ㄷ롸
Анастасия	아나ㅅ따씨아	ㅇㄴㅅ따씐
Арина	아리나	ㅇ륁나
Верочка	비에라ㅊ카	뷕롸ㅊ카

Name (alphabetic)	Modern 한글	한글 (revised)
Виктор	빅또ㄹ/빅또ㄹㄹ	빜또룽
Гена	긔예나	긮나
Даня	다-냐	닽냐
Дарья	다리아	ㄷ뤼
Дмитрий	드미ㅌ리	ㄷ미ㅌ륑
Евгений	예ㅂ기예니	윂뵹긮니
Ирина	이리나	이륑나
Ксения	ㅋ씨니아	ㅋ씨닢
Максим	막씸	막씸
Миша	믜샤	믜샤
Надежда	나지예쯔다	ㄴ쥖쯔다/ㄴ뒾쯔다
Николай	닉꼴라이	닉껄랔
Полина	뽈리나	뽈리나
Сергей	쎼ㄹ게이	쎼룽겜
Татьяна	따티야나	따티야나/따튙나
Тёма	티요마	티요마/팀마
أميرة	아미라	후미톼
خليل	칼릴/ㅋ할릴	ㅎㅎ렐
אֵלִיָּהוּ	엘리야우	엘리야

Lady Mondegreen?

People have long used precise pronunciation to distinguish foreigners from native speakers. The Old Testament mentions that 42,000 people were killed for not pronouncing the *sh* sound in *Shibboleth* correctly.[1] This precision in pronunciation has also been used to identify hidden enemies during wars and guess someone's regional origin, even during peaceful times. This historical context might explain why we often feel a certain pressure to pronounce things correctly.

When learning a second or third language, or even our native tongue, we often make funny faces trying to pronounce certain sounds. When we finally master a difficult pronunciation, we feel proud. We may even brag about it. Even we used to say: this sound should be pronounced this way, that sound that way, those pronunciations are naturally different, or some pronunciations are just expected to be known. Sometimes, the ability to pronounce sounds correctly becomes a standard for distinguishing between what is *normal* and what is not.

---

[1] Judges 12:5–6.

Accurate pronunciation, therefore, can also be a handy tool for governance. Even without explicitly defining norms, pronunciation naturally becomes the basis for distinguishing social classes and hierarchies. In addition, the ability to set standards for speech and writing and establish norms through official documents illustrates a powerful, centralized authority. If used effectively, this practice becomes a solid and easy way to reinforce governing power and establish a concrete system. Imagine a simple mispronunciation or writing mistake is used to maintain discipline among the ruling class and to eliminate political rivals or policy dissenters. What could be an easier and simpler tool for governance?

Records of script creation in East Asia can also be viewed from this perspective. The *Khitan* (契丹거란) scripts, created in 920 AD, were used for 270 years. The *Tangut* (西夏서하) script, created in 1036, was used for about 400 years. The *Jin* (金금) of *Jurchen* people created the *Jurchen* script in 1119. The script created in *Tibet* in the mid-7th century had a significant influence on 'Phags-pa script that *Mongolia* created in 1265. Southeast Asia was no different. *Khmer* (i.e., Cambodia) has records of using its own script in the early 7th century, *Burma* (i.e., Myanmar) in the 10th century, and Laos in the 13th century. The *Thai* script is said to have been created in 1283. The 15th century, when 한글 was created, was a time when making scripts by governing powers would have been a long-standing practice in Asia.

The history of East Asian scripts and the history of Korea are intricately intertwined. In the early 7th century, just before the *Tibetan* script was created, two of Korea's ancient Three Kingdoms fell. One of these was the first state to use the name *Korea* (高麗고려),[2] which had lasted for over 800 years. The

---

[2] The initial national designation of the first *Korea* was 高句麗고구려 (a.k.a. *Goguryeo*), later changed to 高麗고려 (a.k.a. *Goryeo*) around the 5th century. Various scholarly theories suggest that its founding date could be 37 BC, 138 BC, or 277 BC. In 668 AD, it succumbed to a coalition of *Tang* (唐당, 618–907) and *Silla* (新羅신라, 57BC–935, refer to Footnote 4) forces, but within a short span of 10–30 years, a second *Korea* was established in the same region, thereby preserving *Korea*'s historical and cultural lineage. Furthermore, numerous tombstones from the ear of the first *Korea* identify themselves as 三韓人삼한인 (lit. *Three Han** people), or 朝鮮人조선인 (lit. *Joseon* people), showing

second *Korea*,[3] which succeeded the first, flourished for about 250 years and fell in 926, shortly after the *Khitan* scripts emerged. At this time, the last of the ancient Three Kingdoms, which had endured for nearly 1,000 years, also collapsed.[4] However, the third *Korea*, which emerged just before the *Khitan* scripts, continued until the 14th century, surviving for nearly 500 years during

---

continuity with the ancient *Joseon* (朝鮮조선, a.k.a. 古朝鮮 고조선; *Gojoseon*; lit. Old *Joseon*, ?–108BC). Additionally, there are records indicating that this nation was referred to as *Mucri*** in medieval Greek (refer to Whitby & Whitby *trans.*, *The History of Theophylact Simocatta*, Oxford Univ. Press, 1986: 7–12 of Book 7).

*삼한 (*Three Han*): One of the several names for ancient Korea, from which the modern official name 한국 derives. **莫離막리 presumed to be the highest official rank in the first *Korea*, it is believed to be the source of *Mucri*.

[3] The second *Korea* initially declared itself the successor to the first one, resulting in strained relations with 당 and 신라 (refer to Footnotes 2 and 4). Various theories exist regarding its early national titles, such as 震旦진단 or 振國진국, and it is said that, after its establishment (678 or 698), the nation changed its name to 渤海발해 (*Balhae*, a.k.a. *Bohai*) in 713, following 당's recommendation, in order to seek diplomatic ties with 당. However, after Japan sent correspondence to the 渤海郡王발해군왕 (lit. King of *Balhae* province) in 728, a diplomatic reply was sent by letter in 759 with the king self-identifying as 高麗國王고려국왕 (lit. King of *Korea*). This event, recorded in Japanese history,** confirms that the name *Korea* was actively used as the state name during that period. The second *Korea* engaged in over a decade of conflict with the emerging Khitanese 遼요 (*Liao*, 916–1125) until collapsing in 926.

*続日本紀 (*Shoku Nihongi*), Book No. 10, Apr. 16th 728, *The Emperor of Japan sends greetings to the King of Balhae province* (天皇敬問渤海郡王). **ibid., Book No. 22, Jan. 3rd 759, 고려국왕 대흠무 *sends his greetings* (高麗國王大欽茂言); 대흠무 is the name of the 3rd king who ruled the second *Korea* from 737–793.

[4] 新羅신라 (*Silla*, 57BC–935) was known by several names, such as 斯盧사로 (*Saro*), 尸羅시라 (*Sira*), and 斯羅사라 (*Sara*) over the centuries, before officially adopting the name 신라 in 503. The title for its rulers was 간 (干; *Kan*; *Gan*), which intriguingly resembles the title 칸 (汗; *Khan*; *Qan*; *Han*) used by later nomadic states. 신라 was renowned for its extensive trade and cultural exchanges, engaging actively not only with China, Japan, and India, but also with Southeast Asia, Persia, and the Arab regions. Remarkably, a 14th-century manuscript of an 11th-century Persian epic refers to it as *Besila* (Iranshah, *ed.* Hee-Soo. Lee, *trans.* K. Hemmat, *The Kushnameh: The Persian Epic of Kush the Tusked*, Univ. of California Press, 2022: p. 124 and many other pages).

the period when the *Tangut, Jurchen*, and *'Phags-pa* scripts appeared.[5] Thus, the state name *Korea* has been carried on for over 1,400 years in East Asia.[6]

The third *Korea* resisted the Mongol invasions for nearly 30 years before surrendering. Unlike in their direct rule over the southern region under the *Yangtze River*, where they placed the surviving people in the lowest social class, the Mongols respected the *Korean* royal family and recognized their governance. They did not force *Korea* to change its customs and culture to follow the Mongolian way. However, they did not forgo the spoils of victory. For over a hundred years, exploitation and plundering continued through *Korea*'s governmental system. This significantly tarnished the dignity that *Korea* had maintained for over a thousand years. It wouldn't be an exaggeration to say that during its last century, the third *Korea* was rotting from within.

At that time, a new country, *Ming* (明명), emerged in the *Yangtze basin*, pushing the Mongols northward. With a power vacuum created north of the *Yellow River* and in Manchuria, *Korea*'s ruling powers recognized an

---

[5] The third *Korea*, 高麗고려 (918–1392, a.k.a. *Goryeo*), proclaimed itself the successor to the previous *Korea* in name from its beginning. In 935, it brought 신라 under its control, and by 936, it had also subdued factions that aimed to revive 百濟백제 (*Baekje*, 18BC or 28BC–660), one of the ancient Three, thereby achieving regional unification. This *Korea* engaged in three conflicts against the Khitanese 요 (refer to Footnote 3) in 993, 1010, and 1018 (or 1019), who had earlier overthrown the second *Korea*. This time, *Korea* won each encounter and subsequently enjoyed a century of prosperity. However, internal divisions among the aristocracy and a military coup in 1170 eroded its strength, leading to prolonged resistance against Mongol invasions starting in 1231 and culminating in *Korea*'s surrender in 1259. The era of the third *Korea* concluded with the rise of 朝鮮조선 (*Joseon*, 1392–1897, a.k.a. *Chosun* or *Joseon*).

[6] The name 高麗고려 (or 고리) was known as 까우례 (or 꺼우리) in Chinese, 코라이 in Japanese, or 케우리 in Tibetan, before being introduced to Europe in the 13th century as *Caule* (1255) and *Cauli* (1295). Following the establishment of 조선, European references included *Gori* (1514), *Coree* (1549), and *Coria* (1578). The name *Korea* first appeared in the German edition of *Hamel's journal* (1672, refer to Footnote 29 of Chapter III). Subsequently, Germany and Russia adopted the names *Korea* and Корея, respectively. French-speaking areas referred to the country as *Corée*, Spanish-speaking regions used *Corea*, and by the 20th century, the Anglophone world had standardized the name to *Korea*, which is still used today.

opportunity for recovery and expansion. Meanwhile, another political faction emerged within *Korea*. This faction wanted to establish a new world order with Neo-Confucianism as the state ideology, and to ally with 명. They rebelled against the ruling powers' calls for the recovery and expansion of *Korea*'s glorious reign and founded a new state, *Joseon* (朝鮮조선). The fourth king of this new country was 세종.

In the 14th century, the relationship between the Korean 조선 and Chinese 명 was unusually close in the context of the long history of both peoples. The Chinese, having been freed from direct Mongol rule, wanted to eliminate everything associated with the Mongols. Similarly, the founders of 조선 wanted to clear away the remnants of the previous era. However, for 조선's founders, treating 명 like *Mongolia* would have undermined the legitimacy of the newly founded nation. This historical context explains the compilation of a Chinese standard pronunciation book in 명 in 1375,[7] and the creation of a new script in 조선 in 1443. But then, regardless of that context, something unexpected happened: the newly created writing system was so easy and convenient that it swept across the entire country like a *tsunami*.

한글 spread rapidly throughout Korean society. Just forty years after its creation, a soldier serving on the frontier sent a letter in 한글 to his wife at home. A grieving widow buried a heartfelt letter written in 한글 with her deceased husband. Children learned to read and write in 한글. A young prince wrote an adorable 한글 letter to his aunt. Officials responsible for translation learned foreign languages using 한글. 한글 documents were used in local government affairs and matters of family inheritance. Koreans could now record and convey their thoughts without learning tens of thousands of ideograms. They could document their hardships and request help. Koreans lived a richer linguistic life than any other people of their time, skillfully using both *Hanja* and 한글 together.

Chinese 명 had fallen after less than 300 years, and the Manchurian 청 (*Qing*; 淸), which followed, was teetering, though it had only existed for just

---

[7] Refer to Footnote 8 in Chapter II.

over 200 years. After enduring for 500 years, Korean 조선 was also in decline. In January 1919, nine years after Japan annexed Korea, the last king who directly ruled the state suddenly passed away.[8] His funeral, held two months later, became a catalyst for unarmed citizens across the country to pour into the streets and demand independence. Leaders from various sectors of society gathered to declare *Korea*'s independence. Following this declaration, the *Korean Provisional Government*'s organizations were established in Shanghai, Chongqing, Manchuria, Hawaii, and other locations outside the Korean peninsula. These organizations fought the Japanese military from outside the country's borders and disrupted colonial governance within homeland, targeting key figures. In July 1941, one of the cabinet members from the provisional government published a book in *New York* to raise awareness of Japan as a threat to the rest of the civilized world.[9] When the Pacific War broke out five months later, the book became a bestseller. This was an era when the colonial government imposed and enforced restrictions on 한글 orthography and eventually banned the use of the Korean language and 한글 altogether.

---

[8] 高宗고종 (*Gojong*, 1852–1919, reigned 1864–1907) founded 대한제국 (大韓帝國; *Empire of Korea*, 1897–1910) and ascended as its first emperor. Through the 광무개혁 (光武改革; *Gwangmu* Reform), he achieved significant improvements in the economy, education, and social infrastructure. Despite these gains, his focus on enhancing imperial power and increasing royal finances failed in unifying domestic political factions. He actively resisted Japanese influence until the end, sending secret envoys to *The Hague* in 1907 and covertly supporting armed resistance both domestically and internationally. His sudden death on January 21, 1919, seemed to be due to poisoning, considering his extreme swelling and complete loss of teeth, igniting a sequence of events that included the *March 1ˢᵗ Movement* and the *Declaration of Independence*, and the establishment of the *Provisional Government of the Republic of Korea* abroad (April 11ᵗʰ, 1919).

[9] Syngman Rhee,* *Japan Inside Out: The Challenge of Today*, Fleming H. Revell Company, June 1941. In this book, the author argues that, for peace in East Asia, the United States must form an alliance with *Korea* to contain Japan. He criticizes the US for having initially established a certain relationship with Korea in 1882 only to unilaterally terminate it in 1905, which led to a worsening geopolitical crisis. Later, as the first President of South *Korea*, he took a significant step toward realizing his idea by signing the *Mutual Defense Treaty* with the United States.

*이승만 (李承晚, 1875–1965).

At that time, everything about Korea was considered inferior to Japan. 한글 was also deemed in need of *improvement*. This was when 한글 lost *the sky*. Stories spread widely that Korea's ruling class had disregarded and neglected 한글 for centuries. Indeed, this was far from the truth. 조선 was a state that adhered faithfully to Neo-Confucianist principles, which valued filial piety to parents above life itself. 세종, who created 한글, was the father and grandfather of all later kings. While there may have been exceptions over such a vast span of time, the narratives that the creations of a forefather king were openly despised by subsequent royalty, the ruling class, or even the entire society for hundreds of years in 조선 fundamentally conflict cultural understandings based on the extensive historical record.

Although the colonial period lasted only 36 years, young people growing up during this time, who were taught to believe such fictional narratives as truths, experienced significant confusion. One novelist recalled how difficult it was to write in the Korean language when thoughts naturally came in Japanese.[10] Indeed, the individuals who resisted colonial rule and strove to preserve Korean identity, including modern *Korea*'s first president, were mostly born in the late 19th century.[11] The young people who grew up seeing

---

[10] This is what novelist 김동인 (金東仁; *Kim Dong-in*, 1900–1951) said in published contents from March 1948 to August 1949 in the monthly magazine 新天地신천지 under the title 문단 30년의 자취 *(lit. The Trace of 30 Years in the Literary World)*. Despite his position as a significant figure in early 20th-century *Korean* literature, he is criticized for inappropriate behaviors, such as adopting the Japanese name 金東가네히가시 文仁후미히토 during the Second Sino-Japanese War (1937–1945) and actively promoting the colonial conscription policy. His actions contrast with those of contemporaries such as 현진건 (玄鎮健; *Hyun Jin-geon*, 1900–1943), 황순원 (黃順元; *Hwang Sun-won*, 1915–2000), 채만식 (蔡萬植; *Chae Man-sik*, 1902–1950), 이효석 (李孝石; *Yi Hyoseok*, 1907–1942), or 염상섭 (廉想涉; *Yeom Sang-seop*, 1897–1963), who either refused or even regretted one-off collaborations forced by the colonial government. His well-known works include 배따라기 in 1921, 감자 in 1925, and 운현궁의 봄 in 1933.

[11] The leaders of the Provisional Government of the Republic of *Korea* (1919–1948) were primarily individuals born in the late 19th century, including 박은식 (朴殷植; *Park Eun-sik*, 1859–1925), 이승만 (refer to Footnote 9), 김구 (金九; *Kim Ku*, 1876–1949), and 안창호 (安昌浩; *Ahn Chang-Ho*, 1878–1938). Key independence activists, including

only a colonized homeland, and then took the lead in rebuilding the nation after the 1950s, were of the same generation as the aforementioned novelist.[12]

After the Pacific War ended, *Korea* was freed from colonial rule, though it was soon divided into North and South. From 1950 to 1953, a devastating civil war ensued. In 1961, a military coup occurred in the democratic and capitalistic South. The military dictatorship that followed lasted 18 years, ending in October 1979, when the president, who couped and long ruled the nation alone, was assassinated by his close aide. Soon after, another military coup took place in December of the same year. It wasn't until 1987 that a direct presidential election system was reinstated,[13] and in 1993, a civilian politician, not from the military, was elected president. In 1998, a president from the opposition party was elected for the first time in Korea's modern history. Thus, the length of the period during which militarism and authoritarianism took root in Korean society far exceeds that of democracy and modern capitalism.

안중근 (安重根; *An Jung-geun*, 1879–1910), 김좌진 (金佐鎮; *Kim Chwa-chin*, 1889–1930), 김상옥 (金相玉; *Kim Sang-ok*, 1890–1923), 김원봉 (金元鳳; *Kim Won-bong*, 1898–1958), and 윤봉길 (尹奉吉; *Yun Bong-gil*, 1908–1932) were also predominantly born around the end of the 19th century.

[12] Since the 1950s, several key figures have led South *Korea*. In the political sphere, notable leaders include 장면 (張勉; *Chang Myon*, 1899–1966), 박정희 (朴正熙; *Park Chung-Hee*, 1917–1979), 김대중 (金大中; *Kim Dae-jung*, 1924–2009), 김종필 (金鍾泌; *Kim Jong-pil*, 1926–2018), and 김영삼 (金泳三; *Kim Young-sam*, 1929–2015). In the economic sector, influential individuals such as 구인회 (具仁會; *Koo In-hwoi*, 1905–1986, founded *LG*), 이병철 (李秉喆; *Lee Byung-chul*, 1910–1987, founded *Samsung*), 정주영 (鄭周永; *Chung Ju-yung*, 1915–2001, founded *Hyundai*), and 김우중 (金宇中; *Kim Woo-choong*, 1936–2019, founded *Daewoo*) have been pivotal. In addition, 백두진 (白斗鎮; *Paik Too-chin*, 1908–1993) and 장준하 (張俊河; *Chang Chun-ha*, 1918–1975) were key figures in the early governmental policies for economic growth and social infrastructure. Almost all were born and raised in colonial Korea (1910–1945).

[13] The Republic of *Korea* initially adopted an indirect election system for selecting its presidents in 1948 under the U.S. military government. This system was replaced by a direct presidential election following a constitutional amendment in 1952 during the *Korean War*. Despite a military coup in 1961, the direct election system was maintained

Koreans who endured these times often create a curious and grand *collage*, blending nationalism, fascism, militarism, authoritarianism, modern capitalism, democracy, and various philosophies and religions, including Buddhism, Confucianism, and Christianity, like a 비빔밥*bibimbap*. For instance, most modern *Koreans*——or the *fourth Korean*, so to speak—— revere 세종, possibly more than the people of his time. They are genuinely moved by his actions, wondering, *How much must the king have cared for and loved his people to create such an excellent script like* 한글? If someone suggests that 한글 resembles the *'Phags-pa* script or claims that it was created to transcribe Chinese pronunciation, they might react as if hearing blasphemy.

However, these words should not automatically provoke anger. They can be analyzed and evaluated academically. The 한글 writing system was created while Korea was ushering in a new era and looking toward the future of a new nation. It would have been unusual if they hadn't referenced all known contemporary scripts and systems, including *'Phags-pa* or *Sanskrit*. It would certainly be problematic if the system claimed to represent every spoken sound but failed to consider the language of the nearest friendly country. Many scripts had disappeared; that friendly country had long since fallen already; and Korea had even endured the colonial period when it lost its sovereignty, and the language was nearly stripped away. The creation of 한글 alone is an incredibly remarkable achievement of 세종 *The Great*.

More research and diverse interpretations are needed in order for us to ever fulfill the intended role of 한글 properly. Scholars from various countries should scrutinize it in multiple languages. The standards or norms of 한글 that have been added in later generations should be examined objectively along with the temporal signatures or influences present when specific criteria were widely accepted. Most importantly, 한글 should be convenient and easy to use for people across different language regions. This is the correct path for 한글, for us to sift out national and political biases and focus solely on the benefits it provides to the people. Writing systems are more essential for sharing

---

until 1972 when it reverted to an indirect system. A constitutional amendment in 1987 restored the direct election system, which remains in effect today.

and conveying ideas than for governing people. Therefore, the methods and standards for reading and writing should not be too strict or decisive, as if they are trying to single out powerful groups or superior individuals. In using 한글, we should strive to communicate comfortably with each other, effectively conveying the principles and spirit embedded in its creation.

In fact, we are not always strict about pronunciation. Even without recalling a memory at the age of four like Mrs. *Wright*, many of us are familiar with experiences like mishearing *laid him on the green* as *Lady Mondegreen*.[14] We generally perceive *auditory illusions* as amusing rather than problematic, and we usually do not blame or scold anyone for them. In addition, despite the vast variety of dialects across languages, we manage to understand enough to get by. Various pronunciations are accepted and spread either generously or out of necessity. It's a widely acknowledged fact that, across languages, even native speakers may not always accurately produce some peculiar pronunciations that challenge foreigners. Therefore, historical incidents, like when people were executed for not correctly pronouncing *Shibboleth*, are not the issues that should have been solved by learning the correct sound.

Of course, organizing and disseminating methods and standards for reading and writing is crucial for linguistic life. This process is necessary for the efficiency of communication that society as a whole must maintain. However, the organization and dissemination of information fundamentally differs from permitting and prohibiting peoples' behaviors. Especially in government, broadcasting, or education, the implications of this distinction are significant. Moreover, regardless of how vital some standards may be, isn't

---

[14] American writer Sylvia Wright (1917–1981) is credited with coining the term *mondegreen* in 1954, based on a story* about her own experience related to the name *Lady Mondegreen*. She defined it as an *auditory illusion* in which an often-misheard word or phrase in music or poetry creates a new, unintended meaning. *Mondegreen* highlights how our perception reconstructs sound, illustrating the brain's crucial role in interpreting auditory input. *Auditory illusions* also include several other phenomena that stem from the complexity of aural perception, such as mistaking patterns of sound (i.e., Shepard Tone) or the intersection of sight and sound that leads to misunderstandings (i.e., the McGurk effect), independent of misperceiving words or lyrics.

* Sylvia Wright, *Get Away from Me with Those Christmas Gifts*, 1957: p. 105–112.

it best to call someone by the name that they prefer? I write this book hoping that 한글 might provide even the slightest assistance in this respect.

Above all, 한글's greatest attribute lies in its emphasis on *allowing*. The importance of enabling everyone to easily use written characters, record messages, and distribute documents cannot be emphasized enough. To all who read this book, I hope that the value of *allowing* conveyed by 한글, and the blessing of fostering a world where we can communicate comfortably with each other, will accompany you.

Albert Jung 핼벌ㅌ 융

P.S.: To those kind enough to read this far, I am adding a few of my favorite songs transcribed in 한글, as a gift. Sharing the emotion of singing together, even without learning several languages, represents one of the best uses of 한글. I've also included key information about the songs to make them easy to find. Thank you.

OBAA,* sung by *Isamu Shimoji*

おばぁ오바아 (下地 勇시모지 이사무)

*Obaa (おばぁ) is a term of endearment for a grandmother, similar to *Granny*.

This song is performed in the *Miyakoan* language, a dialect from the *Miyako* Islands in southern Okinawa, Japan. The *Miyako* language is endangered, with fewer than 50,000 speakers remaining. *Isamu Shimoji* (下地 勇시모지 이사무) is the only singer who performs in this language. He released this song in 2007, and it also appears on his 2018 album, *Marking Out* (track No. 15) (Japanese lyrics refer to J-lyric.net).

I-1. 으햐 노티 방카이 피햐디티마히 냐다나하
貴方の一てぃ我かい ぴらでぃてぃまいにゃーだな
Why did you leave without even saying goodbye,

바누후 탈게 후ㅊ기 사다링 피△가티
我ぬぅ一人置つぎー 先りーぴずがてぃ
Why are you going away, leaving me alone?

ㅉ링히 피△ 오치가 미파나유 나디
冷りーぴすおじいが 顔ゆ撫でぃ
As she strokes, his face gets colder,

오바가ᅙ 미히카라하 나다누 우티 피△
おばぁが目から 涙ぬ落てぃーぴす
Tears fall from Granny's eyes.

I-2. 이ㅊ누 투캬흔마히 퓽따△ 마ㅊ키히
いつぬ時んまい 二人まーつき
The two of us always

큐가미히 아ㅅ키 ㅉ띠 노티가
今日がみ歩きー来てぃ のーてぃがー
walked together until today, why now?

야누 후마카마 우햐가 카쟎-나다 누쿠링-우
家ぬうまかま 貴方が香ざ 未だ残りうー
Throughout the house, your scent still lingers

노티 으햐 스나시 사다링 피△가
のーてぃ 貴方すなーし 先りぴずがー
Why did you leave without a word?

M1. 뱌가 히비타 부△마 미바카링후타 파링마
貴方が植びたーブーギまい 見守りうたー畑まい
The sugarcane you planted, the field you watched over,

ㅊ카나후타 누마마 핀△마마히
つかないうたー馬まい山羊まい
the horses and goats you raised.

뱌가 미당카 노바시 스디가
貴方がみーだか のーばしすーでぃが
How will I cope without you?

우키루 우키티바가미파나유미 하마 핑히루
起きる，起きてぃ我が顔ゆ見い 笑いふぃーる
Wake up, wake up, look at my face and smile.

우우우 후 후 후

2. 오지가 민푸 나링가라 누마마 핀△마 우뱌렝 피링
おじいがみーんふなりから 馬まい山羊まい売うぁれーぴりー
After Grandfather passed, the horses and goats were sold

우누 얀나 오바가 푸칸나 토마 민푸 나링
うぬ家んなおばぁが他んな 誰まいみーんふなりー
There's no one in this house but Granny.

유넨 나△치카 탈케 유수유 포ㅋ투누
夜なすちかー人 夕飯ゆ喰うー事ぬ
At night, she eats dinner alone,

아티 사비ㅅ카바 마히니ㅊ 나키흐타
あてぃ淋すかーば 毎日泣きうたー
In bitter loneliness, crying every day.

M2. 뱌가 ㅊ푸-수누 마수니누 히ㅊ반 빠무누치
汝が作ふ 魚ぬ塩煮ぬ 一番んまむぬてぃ
Your steamed fish is the best, he said

사키가마 눔샤나 하마이후타ㅋ투

酒小飲んしゃーな 笑いうたーくとぅ

Laughing, and drinking Awamori*——those moments

*Okinawan traditional liquor

ㅉ누누 쿠툰다카릥 우무△디뤧ㅋ시

昨日ぬ事んだかり 思す出れーきし

Seem like they were just yesterday

이꾸라맏 니핑디 봐가 무두릥 쿠디 야ㅊ카

「いくらまい煮いふぃーでぃ 貴方が戻り来うでぃやてぃかー」

"I'll make it for you, as long as you come back here."

아아아 하 하 하

3. ㅍ카ㅈ야 마타 수기 피릥 쓰다스 팡카지누풍키ㅋ시바

日数やまた過ぎぴりー 涼す南風ぬ吹きーきしば

Times flies by, a cool southern breeze blows in,

오바야 마가릥 핑△ ㅋ쑤유 무타기 파스미

おばぁや 曲がりーぴす腰ゆ持たぎ始み

Granny straightens her back and stands up

퐈누캬 마가누캬 바가 미바카릥 이까다까하 나랗ㄴ치

子供達 孫達 我が見守りいかだかならんてぃ

Children and grandchildren, I'll take care of them.

킫맏 푸카라ㅅ키 나릥 하마이후

今日まい 嬉すきなり笑いーうー

Today, I'm happy to hear smiling

M3. 오바하 푸지 나마까하랏맏 간수카릥 우티

おばぁ ぷじ 今からまい 元気かりうーてぃ

I hope you stay healthy, Granny

이ㅉ가미맏 이ㅉ가미맏 나가이키유 시 핑사마치

いつがみまい いつがみまい 長生きゆしーふぃーさまち

Stay with us for a long, long, long time

RUN TO THE FUTURE DAYS, sung by *Leslie Cheung*
奔向未來日子 빤횡메루엿지 (張國榮 쩡궈윙)

This song is the theme for the 1987 film *A Better Tomorrow II*, a hallmark of the 1980s *Hong Kong noir* genre. It was performed by *Leslie Cheung* (張國榮 쩡궈윙), a renowned actor and singer whose life tragically ended too early. *Cheung* was a pioneering figure in the Cantopop music scene, and his influence is still felt today. This *Cantonese* version featured in the movie also appears on his tribute album, *Four Seasons* (track No. 9), released in 2011.

I.
목와만워 껌틴딕씨
無謂問我 今天的事
Asking me about today's things is meaningless

무와휘쩨 빤위만이이
無謂去知 不要問意義
There's no point in knowing, so no need to ask what they mean.

얏이이 목이이 짬머뗑뿐
有意義 無意義 怎麼定判
How can anyone know if there's a meaning or not?

빠씀 빠흐낀 빠찌
不想 不記 不知
Don't remember, don't look back, don't try to know.

2.
목와만워 얏썽딕씨
無謂問我 一生的事
Asking me about my life is meaningless

쒸원이공 쓰흣롱윙씨
誰願意講 失落往事
Who wants to talk about the past?

야우칭 모우칭 빳위만워
有情 無情 不要問我
There's no need to ask me if my heart is warm or cold.

빳레워 빳쪄푸 빳까씩이씨
不理會 不追悔 不解釋意思
Don't understand, don't regret, don't try to explain

M. 목루 목원
無淚 無言
Without tears, without words,

쏨쭝씬휘겡좃 빵윈너찌
心中鮮血傾出 不願你知
Red blood pouring out from my heart, don't try to know

얏쏨얏이 빤황나멜루엿지
一心一意 奔向那未來日子
With one accord, we run to future days

워이한푸네 춈멕후꾸씨
我以後陪你尋覓好故事
Later, with me, we reminisce about the good old things together

3. 목와만워 쓴쏨ㅁ씨
無謂問我 傷心的事
Asking me about heartbreaking things is meaningless

목와휘쒹 빳쭈씌웡씨
無謂去想 不再是往事
It's all vain thoughts, irreversible.

야우씨 약찬씨 빳딱이
有時 有陣時 不得已
Whether time remains or not, there's nothing to gain

쭝깐낑궈빳훠찌 빳훠치
中間經過不會知 不會知
Path gone by, never come back, never come back

REFRAIN 2, M, AND 3.

HAVANA허해나, sung by *Camila Cabello*까밀라 까베요

This song won't need an explanation. The *Spanglish Solo* version below offers a fascinating *Spanish* accents from world-famous, talented Latin artist, *Camilla Cabello*까밀라 까베요. Enjoy her singing, while singing alongside 한글.

MI.   허해나, 운ㄴ나 (하)
Havana, ooh na-na (ayy)

햂올 ㅁ하ㄹ씬 허해나, 운ㄴ나 (하하)
Half of my heart is in Havana, ooh na-na (ayy, ayy)

히툭미 백투 이ㅅ탵래너, ㄴㄴ나, 하
He took me back to East Atlanta, na-na-na

하올 ㅁ하ㄹ씬 허해나 (하), 췔썸띤부ㄹㅣㅅ 매널ㅅ (허허)
Oh, but my heart is in Havana (ayy), There's somethin' 'bout his manners (uh huh)

허해나, 운ㄴ나 (ㅎ)
Havana, ooh na-na (uh)

1.   엘 ㅂㅣㄴㅜ부ㅅ 까릉메아 이로쑤뻬 (ㅎ) (ㅂㅣ ㄲ라라하 싹띠뚣)
Él vino a buscarme y ahí lo supe (uh) (Vi clara su actitud)
He came looking for me and I knew it then (uh) (His attitude was clear to me)

메 디쿄: "쏜 딴따ㅅ라ㅅ 께잇뚜워" (허) (뻬로 메 팥따ㅅ뚜)
Me dijo: "son tantas las que ya tuve" (uh) (Pero me faltas tú)
He told me: "I've had so many girls" (uh) (But I'm missing you)

노 뿱도 쏠따릉떼, 노 세아ㅅ딴ㄱ뤨 (헹) (데ㅅ데싸 노첼쑬)
No puedo soltarte, no seas tan cruel (hey) (Desde esa noche azul)
I can't let you go, don't be so cruel (hey) (Ever since that blue night)

미 빠빠 메 디쎄 께 마로 에셀 (ㅎ) 께 마ㅆ쀌하쎄?
Mi papa me dice que malo es él (uh) ¿Qué más puedo hacer?
My dad tells me that he's bad (uh) What else can I do?

후우우우후우우, 로 쑵뻰눈세운도, 엘 깜빈륌미 문도, 야노뿨로마ㅅ
Ooh-ooh-ooh, lo supe en un segundo, él cambiaría mi mundo, ya no puedo más
Ooh-ooh-ooh, I knew it within one second, he would change my world, I can't go on

후우우우후우우, 하이에ㅅ 껨메둟레 뭇죠, 데씨랴도ㅅ, 오 나나나나나
Ooh-ooh-ooh, es que me duele mucho, decir adiós, oh na-na-na-na-na
Ooh-ooh-ooh, it hurts me so much, to say goodbye, oh na-na-na-na-na

M2. 허해나, 운ㄴ나 (하학)
Havana, ooh na-na (ayy, ayy)

핳올 마하리씬 허해나, 운ㄴ나 (하학)
Half of my heart is in Havana, ooh na-na (ayy, ayy)

히툭미 백투 이ㅅ탙래너 (허허), ㄴㄴ나
He took me back to East Atlanta (uh huh), na-na-na

하볼 마하리씬 허해나, 마하리씬 허해나 (학)
Oh, but my heart is in Havana, my heart is in Havana (ayy)

허해나, 운ㄴ나
Havana, ooh na-na

2. 아 누와워ㅅ뎨 웬아헤엔더싼 (ㅎㅎ) (웰컴투 라윰마)
I knew I was there when I read the sign (Welcome to La Yuma)

안 누윗워쉼 웨니억ㅍ럼비한 (허) (잇게ㅆ미 엘리툼)
I knew it was him when he hugged from behind (It gets me every time)

ㅇ 히ㅅ뿌론웕, 버리ㅣ씨인더ㅅ트맅 (히샌: "궐, 캔위롹ㄷ?")
He's put in work, but it's in the streets (He said: "girl, can you ride?")

앤 디ㅣ씨ㅿ더팥 탵마대히톰미 (톰미). 히 금미 필릴랔
And this is the part that my daddy told me. He got me feelin' like

후우우우후우우, 안누윗웨남메림 핳럱딤 웨나뛜틈. 금미필릴랔
Ooh-ooh-ooh, I knew it when I met him I loved him when I left him. Got me feelin' like

후우우우후우우, 핸뒈나해듯테름 하핸투고욷, 오 나나나나나
Ooh-ooh-ooh, and then I had to tell him I had to go, oh na-na-na-na-na

M3. 허해나, 운느나 (하'하')
Havana, ooh na-na (ayy, ayy)

핼올 마하'리씬 허해나, 운느나 (호오오) (하'하')
Half of my heart is in Havana, ooh na-na (ayy, ayy)

히툭미 백투 이ㅅ탵래너 (허허), 느느나 (호우 노오우)
He took me back to East Atlanta (uh huh), na-na-na

하볼 마하'리씬 허해나, 마하'리씬 허해나 (하')
Oh, but my heart is in Havana, my heart is in Havana (ayy)

허해나, 운느나
Havana, ooh na-na

CHOR. 우느느, 오느느나
Ooh na-na, oh na-na-na

텤미 백백백랔
Take me back, back, back like

(REPEAT 3 TIMES MORE)

후우우우후우우, 후우우우후우우 (텤미 백낀마 허해나, 운느나)
Ooh-ooh-ooh, ooh-ooh-ooh... (Take me back in my Havana, ooh na-na)

M4. 허해나, 운느나
Havana, ooh na-na

핼올 마하'리씬 허해나, 운느나 (하', 잎ㅎ)
Half of my heart is in Havana, ooh na-na (oh, yeah)

히툭미 백투 이ㅅ탵래너, 느느나
He took me back to East Atlanta, na-na-na

하볼 마하'리씬 허해나, 마하'리씬 허해나 (하')
Oh, but my heart is in Havana, my heart is in Havana (ayy)

허해나, 운느나.
Havana, ooh na-na.

SNOWMAN 스노맨, sung by *Sia* 씨아

This song highlights the exceptional vocal talent and charm of Australian singer, *Sia* 씨아. Featured on her 2017 Christmas album titled *Everyday is Christmas* (track No. 3), *Sia* 씨아's unique vocal style in this song, where she seems to be singing with rounded pursed lips, is unforgettably pleasing and mellow.

I.

돈 ㅋ롸, ㅅ노맨, 놑인 ㅍ론욜 뮈
Don't cry, snowman, not in front of me

후 갯츄 티을ㅅ퓨 퀸 캐ㅊ미, 달힝?
Who'll catch your tears if you can't catch me, darling?

이퓨 퀸 캩ㅊ미, 달렝
If you can't catch me, darling

(ㄴ)돈 ㅋ롸, ㅅ노맨, 돈릴ㅁ히ㅅ웨
Don't cry, snowman, don't leave me this way

(ㅎ)뻐롤 얼워럴 캔 홀메 ㅋ롶ㅅ, 밷베
A puddle of water can't hold me close, baby

캔 홀메 ㅋ로ㅅ, 벧베
Can't hold me close, baby

M1.

하 원칱툰누 해람네볼리붕
I want you to know that I'm never leaving

걸움ㅁ쓰ㅅ노, 틀델월비ㅍ릥승, 왜
'Cause I'm Mrs. Snow, 'til death we'll be freezing, yeah

위움마ㅎ움 마홈ㅍ헐씌슨
You are my home, my home for all seasons

쏘 컴 올 렡ㅆ 꼬
So come on, let's go

M2.

레ㅆ 고빌로ㅅ롶 흔핟ㅍ럼더쒼
Let's go below zero and hide from the sun

한 러뷔퍼허해허 워월햅씜펀, 잎ㅅ

I love you forever where we'll have some fun, yes

렛츠 힛허넗폴랜 맅햅뿔뤼

Let's hit the North Pole and live happily

ㅂ뤼ㅅ, 동크롹노틸ㅅ낙, 잇츠 크뤼ㅅ므ㅅ, 뷔뷔

Please, don't cry no tears now, it's Christmas, baby

마 ㅅ누맨 앤 미 엔

My snowman and me

마 ㅅ누맨 앤 미 이이이, 뱁뷔

My snowman and me, baby

2. 돈 크롹, ㅅ누맨, 돈츌 뤼을드썬

Don't cry, snowman, don't you fear the sun

후으 깨릐믜 위퇏렉ㅅ뚜런, 헌뉘?

Who'll carry me without legs to run, honey?

위퇏뗵ㅅ뚜런, 헌뉘

Without legs to run, honey

도언 크롹, ㅅ누맨, 돈슈 (ㅅ)셔릐티

Don't cry, snowman, don't you shed a tear

홀 뤎맡ㅆㅣ크르츼뮤 돈햅의릉ㅅ, 배이뷔?

Who'll hear my secrets if you don't have ears, baby?

이퓨 돈햅윌ㅅ, 벱비

If you don't have ears, baby

Refrain M1 & M2.

Катюша까뜌샤, sung by *Various Artists*

Often considered a Russian folk song, Катюша까뜌샤 was composed by Матвей Блантер 므뜨비| ㅂ란뜨룽 (*Matvey Blanter*, 1903~1990) with lyrics by Михаил Исаковский미하일 이삭콜ㅅ끼 (*Mikhail Isakovsky*, 1900~1973). Soviet Jazz Singer Валентина Батищева 봉렌티ㄴ 부티셰봉 (*Valentina Batishcheva*) first performed it in Moscow in the fall of 1938, leading to its recognition as a Russian pop song and military march. The song, which captivates with its lyrical charm and poetic beauty, gained significant popularity in Russia during World War II and has been performed by many artists since. In addition, Катюша 까뜌샤 has been translated into several languages, including Polish, German, Greek, Hebrew, and Vietnamese, earning widespread popularity. This version appears on the *Alexandrov Ensemble* album, *Anthology, Part 4* (track No. 11).

1. 걍룽ㅆ븨따뤼 야블루니히 ㄱ룽쉐
Расцветали яблони и груши
Apple trees and pear trees started to bloom

뺀펄릴릐 투마니 ㄴ ㄷ리쿠
Поплыли туманы над рекой
River mists began to float and flow

빙|컹디이봐 ㄴ 비릭 까뜌샤
Выходила на берег Катюша
She came out and went ashore, Katyusha

ㄴ 븨쏘끼 빋븨끄 늑끄룽뚜.
На высокий берег на крутой
On the lofty bank, on the steep shore.

2. 븨컹디ㄹ 뺏ㅅ뉴 즈붕딩봐
Выходила, песню заводила
She came out and sang, she sang about

빠릉 ㅅ팁노붕 씨저벌ᅙᅙ 룽롸
Про степного сизого орла
Her young friend, the bluish eagle from the steppe

빠릉 뜨봉오 끈뜨룽붕 뢱빅뤄
Про того, которого любила
All about the one she dearly loved

뻐룽 뚜로 치 삐씨맙뻬링ㄱ라.

Про того, чьи письма берегла
The one whose letters she treasured and kept.

CHOR. 오우, 띠, 뻬ㅅ냐 뻬셴끄 뒈훠칟
(3.)

Ой, ты, песня, песенка девичья
Hey, a song, the song of the young girl,

띠 릐티 ᅀ 야ㅅ님 쏜씀ㅅ뤠ㅌ

Ты лети за ясным солнцем вслед
Fly out after the bright sun,

이 바쭈우 ㄴ 달늼 뻐ㄱ릉니치

И бойцу на дальнем пограничье
Find a soldier on the distant borderlands

욘 까뜨시 뻬릐단 뻐릥뤄ㅌ.

От Катюши передай привет
Say hello from Katya, long waiting for him.

4.   뿌ㅅ띤 픘뽀ㅁ닜ㄷ 뒈붛ㅅ꾸 뻐룽ㅅ뚜유

Пусть он вспомнит девушку простую
Let him remember the young and simple maiden,

뿌ㅅ뚜스위슌 칵ㅋ날카잌 (ㅌ)

Пусть услышит, как она поёт
Let him hear the song she now sings,

뿌ㅅ뚠ㄴ 쉬ㅁ릏 비릐쇼ㅌ핥누위

Пусть он землю бережёт родную
Let him protect his Motherland,

아 뤼보퐁 까뜨샤 ㅅ뻬릐쇼ㅌ.

А любовь Катюша сбережёт
And Katyusha will protect their love.

REFRAIN 1.

Acknowledgments

This book is the result of the thought, dedication, and hard work of many wonderful people.

First and foremost, I owe heartfelt thanks to my two editors. Oksana Marafioti악싸ㄴ 따롱하퐁!띠, author of *American Gypsy: A Memoir* (2012), reviewed every part of this book with care, refining sentences and phrases while offering valuable insights to make the writing more accessible. Flannery Wise퐁꽤너히 왓△ provided meticulous editing and proofreading, along with steadfast guidance and encouragement throughout the publication process. Without their invaluable contributions, this book might still be unfinished.

Given the nature of this book, which explores the phonological characteristics of multiple languages, the expertise of specialists in each language was essential. I am grateful to Antoine Bargel홍ㄸ완 바ㄶ젤ㄹ for French, Martina Moser무룽티ㄴ 무술 for German, Rowena Galavitz로위ㄴ ㄱ뢒뷜ㅊ for Spanish, and Oksana Marafioti악싸ㄴ 따롱하퐁!띠 for Russian. Their careful review of sample words in their respective languages added depth and precision that this book could not have achieved otherwise.

Special thanks go to Mark Karis말ㅋ 캐히ㅅ for designing a simple yet modern cover that beautifully captures the essence of this work. I am also deeply appreciative of the members of Good Governance Research, who managed the interior design and formatting with skill and creativity, overcoming the complexities of this project. My gratitude also extends to Andy Meaden핸디 미든, whose interest in this project and thoughtful advice on design and formatting were both encouraging and helpful.

Finally, my deepest gratitude goes to my family, whose unwavering support and encouragement have been a constant source of strength. Their love and understanding allowed me to dedicate myself fully to this project, even during the most challenging times. I am forever thankful for their sacrifices and the joy they bring to my life.

About the Author

The author of *What's Your Name?* has chosen to remain in the background, allowing the book and its ideas to take center stage. This intentional anonymity invites readers to focus solely on the potential of *Han'gŭl* as a tool for connection, expression, and understanding.

Driven by a fascination with language and its power to bring people together, the author presents a fresh perspective on this unique script—not just as a Korean script or a linguistic tool, but as a universal system capable of bridging cultural and linguistic divides. *What's Your Name?* explores how this alphabet, designed centuries ago, continues to offer innovative possibilities for the modern world.

If you have comments or would like to share your thoughts about this book, please send them to research@goodgov.info. We welcome your feedback and will share your message with the author.

*This section was prepared by the Good Governance Research team to highlight the author's contributions and vision.

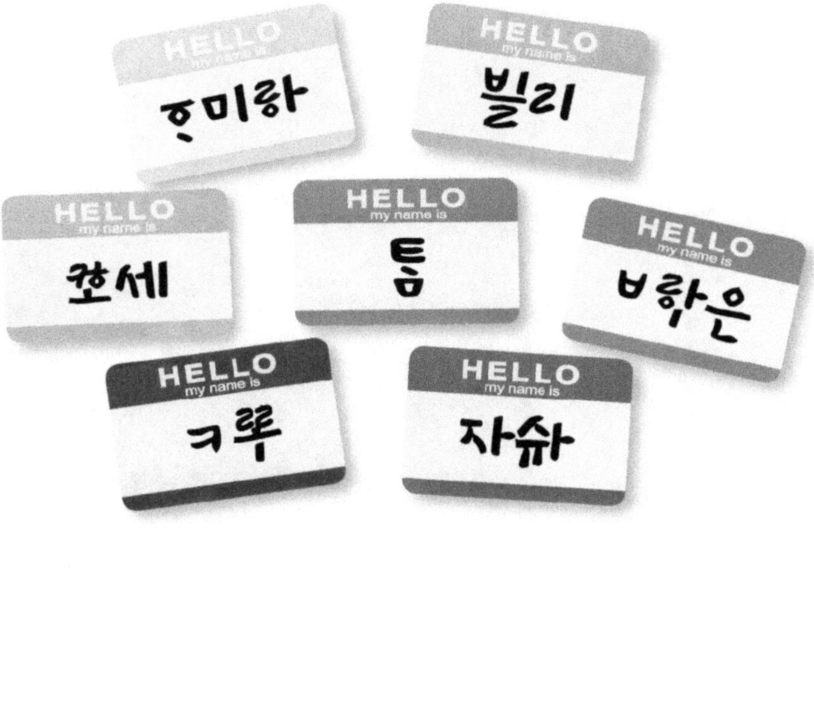